T0209582

The Horse

LAST CHANCE

The Story of a Juvenile Delinquent from the Public
Housing Projects Who Defied the Odds with a
Second Chance at the American Dream

Alvin Miller Sr., D. Min.

WESTBOW
PRESS®
A DIVISION OF THOMAS NELSON
& ZONDERVAN

WestBow Press books may be ordered through booksellers or by contacting:

WestBow Press
A Division of Thomas Nelson & Zondervan
1663 Liberty Drive
Bloomington, IN 47403
www.westbowpress.com
844-714-3454

ISBN: 978-1-6642-6273-7 (sc)
ISBN: 978-1-6642-6274-4 (hc)
ISBN: 978-1-6642-6275-1 (e)

Library of Congress Control Number: 2022906297

Print information available on the last page.

WestBow Press rev. date: 6/9/2022

To Elizabeth Miller, Rita Marie Watson-Johnson,
and Dr. Nolan G. Skinner (deceased)

Contents

Part 4: Lessons Learned on the Migrant Trail

Foreword

This book depicts one boy's challenging and heartfelt journey from poverty to the rank of colonel in the United States Army as a chaplain. He developed a thirst for knowledge as an army officer stationed at Fort Sill, Oklahoma, in the early 1990s. It was during a four-year stint in Oklahoma that Alvin became a doctoral student at Oral Roberts University, where he later graduated with his doctor of ministry degree on May 1, 1999.

Alvin is eager to share with others that one of the greatest moments of his life was when he was chosen to give the invocation for the 44th President of the United States of America, Barack Obama. President Obama made a special visit to the home of the Screaming Eagles Division (Air Assault) for the purpose of addressing the soldiers, sailors, and troops of the 5th Group Special Forces Unit at Fort Campbell, Kentucky, on May 6, 2011. Members of the Special Operations Command, along with US Navy Seals, joined with part of the 160th Special Operations Aviation Regiment (SOAR), also known as the Night Stalkers, at Fort Campbell. The United States Special Operations Command is the team responsible for killing the world's most wanted terrorist at the time: Osama Bin Laden.

Colonel (Ret.) Alvin E. Miller Sr. grew up in the 1960s and 1970s in an agricultural county (St. Lucie) in southeastern Florida, where migrant communities were plentiful. He grew up as a migrant child traveling with his aunts from Florida to states such as South Carolina, Virginia, Maryland, Pennsylvania, and New York. Alvin learned to pick indigenous crops from various states, such as tomatoes, potatoes, apples, cucumbers, peaches, oranges, and other citrus fruit. While living in migrant labor camps, Alvin became even more exposed to the vices of the street life and was put in many situations that compromised his childhood integrity.

When he was not on migrant labor camps, Alvin's performance in elementary school was characterized as dismal and very unproductive.

Other than some kind of sickness or family crisis, what could be going on in a child's life that would cause him to miss nearly ninety days of school during his first and second year? Alvin failed the first-grade during his initial year of school, and for the next seven years, he was sociably promoted to the next grade.

Consequently, Alvin became academically and behaviorally challenged, which led him down the dark roads of illiteracy, crime, truancy, theft, and other community and school violations. This is amazing, because with such a troubled beginning that seemed to be a dead end, many children did not live out the kind of success story Alvin is about to share with you. Believe it or not, there are only a few people (outside of sports and entertainment) who can conceptualize their tumultuous beginning as a juvenile delinquent and explain to other people with sincere, compelling, and convicting candor how they overcame such obstacles before facing an incarcerated life or death, as Alvin does in *The Horse: Last Chance*.

Alvin's appetite for destruction increased as he became more street savvy. As a result of school and community disruptions, Alvin was summoned to juvenile court on numerous occasions. After delivering a verbal thrashing and threats, the St. Lucie County, Florida, juvenile judge warned Alvin that if he did not correct and change his behavior from bad to good, the judge would order his incarceration at Dozier School for Boys in Marianna, Jackson County, Florida. Judge Jack Rogers promised Alvin this would be the judgement if he ever returned to the judge's juvenile courtroom. Alvin's mother stood with him because Judge Rogers had demanded her presence in court. She had to miss a day's work as a laborer in the tomato fields/orange groves.

While Alvin was at Dan McCarty Middle School, the principal contemplated an expulsion packet that recommended Alvin for a one-year school expulsion due to him staying on the suspension list, his belligerent behavior toward teachers and other students, and his lack of respect for authority figures. Instead, the principal asked me to admit Alvin into one of my classes as a means of intervention. At first, the challenge of saving Alvin had its ups and downs because of his cantankerous behavior and determination to resist change. Yet my determination and drive to tackle impossible challenges was the fuel I needed to help save this particular child, who was self-destructing and clueless as to what was taking place as the principal prepared his packet for expulsion from school.

The emergence of this young man is compelling and anecdotal. His story will enlighten and encourage young readers to pursue their dreams and aspirations regardless of circumstance. Retired colonel, bishop, and doctor Alvin E. Miller Sr.'s narrative will also demonstrate to his readers the significance of nurturing, compassionate parents, teachers, extended family members, and community members as children journey through life to become self-actualized.

Currently, Dr. Miller is the pastor at St. John Missionary Baptist Church in Clarksville, Tennessee. He continues to serve on community boards and accumulate accolades from governmental and community agencies because of his selfless service to others. Over the years, he has been recognized for nearly reaching the apex in sports, the military, academia, and the ministry as he excels from the projects of government housing to the pillars of American society. I salute this great American hero for a job well done.

African American Lives Matter!
Rita Watson-Johnson
One of Alvin's seventh-grade teachers and godmother

CELEBRATION FOR THE FORT PIERCE
FIRE HAWKS FOOTBALL TEAM
**SPECIAL SALUTE TO COACH EDDIE DAVIS
AND THE FORT PIERCE, FLORIDA FIRE
HAWKS POP WARNER FOOTBALL TEAM**

CONGRATULATIONS TO THE FORT PIERCE, FL FIRE HAWKS POP WARNER

FOOTBALL TEAM FOR WINNING 2021 POP WARNER SUPER BOWL NATIONAL

CHAMPIONSHIP!

The Fire Hawks Pop Warner Football Team from Fort Pierce, Florida has won The Pop Warner National Super Bowl Championship! Yes, a Pop Warner Football Team from Fort Pierce, Florida (my hometown) is the 2021 Pop Warner National Football Champions with an undefeated record of 17-0! The Fort Pierce Fire Hawks defeated Nevada 38-12 for the National Championship in Orlando, Florida at Camping World Stadium!

After 50 years in the dark, a bright light from Bethlehem has blessed the State of Florida and the City of Fort Pierce with redemption. HOPE has smiled again on another football dynasty like it did in 1971 when Fort Pierce Central High School in Fort Pierce, Florida produced its first undefeated State High School Football Championship Team (Class 4A the largest divisional class at the time)! Congratulations to the Fort Pierce, Florida Fire Hawks Pop Warner Football Team for a job well-done!

'The Boy and The River
That Saved His Life'

A little boy got lost in a dangerous 'Paradox of Life.' He had no vision or map to find his way out. He was in great danger and needed help finding his way to safety.

During the boy's escaped through life, he ran across all sorts of dangerous predators that were determined to devour him. The little boy was gullible and unseasoned about life and the various traps that are lurking in life. Yet he left the only world he knew with the hopes of finding a new world and a new life.

However, during his travel, the little boy ran into an old man that gave him some wise advice about a life sustaining river. The old man told the little boy that if he could find this particular river then he could save his life from destruction. To the old man, the river possessed healing water.

You see the river was constantly occupied by waves and a current that filled the river with the joy of life. At the river, you can witness people coming and going with fun-filled fellowship, social activities, and compassion exploding in the atmosphere like the fourth of July. Also, all participants could find a personal map to enhance their own destinations in life.

For the little boy, Eastern Kentucky University was The River that helped saved his life and offered him a good destiny in the right direction. EKU became the safe-haven that has brought me and many other people a joy beyond measure! #GoBigE

Alvin E. Miller

Eastern Kentucky University Football
Top photo: Alvin at EKU Spring Football Banquet, 1980
Bottom photo: Alvin headed downfield for a touchdown

No one really knows the hurt, pain, shame, or suffering of a child until the child explodes
with some type of destructive action or deviate behavior, or when the child becomes
antisocial or withdraws to a life of isolation or depression. —Alvin E. Miller Sr.

Preface

The Horse: Last Chance is the true story of a little boy who was granted a second chance in life to beat the odds of destruction. From birth, this little boy inherited a losing hand dealt to him by the circumstances of poverty, illiteracy, racial segregation, and a host of other social ills that nearly terminated his existence. Alvin's unbalanced world, his dysfunctional family dynamics, and a racially segregated social structure cast a dark shadow over his life and future.

Early in Alvin's life, things seemed hopeless for the lad, to say the least. Yet by a stroke of faith and hope working together, Alvin was rescued by something much greater than luck. Compassion showed up at his middle school (Dan McCarty Middle School in Fort Pierce, Florida) in the form of his seventh-grade teacher, Mrs. Rita Watson-Johnson. Hope and compassion spread their wings of favor over the young life of Alvin by moving him from the chambers of shame and destruction to the halls of prosperity and the American dream.

The support of his mother, seventh-grade teacher, and middle-school principal, along with Alvin's drive and determination to change, were the ingredients working together to create a beautiful symphony of success. Mrs. Johnson was the engineer who created the environment that fostered the strong pillars of support Alvin needed to usher in his positive change in life from the shackles of shame and poverty to the world of liberation and opportunity.

Alvin realized he was on a journey that he thoroughly enjoyed. He knew his willingness to change his life from destruction to restoration was paramount. He was determined to make the best of the wonderful opportunity granted to him by Mrs. Rita Johnson and Mr. Nolan G. Skinner.

Alvin loved and enjoyed the new respect he was receiving, especially from people who had once looked down on him as a juvenile delinquent. He was determined not to compromise his new position on the social ladder within the Lincoln Park community. Alvin recognized his transformation was only because of his association with Mrs. Johnson, who was a very respected educator in the community.

Believe it or not, Alvin cared more about not letting Mrs. Johnson down than he did about receiving respect from the uppity so-called Negroes, educators, and people who had nothing but negative words and actions for him and his family. When people help rescue you from the dungeons and shackles of destruction, you must have the drive or determination to develop a sincere commitment of loyalty to them as you strive for success. Never allow disappointments to stand between you and them. Somewhere in his heart, Alvin knew this was his only shot at changing from nobody to somebody, and he could not destroy the only opportunity that would set him on the road to success.

The commitment of his seventh-grade teacher, Mrs. Rita Watson-Johnson, to Alvin's life brought the improvement he needed to excel in middle school, high school, and beyond. Mrs. Johnson's personal investment in Alvin's life could be witnessed at his extracurricular activities (football, basketball, track, and wrestling) from ninth grade through high school. She never missed a home football or basketball game. She even attended some of his away sporting events.

Mrs. Johnson was the catalyst who got Alvin marching in the right direction and to the right beat. It all started for Alvin during his final semester of seventh grade. He was less than a part-time student in middle school because his name stayed on the school's suspension list while he attended Dan McCarty Middle School in Fort Pierce, Florida.

Yet transformation was in the process of rejuvenating the life of a young boy who was laying the groundwork for a very disruptive future. Little did Alvin know, Mrs. Johnson had been put in his life to help him switch from the role of a pretender to the real McCoy for becoming a quality student where realism, genuineness, and honesty rule like a person's DNA. Even when Alvin attempted to put up a fight, Mrs. Johnson outwitted him. Since she was from the Desire Projects of New Orleans, Louisiana, she often reminded Alvin that if he ever tried to get physical with her, she would overpower him for her protection.

One might ask, how could a child overcome such overwhelming odds without self-destructing? *The Horse: Last Chance* answers some of the most interesting questions about how this lad changed and excelled, going from poverty to the enjoyment of the American Dream. Alvin beat the odds when so many other youth and adults in his neighborhood were not able to survive similar struggles. The ironic thing is, some of the people who did not make it out had a much better support system in their lives than Alvin did.

Some of Alvin's friends and heroes were overcome by the depredation of their own vicious lifestyles and environments. Today, Alvin lives to tell the story of his survival by giving vivid illustrations of how he crossed the finish line while others were disqualified in the race of life. His thrill of victory was a team effort by some unselfish community servants who decided to give helping hands to a boy who was in dire need of a breakthrough in life.

If it had not been for the help of Mrs. Johnson, more than likely, Alvin would have been expelled from middle school. If Alvin had been expelled from middle school, more than likely he would not have made it very far in life. For Alvin, it was a hard journey during his climb to the top of the mountain of transformation. He could have easily been a loser, or in prison, or sitting on death row, or resting in a grave.

The benefits that came with victory made the entire struggle an appreciated event in Alvin's life. When he looked back over the road and saw the mountain of victories versus the hills of disappointments, Alvin said it was a worthwhile and exciting trip for him. His upbringing had equipped him to survive and maneuver in almost any civilized environment known to humanity, to include the ghetto or the hood.

Just think about this picture: While Alvin's life was spiraling out of control during middle school, out of nowhere, Alvin was given an unbelievable gift of hope and restoration by his seventh-grade teacher. He was given one last chance to prove his worth in life by an African American female teacher and a Caucasian male principal. Dr. Nolan G. Skinner had been in the process of preparing Alvin's expulsion packet from the St. Lucie County Public School System. With this second chance, Alvin had to learn how to navigate and carefully chart his survival in a world that at times could be as swift and poisonousness as a venomous snake.

Alvin's adolescent environment in various migrant labor camps was at times like living in a dog-eat-dog world. In Alvin's mind, his fate on the vicious road he was traveling was anxiously waiting to rip him to pieces like a Florida gator destroying its prey. As a boy, Alvin feared drowning or being eaten by an alligator as he swam in the deadly canals of Florida.

As a lad, Alvin often visualized his wayward life as the hopeless scene of an alligator devouring its prey in the unmerciful, brackish water of Florida. Alvin believed that his time as a tyrant was about to run its course without a good ending. Yet he felt powerless against the current of time, like some young boys who were consumed by the ocean and canal currents.

Alvin lived a major portion of his childhood in a box of deception, believing his street savvy would be strong enough to save him from destruction. As a juvenile growing up in public housing (the projects), and with his experience living in some of the most poverty-stricken migrant labor camps on the east coast of the United States, Alvin learned some of the basic trades of entrepreneurship within the red-light district that was located in the migrant labor camps and his hometown.

When Alvin was a child in the 1960s and early 1970s, migrant labor camps were no place for a child who was not under the parental supervision of disciplined adults. No place in the camp was safe for children who had been tricked into thinking they could live life as adults. Migrant labor camps had their share of dysfunctional people as well as other things like some of the machinery, rules of operation, and the strange caste systems amongst the workers.

When a person becomes a victim or a student of the street life, especially when it is no fault of the person, such knowledge can become a two-edged sword for the person's survival. One's wits about the street life could either causes one's demise or save one's life, depending on what one was seeking in life. My advice to anyone reading this book is to always choose life over destruction. Choose right over wrong. Choose good over bad. Choose togetherness over separation. Choose love over hate.

Alvin lived his childhood in an economically depressed environment in the northern part of St. Lucie County, Florida. At that time, there were few opportunities that offered hope for a positive future for poor African American kids. Children without parental supervision and support often stayed in trouble with the law and school officials. Alvin was one of those kids.

In retrospect, Alvin believes his upbringing allowed him to encounter the dangers of a jungle-like environment. He believes he lived out the survival of the fittest from Charles Darwin's theory of evolution. He believes his struggles as a deviant child back in the 1970s and 1960s is still relevant today for the African American child growing up in Northern Fort Pierce, Florida (the Lincoln Park community).

In order to escape the drugs, crime, and poverty of any city across America, one has to have the determination and commitment to excel above the degradation of one's community or situation. Regardless of the obstacles that may get in one's way, one must have a made-up mind to strive to win the battle against all odds. Believe it or not, I have known very few people who were able to leave the tomato fields, orange groves, and potato fields as hand laborers (pickers) and climb to the middle class of the socio-economic ladder in America.

In 2016, Fort Pierce was listed as one of the deadliest and most crime-ridden cities in the state of Florida and the nation. Crime data collected by the FBI, Florida Department of Law Enforcement, Fort Pierce Police Department, and St. Lucie County Sheriff, as reported by neighborhoodscout.com and homesecurityshield.com in 2014 and 2015, revealed that Fort Pierce was ranked among the top ten most dangerous towns in the state of Florida. Yet today, Fort Pierce is one of the most desired cities to live in throughout the state of Florida. A recent report classified Fort Pierce as one of the best-kept secrets in Florida and the nation.

A group of concerned citizens from Fort Pierce and St. Lucie County called Restoring the Village have added to the area's success. Local citizens across Fort Pierce and St. Lucie County are working together to restore the fiber of compassion for neighbors, improve the physical appearance of the neighborhood, provide educational training and information to eradicate crime, provide community service opportunities for youth and willing adults, revitalize existing structures, and improve horticulture ventures within the Lincoln Park community and across Fort Pierce.

The citizens are very excited about working together to make positive changes in Fort Pierce and the Lincoln Park community. Organized by former State Rep. Larry Lee Jr., Restoring the Village has galvanized people from across the county to take a significant bite out of crime, illiteracy, and the pain of shame and embarrassment by providing alternative solutions for the youth to keep them out of trouble and away from drugs, criminal activities, and other deterrents that kill people's hope while they fight to repair their own dysfunctional worlds.

Restoring the Village is giving hope and excitement to the adults and youth of St. Lucie County, Florida. The group is providing the youth with job training and other programs that are improving their education and social skills. Such investment in the lives of our youth will guarantee them brighter futures, where dividends of success will welcome them into a world that will be one with a thriving economy.

Because of Restoring the Village, people across the community and throughout the nation are coming together and encouraging the village within northwest Fort Pierce to galvanize, return to the pride of its roots, and restore the awesomeness of the village many of the leaders and organizers have grown to cherish. Our efforts with Restoring the Village is to restore hope in the lives of people that may have lost hope, and to strengthen those who may need encouragement to push forward in order to 'keep hope alive!'

> *Any live pet is greater than a dead lion; because a dead lion can no longer eat, roar, hunt, or rule! Do good in life while you have time! —Alvin E. Miller*

The Horse: Last Chance is a real-life story about how a middle school teacher saved a young person from destruction, with the cooperation of a single mother who did her best to make ends meet with her eight children in the house at the time. Oh, by the way, the name *'Horse'* was given to Alvin by one of his high school football teammates, Clint Melton. Clint said watching Alvin run the football was like watching a thoroughbred horse galloping with graceful strides as it ran. Also, Clint made mentioned of Alvin's *horse-like gallop* as he ran his quarter on the mile-relay track team at Fort Pierce Central High School under Coach Phil Farinella.

The team of Mrs. Johnson, Dr. Skinner, and Alvin's mother became a united front that refused to allow Alvin to become just another negative statistic. This dream team was determined to keep Alvin from becoming just another sad story about the incarceration or death of another African

American teen. Imagine what the world would be like if every child could have a '*dream team*' like the one Alvin had around the age of thirteen while in middle school at Dan McCarty Middle School in Fort Pierce, FL.

Over forty years later, it is amazing how a youth under the age of thirteen was able to get so far off-track in life. Yet with the cooperation of a small group of educators and his mother, Alvin was put on the right track to success. You never know what is in a child until you inspire that child with genuine compassion, and then you will know the true character of the person.

When children see the real you, they can make the decision to accept you or reject you. Adults, you cannot make children accept or love you, no matter how much you give them, what you buy for them, or to what extent you attempt to befriend them. Young people will oftentimes accept the real you before they contend with the counterfeit. When adults are transparent, set realistic standards and goals, and lead with compassion and conviction, children will consider it an honor to be led by them.

Even to this day, I am still baffled as to what would possess a child so young to acquire dysfunctional behavior in school toward teachers, administrators, and other students. What would motivate an adolescent boy to become so defiant against rules and laws? What possessed a little boy at the age of six years old to take it upon himself to not attend first grade at Garden City Elementary School for almost ninety days? Did someone or some system fail this minor? Or was all the responsibility solely on him to attend school?

Yet when the final bell rang, he was able to defy the odds by becoming an American soldier and defender of the poor and helpless. What an amazing testimony about the effect the American dream has on people's lives. The fact that somebody cared enough to get involved is what changed Alvin's life. Only within America can a child rise from the dungeons of despair while riding on a crash-course of destruction, and excel in the desert of life due to the help of a seventh-grade teacher.

On one end, it seems like someone or something failed Alvin. On the other end, a team of educational first-responders came together and recued Alvin from becoming a loser in life. When compassionate people become deliberate about investing in the lives of other people, especially our youth, it makes all the difference in the world.

It takes good and loving people moved by a power greater than them to help change bad people into good people. Not all people are good people; neither are all people bad. Sometimes we all may need help getting on the right road in life without being labeled as bad or lawless.

In retrospect, Alvin had been pushing the boundaries wherever he went for at least six years (age six to about thirteen) by failing to adhere to various school codes, community rules, and state laws. By this point, Alvin's forecasted future looked dim at best. Many of his teachers and people in the community predicted a destructive end for Alvin if he did not change his reckless behavior. He was constantly told by adults that he would not live to see the age of twenty-one.

The people around Alvin knew he was paving the road for his demise, but very little was done to help him. According to various verbal assessments and testimonies by educators, social service workers, law-enforcement officers, and community members, Alvin was a prime candidate for the school-to-prisons pipeline. It appeared that Alvin's ticket had already been punched for the pipeline, and judging from the opinions of others, time was not on his side.

However, Alvin never showed up for the pipeline roll call. In the minds of some people, his name was on their shortlist for most undesirable, but he never took his place there. The educational dream team changed Alvin's direction from destruction to restoration, and a destination that guaranteed an abundance of wonderful opportunities. The new direction given to Alvin caused him to answer a totally different kind of roll call filled with all kinds of success.

The handwriting of Alvin's destruction seemed to be plastered on the wall of time in gigantic letters that read *Wasted Potential That Could Have Done Great Things Died Here!*" It was known across the Fort Pierce Community that as a child, Alvin refused to obey the rules of life. Many people from across the Fort Pierce community had seen young males destroying their lives before they even got a chance to experience life.

When our youth believe there's more gratification in death than in life, this is more than a frightening experience. Today, we are witnessing more and more youth giving up on life and exchanging it for incarceration or death. These young people have concluded that death by suicide is a way out for them. To lose young lives in such a disheartening manner is one of the most devastating tragedies our society and humanity are witnessing.

As we reflect on the rising suicide rate among our youth, it is evident that we are in a crisis. It seems like with each passing year, we are spending more time trying to prevent our youth from killing themselves rather than spending quality time with them at fun-filled events. There is something seriously wrong when families are spending enormous hours of the day in crisis mode rather than enjoying quality family time with each other. Families are spending more time at hospitals, funeral homes, and cemeteries than at amusement parks.

Even today, our youth population is facing a very short life expectancy. It is a familiar tune that continues to play out like an old, scratched record. The actions and mind-set of deviant males like Alvin will more than likely cause them to end up in prison or on death row. In all actuality, it takes the commitment of the entire village to nurture and save a child from going down the wrong road in life.

In my opinion, as I glance at the social landscape of the inner cities of America, I am of the opinion that many inner-city youth will get caught up by a negative and reckless turbulence in the front end of their lives. Some will be unable to overcome the various pitfalls as they move through life. As concerned and compassionate adults, we need to encourage our young people by providing realistic hope and genuine support for them in a language and with a touch of love that they can see, interpret, feel, and benefit from.

As I previously stated, today we are living in a time where we need more caring adults than ever before. We need compassionate adults to step up to the plate and give more guidance, support, and hope to young people in distressed and desperate communities. Whatever the case may be, we all need to refocus beyond our own boxes in which we dwell.

We need heroes and heroines to take action and lend a helping hand to the millions who are drowning in the turbulent waters of life. One of the greatest tragedies for many of these youth is that they are drowning without any form of life jacket or boat to rescue them from the dangerous sea of life. The more positive help our youth are given, the better chance they have at succeeding in becoming victors, not victims.

In today's world, we probably see more children left to fend for themselves in various communities across America than ever before. When babies become mothers and fathers as teenagers, and uneducated mothers and fathers continue to bring babies into the world without proper guidance, then community organizations, government agencies, social service organizations, and religious communities need to start networking with each other for solutions as to how to bring compassion, guidance, and direction to the crisis of babies having babies. If America is to save its youth from illegal drugs, heinous crimes, and other social ills, concerned organizations need to start pulling their resources together to avoid a national epidemic.

As concerned adults, we must do a better job of expressing the true meaning of compassion to our youth. It is paramount for the youth to know the adults in their lives truly love them regardless of their personal situation or issues, etc. Compassion is a principle that is innate in most human beings, and it is acquired by the observation of those looking on, directly or indirectly. Young people must be able to see, feel, touch, and taste compassion; its purpose must always be authentic and beneficial.

Always remember that love is more contagious than a serious case of the flu. We must be willing to share the extraordinary benefits of love with others, especially our youth! Alvin was shown love, and it is the same compassion that saved him from the claws of destruction. I guarantee you that compassion will work with precision within the environment or person you desire to help transform as a benefit to humanity.

Compassion will work nearly every time when you share it with others. People respond in a greater way to compassion than they do to hate. Throughout my life, I have observed that people respond aggressively against those who display an unconcerned disposition toward them, their needs, and other people seeking respect and love.

If children do not witness compassion, then how can they be expected to duplicate it? For our young people to understand the concept of real compassion, the youth must be overwhelmed with acts of compassion by caring and loving adults. With good examples of expressed love that is visual and felt by the recipient, youth can model the same type of behavior as they develop into caring and compassionate adults.

Believe it or not, many neighborhood citizens in the Lincoln Park community and educators in the St. Lucie County Public School District were convinced Alvin would end up in prison. Some even thought he would end up on death row or worse—in a grave in a Fort Pierce Cemetery. Even when other people give up on you, you must remain focused and keep your eyes on the prize of success. Never allow failure to become your brand in life.

Over the years, Alvin learned that the opinions of others will vary depending on how they feel. Yet a person must continue to strive for success regardless of what the situation looks like or what the critics forecast about one's destiny.

The power to excel is in you. Faith was put in you long before the world came into existence. You must allow your wings to spread so you can rise to the highest mountain. Believe it or not, you control your destiny in life—not your problems, circumstances, or enemies.

Trust me on this: one thing other people do not have in their possession is the power to control your destiny, especially if you decide your positive actions will set the groundwork for your destiny in life. Your destiny is the part of life that belongs to you. Other people can help you, but ultimately, you are in control. So whatever happens in life, you must learn to stay in the saddle and ride that horse until you reach your positive goal.

With the help of his middle school teacher, the hope of a middle school principal, and the unselfish support of his mother, Alvin excelled to a level that was beyond anyone's wildest imagination or dream. Alvin beat the odds that are today destroying the lives of many of the youth across America.

Young people must learn to dream of a world that is beyond the disappointments, pains, and pitfalls that are invading and ravaging their lives. They must be able to stay focused on a place of hope that is much better than their current world of pain and disappointment. If they do not have the drive or determination to rise above the chaos in their current condition, then more than likely those distractions will end up as their greatest defeat. Yet failure does not have to be the final or only end.

As painful as it may seem, if young people are ever going to make it out of their deplorable conditions, they have to dream of a world beyond the things that shackle their minds. If young people—whether rich, middle class, or poor—do not dream beyond their current conditions and world, they will become stagnated by lost dreams and lackadaisical fantasies.

When inner-city especially kids cannot dream about a better world, their doubt and lost hope encourage them to commit serious crimes as a way to survive or get out of the hood.

In retrospect, no one saw what was coming with Alvin's out-of-control juvenile life until it was almost too late. It was like being trapped by an enemy's attack, and there was no way out except death. Yet all of a sudden, out of nowhere, the cavalry showed up and rescued him. What looked like a total loss ended up becoming a victory. This is why it is so important not to ever allow your frustration or situation to force you to give up.

The cavalry will show up and give you a reprieve from a death sentence due to an unfortunate situation. Even to this day, people are baffled and still in disbelief at how a defeated loser could turn his life from destruction to success. The cavalry and Alvin's changed attitude helped him to excel to a level that was beyond the imagination and expectations of people who had counted Alvin out.

Alvin Miller is more than grateful for the opportunity or final chance to prove his self-worth. He is overwhelmed with joy for those who invested so much in keeping him out of trouble and alive. Even to this day, Alvin continues to praise his support team that refused to let him drown in the turbulent waters of life. He believes more youth need a support team similar to the one that helped guide his life in the right direction.

Alvin Miller coming out of the backfield against an opposing football team
Eastern Kentucky University Football
#EKUCOLONELNATION

Everything that looks good to the eyes is not always what is best for the soul. Everything that tastes good to the lips and tongue is not always good for the stomach. Everything that feels good to the body and seems right to the crowd is not always good for your destiny.—Alvin Miller

Eastern Kentucky University Football: Alvin "Horse" Miller hands football to referee after scoring a touchdown. #COLONELPRIDE

You have to step out of your box if you want to see, hear, and grow beyond the walls that control your world.—Alvin E. Miller

Special Acknowledgments

A Salute to …

I would like to salute two big brothers and my dearest childhood friend, who remains one of my nonbiological brothers and friends even to this day. I will discuss each of these young men and their positive impact on my life later in the book. Each continues to play a major role in my life. It is a wonderful asset to have wise women and men come into your life during all stages of your human development. Being accountable to responsible people is one of the greatest gifts of humility and can help people stay out of trouble as they journey through life.

Terry Roosevelt Miller, Larry "Bumpy" Lee Jr., and Jerome "JR" Rhyant helped guide me on my journey to manhood when I was dumb, deaf, blind, and lost in the wilderness of life. These men personally poured into my life so I could live and not die. They became my lifeline during some of the darkest moments of my life. They earned the right to be called my brothers.

Moreover, these men walked with me during times when I did not have the energy or the strength to stand. They refused to allow me to fall by the side of the road. Gentlemen, thank you for being true friends of faith and hope. Thank you for believing in me when I couldn't see my way through some of the darkest clouds and storms of my life.

I have made so many mistakes that I cannot begin to count them. Yet I have been shown so much grace and mercy by the judicial system and life itself. I know I should have been dead like many of my friends and classmates, but Old Man Time had a better plan for my life, and I am most thankful.

In Honor of …

Omega Men of Omega Psi Phi Fraternity, Inc.

Mr. James A. McNeil (deceased), Mr. Arthur T. Johnson Jr. (deceased), Mr. Samuel Gaines, Mr. John Townsend (deceased), Jimmie Johnson, and Harry Belafonte Williams made a significant impact in my life from the days of my youth through adulthood. I am compelled to salute them for the compassion, instruction, and direction they showed me during my life.

I must give a shout-out to my "Battle Buddy," Mr. Rufus Curry Jr.; Brother Charles "Tommy" Walker of Lexington, Kentucky; and Brother Tommie "Tuda" Robinson for making good brothers for the Omega Journey through life. I also want to personally thank all the true soldiers of Omega Psi Phi Fraternity, Inc., from the Delta Sigma Chapter at Eastern Kentucky University for making me the Omega Man I am today.

Finally, I give honor to Dr. Allen L. Malone of Huachuca City, Arizona, for the fatherly love and advice he has given me over the years. Although he was not in my life during my upbringing, he has added so much compassion and guidance to my life as an adult that it would be unjust to not to mention him and his wife. I met Dr. Malone and his wife, Martha, while at a dark place in my life in the Arizona desert. They both breathed life back into me. They gave me the strength and encouragement to run the race of faith and hope.

Dominique Haywood Miller

My wife, Dominique Haywood, has added so much to my life. She continues to be my foundation and encourages me on every end. When I am tired, she sparks energy in me that forces me to go into overdrive to complete the task at hand with jubilation and victory.

She encouraged me to write my life story when I became tired. She picked me up when I could not get up on my own. She is the motivation who helped me get out of the boat and walk on water. I pen this manuscript knowing your love for me is a genuine love until death do us apart. You have been more than a great inspiration to me, and I love you, and that is forever. Thank you very much for your support.

Michael Campbell

Michael Campbell was one of my dearest friends when I was around eight or nine years old. For ten to twelve months, we hung out with each other nearly every day. When I tell you Michael Campbell took care of me like his little brother, I would be making an understatement. Sometimes when his parents would go to sleep, especially on the weekends, Michael would sneak me into the house to feed me and let me spend the night.

Yes, Michael treated me like a little brother, and I love him like a big brother. I always thought of Michael Campbell as my guardian angel who watched over me during a very rough time in my life. He was a very compassionate person who stood up for an underdog like me. Thank you, Michael Campbell!

Special Acknowledgement

To the Eastern Kentucky University library archives, where all of the Colonel Nation Football photos were discovered for publishing.

Thank You!

#COLONELNATION

Remember to bring others across the finish line with you, so everyone can enjoy the celebration of victory together!—Alvin E. Miller

Special thanks to:

Ashley Thacker of the EKU special collections and archives department, thank you for researching university football photos. Deacon Brian Hayes and Trustee Shawntai Riley, a shout-out goes to both of you for helping me to navigate in the world Excel spreadsheets and Microsoft Word documents

Brian Hayes, I salute you in particular for being chosen as the most valuable player (MVP) of this entire project! You are the man of the hour who helped me, supported me regardless of the mission, and told me the impossible was within hand's reach. You made the impossible simple. You made my hard computer language understandable, or shall I say, translatable. Brian, thank you for helping me with my Google Drive link for the book! Without your support, this book would probably still be on a computer screen. Again, thank you for all you do for me and the mission that I have the oversight to mend.

My Biological Siblings from Elizabeth Miller Side of the Family, from Oldest to Youngest

Gary Jerome Miller (deceased)
*

Ruthie Mae Purdue
Gene Miller (deceased)
James Edward Miller
Michel Lee Avant
Tamie Elizabeth Miller
Charles Franklin Salem, III
Fredinard Leon Salem (deceased)
Robert Bradley Miller

*Alvin, second oldest child of ten

Introduction

I liken myself to the protagonist in Robert Frost's famous 1916 poem entitled "The Road Not Taken." I stood at the edge of a divided road in life without any inclination of what to do. I was around thirteen years old when it dawned on me that I was deeply lost. To make matters worse, I was traveling without a road map that could possibly lead me to a safe haven.

Yes, I stood at the fork of a divided road in life. I did not know which way to go. *Wrongness* was speaking to my mind, telling me to follow its direction where so many of my friends were traveling. On the other hand, *doing right* was speaking to my heart and pleading with me to following its narrow directional path.

All I can say is whenever your small and ignorant bank of knowledge as a child is polluted by immoral and bad examples, and a heart of disobedience, you probably will end up like me. I was always in trouble with the law and school officials when I was in elementary and middle school. Many of the bad choices I made early in life had a lot to do with my rebellious spirit, which partly derived from my interpersonal hurt, shame, and embarrassment.

As a lad, I had limited understanding and intellectual training, and a scarce list of examples I could draw from in terms of doing the right thing in life. It is a very difficult task to walk and find your way in the dark without the proper instrument to guide you. I was attempting to walk in darkness without an instrument that could give me light. I thought I knew my way, while all the time I was lost.

My constant rebellion as a juvenile nearly bankrupted me when it came to doing the right thing in life. The best thing about my life when I was in the seventh grade was that there were enough people willing to give me one last chance to make good in life, even after failing to produce good fruit. They not only gave me the opportunity to correct the wrong way

I was traveling but also gave me an opportunity to acquire success that I just could not refuse.

My super-team gave me the help I needed to change my wayward thinking and destructive behavior. They gave me the chance to jump-start my life. They gave me the opportunity to transition from bad to good. They allowed me to see a vision I had never glimpsed. Oh my, what a beautiful sight to behold. I received a vision that I could become the change agent I had dreamed about when I was running around the world without light, inspiration, discipline, and self-respect.

They offered me a golden token to walk on the streets of respect rather than live on the frail streets of disrespect and humiliation. All I can say is, I am so glad Mrs. Johnson came into the lives of me and my mom at the right time. Mrs. Johnson's unselfish investment helped me change my life from a waste dump to an oasis of productivity while living in the desert of poverty. One of my brothers told Mrs. Johnson that he wished she could have helped him like she helped me, because he would not have gotten entangled in a life of confusion and disappointment.

One teacher's *yes* response to help a child in need changed the world for this one child and motivated others to see that there is a light at the end of the tunnel if you want success bad enough. A compassionate teacher saying *yes* when she could have easily said *no* changed and reshaped my entire life and the lives of those I have embraced over the years.

My transformative life from misery to joy is one of the greatest fulfillments and thrills I have ever felt. Mrs. Johnson stepping up to the plate helped change my mother's life as well as mine. I have been able to become a beacon of hope for family members and other people to use as a positive example of how to beat the odds when the deck is stacked against you.

For the most part, my childhood was like a dead battery in a vehicle that will not start. No matter how many times I turned the key in my mind for a fresh start, I could not start it. Because of my inability to jump-start my engine to do right, many people had the attitude that since I was a dead battery and did not have enough strength in the battery to change, then in the life of the vehicle (community), I needed to be discarded and put off into a controlled environment (juvenile detention or reformatory school).

Yet there was this particular group of three people who came to my defense and said, "Do not discard this battery to the vultures of life." Mrs. Johnson and Dr. Skinner saw the glimpse of hope in me that I was unable to see. Dr. Nolan Skinner saw that the battery only needed a jump or boost from a live battery, so he put me in Mrs. Johnson's class until he could finish an administrative task. Mrs. Rita Johnson was the live battery that the cables attached to my nearly dead battery. Rita Johnson, Nolan Skinner, and Elizabeth Miller became the cells in the battery that brought energy to my barren life at the time. I am forever thankful to such a wonderful and awesome dream team.

At first, I refused to humble myself and allow someone to lead me in the right direction. I was torn between the two roads until I began to see things more clearly after meeting my seventh-grade teacher, Mrs. Rita Marie Watson-Johnson. As I zoomed in and took notice of the people traveling on each of the roads as they came and went, I noticed the reactions and behavior of people depended on which road they were traveling: the road on the right or the road on the left.

I learned that a one's directional travel was somewhat connected to one's attitude and overall disposition toward others. It had a lot to do with determining the various rewards or punishment one achieves during one's journey in life. People who tended to travel the road on the right seemed to end up with an abundance of accolades and joy.

I noticed that among the huge crowds of people going down the road on the left, some were holding up signs that read *It's All About Me* and *Living for the Moment* and *Do It Your Own Way If It Makes You Happy!* As I examined the road on the left more closely, there seemed to be lots of noise coming from that direction. It sounded like confusion in the atmosphere. I never could understand what the people were saying to each other as they shouted out.

The air around the road on the left was filled with the smell of death, like an unkempt cemetery where the stench of dead corpses permeated the atmosphere. But it had some good-sounding music, many fun-looking props/floats, and enough attractions to keep people busy and amused for a lifetime. It was like a grand tour of a phony fun world with all sorts of games, rides, tricks, and laughter from the initial glance.

My first impulse was to take the road on the left. I noticed some of my friends traveling on it, and they seemed to be having lots of fun. Yet it dawned on me that they were wearing masks. Underneath the masks, I could see how unhappy and depressed they were while riding and playing the game of life. I asked myself, *Am I already traveling the road on the left? Or am I at a standstill at the place where the two roads divide?*

One thing was for sure: I was too afraid to make a drastic decision without some deep and sincere thought. I knew I had to make the right choice or else end up as a lost dream. While standing there gazing at the future, I became very nervous, and a breeze of fear came over me. I felt like my foundation was shaking.

Fear and Confusion came over me and attempted to bully me. Fear told me to take the road I was accustomed to traveling, because I knew that way so well. Then one of Fear's best friends, Doubt, jumped on my neck to strong-arm me into bowing down to the ground. As I wrestled with Doubt, he told me that if I decided to take a new direction in life, it would not work for me. Doubt assured me that if I made the decision not to go left, I was going to lose my friends and the false sense of clout that came with them.

Yet in the midst of my nervousness, I knew that whatever was not working for me was not going to ever work for me. I was just spinning my wheel and getting nowhere in life. I knew a change was knocking at my door, like when Old Man Winter knocks on the door of the fall season. The knock for positive change in my life came like it was sending me a message that it was my last opportunity to turn in the right direction.

I sensed that the game clock was about to run out and the buzzer was about to ring. I knew I had pulled the last straw. I needed to decide what I was going to do about the storm that was headed my way. At the moment of truth, I knew that if I did not hurry up and make the decision to change my destructive ways, life would end up cashing in my lot forever.

My friends and I would often talk about how dysfunctional our lives were as children. It's like we were in a make-believe world without a care or concern for doing what was right and correct. We would be walking along the dirt roads of Fort Pierce, and we would pick up a wooden stick and start playing this game called the magician (made up by the group), as though we had some magical powers to make things appear and disappear out of thin air.

To some degree, we knew our lives were different, but we did not fully comprehend how poor and dysfunctional we were at the time. We were miserable with our young lives, but we did not know where to start with rectifying our problems. It's like we were being attacked and stung by a swarm of bees, yet we could not figure out which way to turn to defend ourselves or ask for help. When a community rejects and neglects its most vulnerable citizens (youth, senior citizens, disabled, and needy), if it is not careful, it will create an unbalanced caste system where the haves get more and the have nots get less.

We did not have the training, experience, or skills to diagnose our official state of mind or the symptoms of trauma or depression. I believe we were experiencing some type of PTSD; the shame and embarrassment of growing up in poverty took its toll on our young lives. We were living in a nightmare that we could not wake up from no matter what we pretended or attempted to do. The more we fought to wake up and run away, the harder the culprit called Failure would fight to drag us back down.

Somehow or some way, we knew we needed to change our ways if we had any chance of experiencing better lives. We agreed we all wanted better lives than our parents', but none of us knew how to go about acquiring a better life for ourselves. It was very frustrating knowing something was wrong but not having the necessary tools or power to diagnose the problem and establish a plan of action to rectify, repair, or fix it.

As I stood at the crossroads of life, I reflected over my own existence. I even attempted to put together some of the foggy mental pieces of my own destiny; but because of the lack of wisdom and knowledge, I was unable to do so. I knew that if I did not make the right decision concerning which road to travel, my life would continue in the wrong direction. The crucial decision for me was to change or self-destruct. I so desperately wanted to live and not die.

I remember some of the arguments I'd had with my friends about needing to change our ways before it was too late. We were like desperate little rats looking for cheese yet hoping we would not wander into the trap. I had this eerie feeling that time was running out on me, and I needed to make a positive change before destruction greeted me.

Not one of us had the guts to step outside of ourselves and connect the dots to our demise if we did not change soon. The urgency to make a positive change was pressing upon us, but our deviant behaviors were demanding we heed the cheers of an audience that was leading us to do wrong. Keep in mind, knowing what is right and doing what is right are a world apart. Many young people and adults have difficulty distinguishing the difference between the two simply because they both have the ability to come to you as a friend—yet only one (doing the right thing) is your friend.

None of us was bold enough nor had enough assurance to know the right steps to take in order to begin facilitating the positive change we needed in our lives. We were too afraid of the unknown to become good. No one wanted to be the first to break the ranks from the norms that we were accustomed to living. With the help of my seventh-grade teacher, Mrs. Rita M. Johnson, a few years later I was able to break ranks and pull away from the unstable ideology of the group for an American dream that I was totally unaware of at the time.

My neighborhood friends and I were traveling on the left side of the road, with no idea or care as to where the road would lead us. From some of the conversations on the left side of the road, it was obvious everyone was just traveling through life without any real purpose or destiny in mind. These were the kind of people who were willing to fit in wherever they could get in.

The people traveling on the left side of the road seemed to know they were lost and were not concerned about where they would end up. They had a nonchalant attitude about the direction they were traveling in as long as their physical needs were being met. They traveled as people with no urgency to get anywhere in a hurry. They were only on the journey for the enjoyment of the ride and to pass the time.

These people seemed not care where their ride would end up. This thought process seems very common in people who have no personal vision and no concept of their true purpose for living. They lack the motivation to excel in life for the betterment of themselves and humanity.

The travelers on the left side of the road seemed to live only for the moment. Based on their own conversations, they had no plans of what to do once the immediate moment was over. Watching the people on the left side of the road made me aware of the destructive path I was going down. I was not aware that the tragic image I was witnessing was a true reflection of the road my friends and I were on, wasting our young lives away on nothing. What a devastating tragedy for a group of misguided children!

Over the years, I have learned that people without direction and vision are like an airplane flying in a storm without proper navigational tools and equipment. No matter how you look at it, destruction is bound to happen sooner or later when a person is failing to follow rules that are safe, right, fair, just, and healthy for society's survival. Having vision and understanding helps makes it easier for a person to find direction and purpose in life. Every society should have a road map that is understandable, free of stumbling blocks, easy to access, easy to read, and a joyful destination when traveling by the rules and directions of the map.

A person with vision and goals has a targeted site of inspiration to consistently aim for as a landing pad. Having a clear picture of your purpose in life is part of the power source that allows a person to achieve mountaintop experiences and desired successes in life despite the odds or obstacles. Whatever intentions you have for your life, young or old, remember to always make realistic and achievable goals for yourself. Setting goals is one of the ways you can know for sure that you are taking the road less traveled.

While standing in the middle of the divided intersection, I began to examine my own life and the direction I was traveling. It seemed like for a split second, my own mortality flashed before my eyes. As the end of the flash was bringing me back to reality, I came to grips with the direction I was traveling with my youthful life. I realized I was lost in a world of chaos and desperately needed help to rescue me from destruction.

At the moment when the flash was ending, I began to realize that during my short life span, I had been traveling on the left side of the road with the rest of the wayward and lost people. I came to the conclusion that I needed to change my directional flow. Not only was I on the wrong side of the road, I was speeding in the wrong direction. I desired to get on the right side of the road so I could slow down, but I did not know how to make the correct transition without proper guidance and influence from someone who was willing to invest love.

As time passed, somewhere it dawned on me that I was one of the prime candidates for standing in line with the lonely and lost people. All of us standing in line seemed to be in search of something. Yet none of us had any clue as to what we were actually seeking to quench our thirst in life. Attempting to go somewhere but unsure where you are going is not a good way to live. I had a first-class seat on this particular train.

I became so convicted about my wayward life and the way I had lived as a reckless and disobedient child that I admitted I wanted to do better and make a positive change for myself. No longer did I want my life to slip down the drain of lost hope. A seed was planted in my heart for right, even though it may have been on a delayed timer.

I guess one of the beauties of life is that we are granted the ability to dream even if the dream never becomes reality. I was aware that I could not make the positive transition by myself. I needed help from a superhero if I was ever to move from the dungeons to a place of respect in life. I so badly wanted to change my life, but I could not let my friends know anything about my dreams or intended plan of action.

In the past, I experienced the same wishful thinking about getting on the right side of life, only to find myself on the short end of the stick. I needed outside help to save me from the path of destruction on which I was traveling. It's like I was recklessly driving a vehicle without a seat belt or any other safety mechanism to protect me from danger. I knew I was traveling in a danger zone at my own risk while believing it would be the other person getting hurt and not me.

After seeing the people on the left side of the road from the view of a spectator, I reached the conclusion that I needed to make a change to the right direction in my life. I knew if I stayed in my current position, I would continue on the downward spiral I was experiencing on a daily basis. I knew what needed to be done, but the question was, could I do it—and would I do it? The one thing for sure about my life is that I had to make a positive change in order to reap the dividends of joy rather than the pains of sorrow.

I noticed the road on my right side did not have as many travelers as the road on the left. There were no road signs or potholes on the right side of the road as there were on the left. The people traveling on the right side were not in a rushing frenzy like the people on the left. The road on the right seemed to be newly paved, and it had plenty of room for travelers to maneuver.

The most striking things about the people traveling on the right-hand side of the road: they were full of joyous laughter and they had contagious fellowship for each other. There seemed to be a common bond of respect and appreciation for fellow travelers as they conversed with one another. One could easily hear, see, and feel the compassion and peace the travelers on the road to the right had for each other.

The people on the right fellowshipped as though there was some great expectation at their awaited destinations. It was obvious that their journey gave them great excitement instead of dread. The vibes from the people's fellowship made the road seem to vibrate gently as the travelers moved along. It was a beautiful sight to behold.

As I stood at this pivotal point in my life, it seemed as though both time and life were breathing down my neck to make a decision about the direction in which I was going to travel. There I was, standing dead center between the two roads. I sensed my decision would be critical to my destiny as well as to the dreams and hopes I had often envisioned as a little boy. I knew which decision was best for me, but everything around me except my heart was telling me to continue traveling the road on the left with my friends.

It seemed like my mind was telling me I could not make the switch to the road on the right side of life. Yet my heart was saying to me, "You can do it!" In the end, I am so glad I decided to go with my heart.

In conclusion, all I can say is, I truly know I made the right decision. What about you? Which decision will you make to better your today and tomorrow? Although I did not know things would be so wonderful living on the right road, I am glad I decided to travel it.

I have no doubt that if I had continued traveling on the left side of life, I would not have had the opportunity of experiencing the great American dream. I am so happy I made the right decision to travel the road on the right side of life instead of the road on the wrong side. The choice I made back then was the best decision I had ever made in my life at the time. For the first time in my life, I began to feel the peace that comes along with following the right and narrow path.

PART ONE

The Beginning of the Journey

My Guardian Angel

I am more than grateful that my seventh-grade teacher, Mrs. Rita Marie Watson-Johnson, and my mother, Elizabeth Miller, partnered to save my life from the jaws of destruction. It was not by some dynamic military tactical plan that was strategized to the smallest detail. It was an agreement between my mom and Mrs. Johnson, who would become the most significant teacher to ever embrace my life.

Over my elementary academic career, many teachers had attempted to encourage me with words to get on the right and narrow path in life, but only one took the time to actively lead me there with personal examples. Mrs. Johnson's importance to my life and my mom's can never be fully told with mere words, a pen, and paper. Mrs. Johnson did more for me than any mother could have done for her own child. She treated me as if she had conceived, carried, and birthed me herself. Also, she nurtured and tutored me like a big sister caring for her younger brother.

Here is the bottom line: during my years in middle school and high school, Mrs. Johnson became my guardian angel. The genuineness of our relationship was no fly-by-night professional or business transaction between teacher and student. Neither was it a phenomenon that came and went, as it does in many fairy tales. All I can say is we continue to have conversations several times a week, and sometimes several times daily. She and my mother converse often as well.

Yes, nearly a half century later, we continue to encourage, support, and check on each other. During the latter years of our lives, it is a covenant representation that something awesome took place in the life of a young boy that would change his destiny forever. Mrs. Johnson became my superhero who helped save my life. My seventh-grade teacher came into my life for my benefit and to make sure I added to the betterment of humanity beyond anyone's wildest imagination.

* * *

When I was in elementary and middle school, I noticed how teachers and parents had a unique bond of respect for each other. Teachers, educators, and school administrators were community leaders who were given high places on the social spectrum and economic ladder within the local community. Many students admired their teachers so much that some became teachers themselves.

Teachers were in a covenant role; nearly everyone in the community appreciated and loved them for the inspirational role they played in the lives of young and older people. Teachers and educators were immortalized when I was in elementary school. For people like me who grew up without a television at home, our teachers and administrators were our superheroes. I grew up believing my educators were perfect—until one starting mistreating me.

Before we knew about Disney World, Mickey Mouse, Popeye the Sailor Man, Superman, Batman, or the Three Stooges, we knew of the compassion we had for our teachers. Also, the way our teachers and educators adored serving us was second to none. Our teachers and educators were some of the most admired pillars in the community, especially within the African American community.

Teachers back in the 1960s, 1970s, and prior were what professional athletes and world-class entertainers are today. Teachers were the bedrock of the community and were treated as such. Back then, society recognized that communities could not survive and thrive without teachers and educators providing students with life-sustaining tools and skills.

Although I was very deviant in elementary and middle school, I still had a great deal of respect for nearly all my teachers, and other teachers I came across. Even with all the problems I encountered in elementary and middle school, I never attempted to hit or fight a teacher. I respected teachers. I believed teachers, ministers, and educators were some of the most covenant professionals in the communities where they lived, taught, worked, and served.

In retrospect, I even respected teachers who disrespected me. There were a few teachers and educators who reached out to help me when I was in elementary school, but I would not heed their call. I was too tied up in my ignorance and was not thinking about following the rules. I had no concept of learning and the purpose for going to school after my spirit was broken by this one particular teacher.

* * *

Over the years, I have learned the valuable lesson that it is better to follow the rules rather than violate them. Submitting to wholesome and quality leadership has been one of the many things that has helped save my life thus far. Remember to always extend compassionate respect to others; it could be the one thing that saves your life. There are some things we do not have the luxury or wealth to give to people, but everyone can give respect.

Respect is a simple and beautiful jewel we can give to other people without having to break our backs. Respect is very powerful and paramount to every situation because it becomes the foundation for genuine communication and relationships. People tend to thrive in environments where they are respected, regardless of the people, situation, or setting.

As I reflect on my life as a thirteen-year-old child, I can see that Mrs. Johnson and my mom had awesome respect for each other. My mom respected Mrs. Johnson's unselfish desire to help her raise and mentor her son, even though there was no bloodline relationship. Mrs. Johnson gave my mom the utmost respect, because she recognized that my mom was my mother, and anything less than respecting her would have been a moot point.

My mom respected Mrs. Johnson for helping her child get on the right road in life, and she trusted Mrs. Johnson enough to give her complete control over my life and my educational progress. It was a beautiful thing that my mom realized Mrs. Johnson had the ability to help me academically in ways my mom could not. My mother knew I was out of control, and Mrs. Johnson would become the mentor/teacher to help me get on the right side of the road in life—something I desperately needed.

My mother was wise and humble enough to admit that she could not help me connect to the future academically, socially, financially, or culturally. She understood my dire situation well enough to know it would be best for her to step back and allow me to move forward, even at the hands of another woman. To this day, I applaud my mother for her compassion, courage, respect, unselfishness, trust, faith, and humility to allow another woman to help her child turn away from the road of destruction.

My mom allowed this same woman to nurture and guide her second oldest child of nine living children at the time. Meeting Mrs. Johnson was like traveling a highway where some of the most successful crossroads intersected with incredible success. I call it the Wall Street of success. In retrospect, I must say, I thoroughly enjoyed the ride on the train to the city called Unlimited Success: the American dream!

Sometimes in life, we have to trust other people to do things we ourselves cannot do. My mother trusted Mrs. Johnson, and Mrs. Johnson made good on her commitment and promise. She led me in a direction that would be beneficial for everyone in my family, including my siblings and other relatives who came after me.

Some of my relatives were so inspired by my journey in life that they decided to follow in my footsteps with sports, military service, and education—all because of the decision of one teacher who lent a helping hand to help save a misguided youth. Instead of a dream killer, she became the dream maker.

The hope and trust my mother surrendered to Mrs. Johnson paid off with great dividends beyond anyone's imagination. Thank you, Momma, for your unselfish cooperation. I am so glad you did not become jealous or intimidated by the success you witnessed as Mrs. Johnson mentored me.

If you asked my mother today about the impact Mrs. Johnson had on my life, she would give all the credit to Mrs. Johnson. And Mrs. Johnson would turn around and give the credit to my mother for being unselfish and cooperative during the entire process. All I can say is my mom's trust in Mrs. Johnson was like the trust a mother or parent places in a surgeon who has to take the most precious life, a baby, into the operating room. In order to save the baby's life, the mother has to relinquish her fears and rely on trust, faith, and hope to help save a baby who is barely clinging to life. This is what my mother did for me with Mrs. Johnson.

Sometimes in life, we do not know how things will turn out. We have to put our trust and faith in people we do not know, such as when we ride on airplanes or elevators, or eat in restaurants without knowing or seeing the cook. Faith demands that we believe in people and things without knowing the outcome. Faith is trusting in a positive outcome without definitive proof that something will work or fulfill your needs.

* * *

Although much time has passed since my adolescent years, and many seasons have come and gone, there is much that remains unchanged. For example, several times during the year, we all get together, either for the holidays or vacation time, to reflect on the past and celebrate the great joys of today. When I travel to Fort Pierce for the restoring the Village community beautification projects, I always spend time with my mom and Mrs. Johnson.

Sometimes I stay at my mother's home, and sometimes at Mrs. Johnson's. Whenever I decide to stay with my mom, Mrs. Johnson comes over for fun and fellowship as we reminisce about my past. We have conversations about the various educators I encountered during my tenure as a student in the St. Lucie County public school district. We talk about how Mrs. Johnson came to every home game and some out-of-town games to watch me play high school football and basketball.

We also talked about how people believed I was not going to make it out of Fort Pierce, even with the help of Mrs. Johnson. Oh boy, were they wrong! Can you believe some people were waiting around for me to fall to the ground and die like Florida's mangos and oranges, which often fell to the ground and developed brown rot. It is a sad sight to witness good fruit going to waste.

Since my youthful days and years, many things have changed about my life, but there are things that remain the same even to this day. Our love, respect, and bond of compassion for each other remains stronger than ever. Though we find lots of humor as we reminisce about the past, we wish we could relive some of those wonderful moments in time. Yet we all are thankful for our lives in the present and continue to hope that the best is yet to come.

* * *

I am thankful for the opportunities that allowed me to become a "miraculous failure," according to Phil Coffin, staff writer for Louisville, Kentucky's *Courier Journal* newspaper on December 13, 1979, page 13 in the Sports section. Whenever good-hearted people gave me a second chance in life, I did not take the opportunity for granted. As people invested and poured into my life by giving me opportunities to excel in life, I did not take the offers lightly.

With each opportunity, I became more driven to succeed in life. It is wise for you to do the same by taking advantage of every opportunity that comes your way. Make it a part of your DNA that you do whatever you can to ensure you cross the finish line with a story of success, especially when others have invested so much into your life.

You must be willing to take the bull of opportunity by the horns and ride it all the way to success. Make something good happen in your life with every chance or break you are given. Even if you feel like you are not given breaks or opportunities, still rise above your current circumstances and make good things happen in your life, for you and others.

If you try hard enough for good things to happen in your life, good things will come your way. I am a living witness to this truth. In my youth, I wasted too much time focusing on the bad things about my life and not enough making use of the good things I inherited in my life as an American citizen.

Instead of getting angry and complaining about the things that I presumed were wrong in my life, I should have used the good things in my life as stepping-stones to success. I wasted too much time focusing on the bad things that were going on in my life. I challenge you to use the good things as stepping-stones for your life's journey and as symbols of opportunities to help you get to where you want to go in life. Whatever you desire to achieve in life, you cannot afford to dwell on your past failures. They will only hold you up in climbing to the top of the mountain as you excel in life.

Whenever the opportunity for good times presented a chance for us to come together to laugh and joke about some of the crazy things we did to each other and other people, we celebrated these moments. Some of the things I did in my childhood gave me no chance of surviving and excelling in life. Please remember, most people who give a negative forecast about your life do not really know your journey or story. Some people may know some things, but not the whole story.

Some of the people in your circle may not really understand the things you had to endure in your life. They have not been given the authority to serve as the commentators to dictate whether you succeed or fail in life. The odds of me surviving were so severely against me that only hope could save me.

This is why I challenge you to never allow anyone or thing to determine your destiny in life. I charge you to take every good opportunity that comes your way as a gift and a chance for you to succeed. You have to understand that you will either be your best friend or your worst enemy. Let faith, hope, perseverance, determination, and humility lead you to the well of success, where you will never have to thirst again. If I could do it, you most certainly can.

* * *

Keep in mind, your success in life is in your hands. Other people lend a helping hand, but unless you reach out and take hold of that hand, it cannot pull you to safety or success. Remember, your hands hold the key that opens the lock to your success.

Although others may play important roles in the progression of your success story, only you hold the match that can light the candle of fire for your successful journey in life. You must decide how you will use it. Others can only attempt to control your life from the outside. You must control the things in your life that you have the power and ability to control from the inside.

Don't forget: you are the best person to dictate your success in life. You are the person who is driving the bus to success. So please do not allow yourself to become a victim of the many voices around you. Become the victor instead of the victim as you journey through life.

I encourage you to follow the good voice that speaks within you from the depths of your soul. If you want good to come to you, you have to plant, water, and nurture the seeds of good from within you. Other people can give you seeds, but only you have the ability to plant them in good ground if you desire a good harvest.

Lock out the negative things that are disrupting and influencing your life. Do not be afraid to greet the faith and success that stand knocking at the door each day. Every day you are given life, it is a new chance for you to use it to either do good or bad. It's your choice, make the best of it! Take it to do good.

Doing good offers a rewarding feeling that is second to none. Always allow the good within you to reflect outwardly so you and other people can benefit from your good. Do everything within your power to remove anything that is a hindrance to your success. Sometimes when you have to remove people and things, it is painful, but keep in mind that this is a necessary pain for your growth and your entire destination of receiving a fulfilled life of happiness and joy.

Remember, doubt and fear are never friends of your success. You have to establish a partnership with faith and hope. Nothing moves without you first believing in yourself. If you never allow the good within you to embrace the people you encounter in life, you will continue to walk around in a delusional frame of mind.

You are the best promoter of your abilities and capabilities to move mountains, to cross rivers, and to walk through valleys in your life. Always market your wonderful qualities, gifts, talents, and compassion for humanity with overwhelming humility. Self-pity or a prideful spirit will continue knocking you down and keep holding you down until failure and destruction arrive on the scene to finish the job.

In retrospect, I am very much aware that during my time with Mrs. Johnson as my seventh-grade teacher and mentor, any weakness in this team effort between me, my mom, or Mrs. Johnson could have caused a breach of the covenant. Any such breach of trust and commitment could have decimated the entire effort to keep me out of the criminal justice system as a longtime resident. These women established a bond to ensure that I did not become a convicted felon or, worse, establish a permanent residence in a graveyard like many of the people I knew growing up in Fort Pierce. I salute my mom and Mrs. Johnson for their heroic actions.

* * *

As a juvenile in middle school, I felt like something evil was shaping my future. I knew the rough road my life was headed down would eventually bring me to a bad end. I had no doubt that I had begun descending downward from my short and bad trip to the incarceration tunnel within the juvenile penal system in the state of Florida. Deep down within me, I had the strangest feeling that the door of life was about to close on me. I knew I had to change my direction, but I just did not know how to do it. All I knew was that my time was running out.

During my heyday, when I failed to follow the rules, there was a voice within me that often reminded me that if I continued on the road I was traveling, my ending would not be good. I knew I was doing wrong, but I was controlled by a force that was a lot stronger than my willpower. This dark force was controlling my thought process and my drive to rebel.

Whenever I tried to go right, this force made me turn left and do wrong. Whenever I would say no, it overruled me and made me do wrong. It was like I was in a culture of wrongness, and for me to succeed at doing the right things in life, my mindset or culture had to change. As a child between the ages of six and thirteen years old, I was being controlled by a power much greater than my childish mind.

Somehow, I knew there would be some type of negative payback for my unruly behavior in school. I was well aware that I could not continue to violate laws and school rules and not suffer the consequences for my wrong actions. In my short life, I had become a disruption in school and within the neighborhood. I was causing a disturbance in the St. Lucie County public school district in the late 1960s and early 1970s. During my years in elementary school and middle school, my behavior became like a runaway train.

People began to avoid my path because I was a wreck waiting to happen. Outwardly, I did my best to forecast to others that I had no fear of the law or death. Yet I did not want to die. I so desperately wanted to be saved, but no one was willing to make the sacrifice to save me.

There was great fear inside me, like footsteps were chasing me as I ran for my life. I was only afraid of dying whenever I thought about it. So, what I tried to do to block my fear of getting killed was to not think about getting killed while I was doing unapproved things. I was totally oblivious to the Grim Reaper stalking my every move, waiting for the appropriate time to pounce on me like it did with many of my childhood friends.

During my childhood, I carried the feathers of shame and embarrassment in my heart. I grew up with a lot of internal pain and shame that I attempted to hide in a safe spot. Most of my embarrassment I tried to hide with pride, yet it continued to show itself as damaged scars of hurt and pain within me. As I said earlier, I spent too much time being bitter about a situation I had no power or control over.

* * *

It angered me to know I was conceived while my father (now deceased) was married to another woman. I walked around with a chip on my shoulder for many years because of the way I was brought into the world. Yet I had no vote or voice in the matter concerning my conception or birth. I just reported on site at the request of nature.

During my childhood, I felt like I was just another guilty bystander. It is a shameful thing for a man to look at you and have the audacity to tell you he is not your father when all of the physical evidence says otherwise. Prior to him becoming angry with my mother, he even admitted being my father. His story only changed when he became angry with her.

Yet when I started running touchdowns in middle and high school, he claimed ownership of me. He even attempted to persuade me to leave my mother and come live with him. One moment, you are disowned by your dad, and then the next moment, he attempts to have you move in with him. As a child, you wonder, what is behind his change of heart?

It seems like over the course of years, time creates a memory lapse for some people about my troubled childhood. Some either do not know about my bad past or have forgotten those terrible days when I lived as a student of disobedience and disruption and not as a gentleman of light. Yet there still remain people in my hometown who have not forgotten the days when I lived life as a delinquent juvenile. I am overjoyed by the second chance that wisdom granted me.

In retrospect, it was like I was under a dark cloud or some negative influence that was leading me in the wrong direction. As a child with a confused mind and a hurting heart, I was blind to the truth about life and the wonderful possibility that awaited me in the future if I did what was right. As a lad, I thought I was in control of my life, and I was going to live my life as I desired. So I thought at the time!

Today, I know I was just a miserable and unfulfilled child without hope, dreams, and goals. I have come to the knowledge that when people are unfulfilled, they become miserable. When they become miserable, they strive to make other people unhappy and miserable as well.

The old adage says, "Misery loves company." I have seen that when people hate or dislike you, they will do everything to tear you down and make you miserable. They will claim to know you, but they forget that you left that old you back in the dungeons of your past. Although they may still live in those old dungeons, you cannot ever allow them to drag you back in.

* * *

I am amazed that even as a juvenile, I knew I was on a destructive path. Yet I could do nothing on my own to stop the downward slide. I had fallen and could not get up on my own. This is one of the reasons why authentic relationships are so important. When you are about to fall or have fallen, real friends will be at your side to pick you up or rescue you.

I needed help from a source much greater than myself. I desperately needed help because I was chasing a false sense of gratification that did not exist. I needed help but did not have the willpower or knowledge to go about unifying or galvanizing the life-saving network I so desperately needed in order to restructure my life.

My alter ego kept convincing me that I lived in a world where foolish minds were in control. My Professor Ego, as I called him, told me all I needed to do to get my needs met was be slicker than the next person. Somewhere deep down in my heart, I did not want to become this type of person. Matter of fact, these so-called slick people were some of the people I despised as a youth. One day I asked myself, *Am I becoming what I hated?*

Somewhere deep in my heart, I felt like I was building a Trojan Horse that could only offer me a false sense of success. I somehow knew if I did not defeat this Trojan Horse, it would eventually bring me to a decision I would regret for the rest of my life—or it would end up costing me my life. Somehow, I knew the untamed monster I was dealing with was bad news for me. Yet I did not know how to subdue it. It was more than I could handle.

At this point, I felt like my life was a terrible nightmare. At best, it was similar to the reflection of a deadly accident that one may witness taking place in slow motion. You see the accident happening before your very eyes, but you are helpless. You cannot do anything to prevent the accident or help the people involved in it. You are at a loss with your lack of ability to intervene or help. It is a terrible feeling. You try to move out of the way and even yell for help to alert those in harm's way, but with all of your effort, the accident happens anyway. It's like you are a part of something but have no voice to help determine the outcome.

Because of your limited actions, people end up getting hurt, but you have no power or control to prevent the catastrophe. This is a very sad picture to have engraved in your mind, especially the mind of a youth. There are many young people who are carrying around so much grief, shame, hate, pain, embarrassment, hurt, and other psychological experiences that have caused a change to their entire personality. It is like their own experiences have decoded their DNA, causing them to become a totally different person in life.

Remember, all of the moving pieces of the accident happened too fast for your human sensors to respond or react to it. As the event was taking place, you were helpless to prevent it. The evolving process of the accident is similar to the way I was floating downstream in life without any type of life vest or support that would keep me from drowning in a lake of crime and foolishness.

* * *

From my first-grade school year all the way through the beginning of my second semester of seventh grade, I believed my life had been cursed to end in tragedy. I can vividly remember that as a student at Dan McCarty Middle School, I felt like my time was running out. Some days I became very nervous and fearful that the curtain was about to close on me before I could finish.

I kept all of this fear to myself and played it off by acting out with some type of disruption. I knew I was fighting a losing battle against time and the powerful legal system that had the ability to drop the hammer on my life in an instant. I kept lying to myself to the point that I started believing the lie that I was something more than I really was. I attempted to play the game of life, but in all actuality, I really did not know what to do or where to turn for genuine help or guidance.

There were times I wanted to change my life for the good, yet I felt like I was overtaken and ruled by this evil force. Today, I am convinced this force of disobedience was the driver behind my pride. This force I am referring to would entice me to fulfill the disruptive character that other students had encouraged me to display for them. Sometimes I did not want to fight or act out in a negative way; but the crowd that was watching and waiting for my disruption would have been disappointed if I did not put on a show for them. Yes, peer pressure almost got me expelled from middle school.

Sometimes I found myself wanting to be a normal student and obey the classroom rules, but the crowd was watching and demanded otherwise. Please never underestimate the power and influence of peer pressure. For children, peer pressure is like a two-edged sword with a dual purpose: to help or to harm.

Parents have to teach children to navigate around negative peer pressure in life. Parents are the first line of defense in teaching children to have good self-esteem. As parents, we must do everything within our power to teach our children how to resist negative peer pressure while accepting the positive peer pressure life has to offer.

Positive peer pressure serves as a check that brings a balance to the lives for our youth so they will stay on the right track. We must educate our children as to how to make positive peer pressure work for them and not allow peer pressure to force them to work on the behalf of the currents of negative peer pressure. The aim here is to always celebrate the children over the negative peer pressure they will encounter in life.

* * *

Although I was on a reckless course, I somehow knew I needed to get my life in order before it was too late. I was well aware I could have ended up incarcerated in a juvenile detention center, or gotten killed, or drowned in one of the gator-infested canals where we often went swimming. I knew we had no business swimming in the canals where alligators, water moccasins, and deadly currents threatened. It was out of sheer disobedience that we often played dangerously with death by swimming in the murky waters of Florida's deadly canals.

Our parents told us not to go swimming in the canals and creeks, but we did it anyway, without their consent. Some boys did not make it back home, including my oldest cousin, Jerry Miller, who drowned in the Taylor Creek/Header Canal Waterway back in 1959 or 1960. When Mr. Curtis Johnson Sr. rescued his body from the canal for burial, it was discovered that his undershirt had gotten caught on a branch at the bottom of the canal, which ended up trapping him underwater, where he drowned.

As renegade boys, the thrill of swimming in the canals was greater than the thought of being killed by a gator or drowning. Some of my neighborhood friends, my brothers, and I would sneak off and swim in the alligators' death holes (Headers Canal and Taylor Creek) against our mothers' directives and scolding. Probably like the boys who drowned, we never thought we would be the one eaten by an alligator or drowning.

We always thought if someone drowned or got eaten by a gator, it would be one of the other guys that the gator would get, not one of us. How foolish was our thinking back then! We were just too ignorant to know any better. We were blinded by our selfish and silly youthful thinking without any consciousness of right or wrong, life or death.

In retrospect, it seems like the more our parents and guardians told us not to go swimming in Taylor Creek or Headers Canal, the more we did it, risking everything for the thrill of the moment. During this particular time in my life, I felt helpless as far as my hopes of doing the right things. The desire to do wrong and the recognition by peers for doing wrong was too much for my mind to process while in elementary and middle school.

While in elementary school, to include sixth grade and three-fourths of seventh grade, I did not have the right support system, or exposure, or influence to pull it together. I just did not know how to become a model student/citizen within the community. The good examples of doing right in life were not bright lights within my immediate family. When children do not have good examples of impeccable moral standards, where are they to pull from when they are living the lives of truants and petty criminals?

Even when I wanted to do the right thing, something would take over and force me to do wrong. I often say to people, you never have to teach a child to do wrong, but you do have to constantly teach children to do the right things in life. Doing wrong seems to be innate, but doing right is a deliberate learning experience, where action speaks louder than words.

During childhood, my mother was always working in the orange or grapefruit groves or tomato fields, and later as a laborer at a tropical fish farm in Indian River County, Florida. On the nights when my mother came home from her day job, she would go right away to her night job as a waitress at Eddie's Bar and Lounge on Avenue D between 19th and 20th Street in Fort Pierce. Mommy had to work hard because she had no formal education beyond tenth grade, and no husband in the house to help her. The closest thing my mom had to a husband was the State of Florida welfare system.

At this particular time in my life, my mommy had about five children, all under the age of twelve, to feed and clothe. Without the help of my maternal grandmother, Leona Moore Miller, we would not have made it as far as we did as indigent children. My grandmother held down the fort for us and her other grandchildren. She was not a lady of many words, but she got the job done. When I was a little boy, my grandmother was the one who taught me how to hoe, rake, and plant a garden.

My grandmother even taught me how to water and nurture a garden. She was just a country girl from the fertile land of Georgia. From my perspective, the things my grandmother loved most were tending to her garden, baking, cooking, dipping her snuff (during the early years of my life), and playing her numbers. My mother is just like her when it comes to gardening. My mom is now eighty years old, and even to this day, you can find her spending the majority of her day working in her garden in Fort Pierce.

When a person is poverty-stricken and forced to grow up in government housing projects or dilapidated rental shacks or in migrant camps, believe me, you get very little or no respect from people who think they are much better than you and your family. We were so poverty-stricken that the poorest of the poor did not give us respect. Although my mommy did her best with the limited resources she had, it was Grandma who stepped in to help save the day for everyone.

My grandma was the MVP for the Miller, Moore, and Martin clan living in the Fort Pierce area. I can remember my grandmother making quilts with patches from various old clothing. I still can smell the aroma of the sweet potato pies and pound cakes she would bake. Sometimes I would be so close on Grandma in that little kitchen at 505 North 18th Street that she would nearly trip over me. She would yell, "Boy, get back—you almost made me trip over you!"

* * *

Alvin Miller Sr., D. Min.

As I look back over my childhood years, I realize we were in a terrible socio-economic condition, which created a mess for the entire family. It would take the power of a superhero to change the course of history for my mother and her children. Poverty by itself has the ability to scar the psyche of a child for life.

For me, being poor was one of the most devastating things I could encounter in life. It is probably the most embarrassing thing I have had to endure. I watched, heard, and felt the pain as people picked on and made fun of me, my mommy, and my brothers while we boys were growing up in Fort Pierce.

Poverty is a contagious disease that teaches and encourages a person's mind to continue perpetuating a culture of poverty. This process of shaping the mind to embrace poverty is a vicious cycle that goes on for generations. The cycle of poverty will continue to tantalize people until someone from within the family rises up and conquers the cycle of poverty from its roots. Once one defeats the poverty disease, one has to make sure the message of prosperity is passed on to other family members so they too can become liberated.

Although my mother could have abandoned us, she never did. She stayed and never complained about her predicament. My brothers and I gave my mother plenty of reasons to abandon ship and jump overboard; but she stayed onboard like a devoted captain of her vessel. She brought the ship safely to shore, even in the midst of tumultuous storms.

* * *

My life growing up was so difficult and painful that I find it very hard to write this book without tearing up. This has proven to be the most difficult writing assignment I have ever encountered. It is forcing me to deal with some of the issues and things I thought I had buried in the back pages of my mind.

Yes, I feel there is something in my life that could possibly help other people. I cannot help but think about the children who are dealing with some of the same issues I had to endure and deal with. One of the goals for writing my life story is to help our youth as well as adults overcome obstacles and hurdles similar to those I had to overcome. I am willing to become a sacrificial lamb, putting myself in a position of vulnerability just to save someone else's life. Other people put themselves in vulnerable positions to help save my life; therefore, I must be willing to return the favor by helping persons in need of good guidance and powerful encouragement.

The writing of this book proves I am willing to give back to the community in such a way that I become a stepping-stone for others to climb upon. I believe it would be a very selfish and an act of treason against humanity if I refused to give back when so many people have freely given themselves to me. People invested resources in me that I can never repay. I believe they would want me to pass on such liberating methods and techniques to others who could possibly be saved from their shackles.

Many of the things I went through as a child should be locked away so no other child has to encounter them. Although I wish I could share more, some things you just have to take to the grave with you. Only over the past few years have I gotten enough courage and strength to share some of the most private and venerable treasures I have to offer to others, especially youth.

My time in elementary and middle school was disastrous for me. Over the years, I have tried to block so many horrible experiences from my memory bank. Yet my memory chip will not allow me to erase the contents of the disk. I am convinced the reason I cannot erase the information is because maybe you are a person who will benefit from some of the things in this book about my life story.

* * *

While I was attending Dan McCarty Middle School, one day I began to daydream about being a person who people no longer looked down on. I was wishing to be smart like the other kids in my class. Yet knowing how to read with precision and work math problems like a miniature calculator seemed to be a distant dream for me. I wanted to speak with a command of the English language, as if my parents were educators or professionals, but I did not know how to make my verb and subject agree.

I wanted my mommy to attend PTA meetings, but it never happened; she was always at work. I wanted my daddy to take me fishing or hunting, but it never happened. I was disowned by my dad—until I started playing football in ninth grade. More than anything, I wanted my daddy to give me his name; but it never happened. My father and I never established a father-son relationship. It was more like two strangers sitting next to each other and having nothing to talk about while on this long train ride.

Me and my daddy had nothing in common except a bloodline connection without any value. I wish we could have had more in common, but he was only a small foggy glimpse in my past. I went to live with him (and my older sister Jennette) for a few weeks during the summer of 1973 or 1974. Other than this, our communication was in passing, like two strangers on the same airplane ride.

I knew I could not keep disrupting class and fighting in school without facing severe punishment for my actions. I felt like the hands of time were against me. I was out of control and on a very bad course in life. Something positive needed to happen in my life that was pretty much beyond my control. Sometimes I became my worst enemy when it looked like I was about to turn the corner on a good note.

Some days during my middle school tenure, I could feel the cold chill of devastation and destruction running down my neck and back. I was running in the shadow of fear to the point where it felt like I could hear the sound of a clock ticking in my ears. It was as if time was running out if I continued to travel in the wrong direction.

As I have stated, during elementary and middle school, my thoughts were not good, and my actions were not commendable. I was out of control, with no intention of changing direction on my own. My life was paving a path of confusion and turmoil from the age of six through thirteen.

Given the destructive road I was traveling, sooner or later I felt like fate was going to deal me a hand that would seal my downfall forever. I knew once this slick and unmerciful dealer dealt me my hand of devastation, I had to continue playing the game of life with the hand I was dealt. Of course, I was well aware of the fact that whatever the hand dealt to me, I deserved it. I knew I was the guilty one. Even the mirror on the wall with its dim reflection knew I was guilty.

You see, I realized it was me who sat down at the table to play the game of Russian roulette with my life. The rules of this game are cruel, vicious, and deadly. The rules love no one, regardless of age, gender, ethnicity, or nationality. Only a few people have lived to tell the story of triumph and how they became victors instead of victims after surviving the biggest gamble of their lives. I recognize that I am one of those persons who survived this most deadly gamble. I promise you that I will never again attempt to complete such a lethal journey. How I made it out is left up to fate.

Most people do not escape the deadly game of Russian roulette. I was aware that whatever cards I received in life at the time as a delinquent juvenile were the result of my actions. I knew I had to make a decision to play by the rules of the game or end up finding myself in a worse predicament. Time was running out on my misfortunes, and I needed to do something about redeeming the precious time I had lost in the wilderness of life. Deep down within me, I was searching for a way out of a world of destruction, but it seemed all doors were closed until the second semester of my seventh-grade year at Dan McCarty Middle School when I met Mrs. Rita M. Johnson.

In the year 1972, while I was in the seventh-grade, little did I know my entire life was about to make a dramatic shift in the right direction. The transition taking place would end up changing my life and world forever. It happened so fast that I did not have time to react to the positive changes that were occurring. She outplayed me in a game I thought I knew so well.

The transition rocked my world as I knew it. I was in a daze for three to six weeks after the abrupt change to my class schedule, which ended up rocking my entire life and world. The old adage that says "Ask and you shall receive" came true in my life. I had been asking for help and a way out of the life of destruction I was living. Believe me, change came sooner rather than later! Yes, the mail I had been requesting from life finally showed up in a certified envelope.

Prior to the spring of my seventh-grade year, I was used to handling things the reckless way I thought they should be handled. I did not believe in following the systematic rules of justice that most law-abiding citizens conformed to. Now, the question that convicted me was, *How do I respond to the good that is occurring in my life?* A transformation was in full swing, but at that time in my life, I had never heard the word *transformation*, and neither did I understand what it meant.

To me, it seemed like I was losing control of my little delinquent juvenile playhouse that I had lived in all through elementary school and most of middle school. I seemed to have no control over the things that were taking place in my life once the transformational process was in motion. I was caught up in a whirlwind that gave me very little choice as to the path I was traveling.

Moreover, I felt powerless, because deep down within the core of my soul, I wanted someone to come along and help me change from the negative direction my life was headed. I felt like a victim drowning in water while calling for help, but no one could hear me or was able to come to my rescue. Yet at the last hour, help arrived. So now, what would I do to embrace that help?

The world and culture I had come to know did not want to let me go from its destructive claws. Like a tick on an animal, *wrong* wanted to stay stuck on me. It had every intention of draining me of all things that gave me life. I had been one of trouble's most loyal and destructive subjects for at least six or seven years as a lad. I was somewhat afraid of letting go of the only life I had grown to know so very well.

It is amazing how fear tried to intimidate me into not pursuing a better life for myself. Fear told me I could not handle things and situations on the road to a positive change. Fear told me to turn around, because I was making the wrong choice at the crossroads of life. On the other hand, a small voice inside kept telling me, *You are headed in the right direction; do not turn around.*

It is like I was predestined to experience a transformation that would continue to mold and shape my life even to this day. When the initial change began to occur, many people could not believe what they were witnessing. Some began to make negative comments like, "It's only a matter of time before the old Alvin returns" or "This boy will never amount to anything" or "He is a waste of time like the other ones people tried to help."

Believe it or not, nearly fifty years later, some of the same people are still in awe of the positive strides I have taken in my life. No matter what I do in life or how far I have come, some people will never accept the success that has graciously embraced my life. Always remember that when people hate the good you do, they will never congratulate you for the victories you achieve. This is why it is important for you to love and appreciate yourself and the life you have been given as a jewel. Appreciate and celebrate yourself even if no one else celebrates you.

Sometimes I catch myself daydreaming and hoping that I will never wake up from the life I am currently living and enjoying. I would be the first to admit I love all the wonderful things occurring in my life, from the time I met Mrs. Johnson until today. Oftentimes, in the midst of daydreaming, I catch and remind myself that I am not dreaming but actually living in a world where people are celebrated for doing right in life.

The journey from poverty and juvenile delinquency to the American dream has been long and hard. My ride has been filled with joys that outweigh all of the stumbling blocks and setbacks that have occurred along my life's journey. I encourage anyone to make the decision to walk on the right side of life, because it pays great dividends, including the joy of hope.

* * *

I often say to myself, *Am I really living the American dream with joy and unlimited fulfillment?* I enjoy the place of tranquility where my change of attitude and positive dreams have brought me. I will take this kind of lifestyle any day over the potato and cucumber fields of Virginia, or over the apple and peach orchards of New York State, or over the rocky tomato fields of Pennsylvania, or over the orange, grapefruit, and lemon groves of Florida. Finally, I would take living the American dream over the green tomato fields of South Carolina near John's Island and Beaufort.

The conversation below is part of a response to a dialogue between myself and another child whose parents were migrant workers from the same Fort Pierce, Florida, where I grew up:

> "Hey, Lugger, you know the drill! Don't hold up my money! Come on and get my basket! You are taking too long! Hey Water-boy, bring me a drink of water." This is the sound of men and women working in the *matoe* or *madah* fields. "Are you picking by the day or piece? Are you paying 10 cents a basket or 15 cents? Are you paying $5 or $8 a day? Do you need a field-walker or a loader? What time will you leave the loading ground tomorrow morning?" You will know this language if you've been there. Portable what? Outhouse what? Child labor laws, what? Green tomato sandwich from some borrowed bread in the sweltering heat on those mile-long rows working

either bent over or on your knees from early morning to late, late in the afternoon, just before evening made its way home for the day.

We'd arrive back at the loading ground after sunset only to get up the next morning for work at around three or four in the morning to get ready for the loading ground and another field day experience all over again.

You say "child labor laws," and I say, "Where were they?" Because we didn't have them in the migrant labor camps where I lived in South Carolina, Virginia, Pennsylvania, and New York State. I had to work so hard in the vegetable fields and fruit groves because I had a permanent address on the suspension list prior to my high school days. With unyielding help from Mrs. Rita Marie Watson-Johnson and my mother working together as a team, the odds of me turning my life around became more evident than ever before. The teamwork between these two ladies was more than amazing, to say the least.

I often reflect on how other kids, parents, and adults made fun of me and my brothers during our elementary school days. Can you believe decent human beings would make fun of other people simply because they are too poor to afford adequate or so-called *decent* clothing for school? My mother worked very hard, but it was not enough to satisfy the demands of her family.

As I reminisce over some of my past hurt as a child, I will be the first to say maybe some of the laughing and picking from other people paid off in positive ways. Once I got my bearings and balance straight after the big letdown as a youth, the ridicule from others taught me how to excel when it came to achieving productive things in life. I became motivated by some of the painful hardships I experienced as a young child.

It was during my time as a migrant worker that I developed the belief that hard and honest work builds character. My experience as a migrant worker and living in migrant camps instill in me a great sense of pride and dedication to hard work. Once you learn the art of hard work, it is a lesson you will never forget. Good work ethic is a jewel of success no matter where you go in life. People all over the world have a great deal of respect for hard-working people regardless of their nationality or ethnicity.

Remember, as you excel in life from hard and honest work, you will pass by some of the same people who made fun of you, or looked down on you, or are forever looking for the easy and cheap way out of life. Always keep in mind that there is nothing cheap about success. I am honored that a country like America gave me an opportunity and another chance to grow up in a migrant town on the east coast of Florida called Fort Pierce, the Sunrise City.

Every day was not easy, but I am here by the goodwill of others who invested their time, unselfish energy, and personal resources into my life. Their investment encouraged me to see a better world beyond the dark shadow of my own world, which was phenomenal to say the least. My childhood story shows that when people and organizational systems within a community or culture work together for the good of youth, success is inevitable. As someone once said, "Teamwork makes the dream work!" This statement is a covenant oath in my life as I serve communities across the United States and throughout the world.

* * *

Children will excel in environments where positive energy, proactive actions, and the spirit of compassion embrace them. I salute the people (deceased and living) who poured into my life, whether it was positive or negative. All my past encounters were motivating factors that helped propel me to the next level of success.

My mother and Mrs. Rita Johnson banding together as a support team is an example of the commitment that gave me an opportunity to experience a much better life. The successful venture to transform me from a juvenile criminal to the rank of colonel in the United States Army was the teamwork of a community working together with my mother and Mrs. Johnson. I am more than grateful for the help of Mrs. Johnson and my mother. It is because of their devoted help that I did not end up as a negative statistic like many African American males coming from homes and environments similar to my upbringing.

In the environment where I grew up, many of the homes were operated by single-parent mothers who were not financially stable enough to provide for their children. Such an environment could be devastating to the self-esteem of children. Growing up in poverty was not a good feeling for me. When I realized how poor we were, it was very embarrassing.

It is very disheartening for a child when parents are not educationally equipped to help with homework. Growing up poor was no joke for me, especially when it seemed like nearly everyone outside the project housing development knew you were on social welfare and other governmental programs. Even other poor kids made fun of you when they found out you and your family needed governmental assistance to survive.

I lived through this humiliation and embarrassment with my mother and siblings. The entire process is part of the madness of many of the out-of-control children and adults in America today. Like me, their rage starts during childhood and becomes out of control during adulthood, a time when it is more than likely too late to try to intervene or rehabilitate. It is like letting cancer go too long undetected and untreated, and now you are in stage four, when hospice is called to the scene.

When people put themselves in the way to give you their most valuable gifts and resources (themselves), it is not the time to fail. It is time to excel with enthusiasm because someone cares about your destiny enough to help you. Once I got off the winding road to destruction and started traveling on the right side of life, I was determined not to let my mom and Mrs. Johnson down by not taking full advantage of the gift that was given to me.

I had a burning determination to succeed and prove my critics wrong. There were so many people talking against me and waiting to see how long I would last with my new attitude of doing the right things in life. You will probably always have some people waiting for your failure in life. I was determined not to allow negative people to influence my destiny and my decisions. I made a choice that I was going to travel the straight and narrow path.

There are always people who will attempt to dig beyond the grave to find negative information about you. This is just the nature of the beast, called haters on the scene. Regardless of how successful you become, you will always have those who are jealous of you and hate you because of the success you achieve in life. So let them talk and never attempt to defend yourself to people who did not help you achieve success in life.

Here is the bottom line: some people you meet in life are like rats looking for scraps (negativism) so they can devour your good name and reputation. Do not allow these people with such great hate toward you to consume you simply because they cannot eat anything else. My advice is to keep your head up, do not look back, and keep walking forward in your positive life.

I became more motivated to succeed when I witnessed the excitement Mrs. Johnson and my mom had for the transformation taking place and shaping my future. Mrs. Johnson was a bright light of hope and a straight road that would lead me out of poverty, shame, and destruction. Mrs. Rita Watson-Johnson was the bold one who lit the match that started the fire of hope for me and my mother. The fire of hope continues to burn even to this day.

Each day I wake up, I am still amazed and appreciative for the wonderful things that have occurred in my life since I decided to stay out of trouble and go the right way. Now, when it looks like my day is not going according to my plans or expectations, I remind myself that whatever is going on in my life, it sure beats waking up in a jail or prison cell, or worse! After I made the decision to change my life for good, so many positive and great things happened for me. I am still astonished about all of the wonderful things that have occurred in my life since I decided to switch to the right side.

Each day, my mind is blown by the many acts of kindness bestowed upon me by other people. I live in a state of great amazement. Each day waking up for me is like a kid waking up with the excitement of being at an amusement park or toy world with unlimited gifts. I can testify that there is a greater magnitude of rewards on the right side of life than the empty carts located on the wrong side of life.

After witnessing the positive things occurring in my life once I decided to turn from bad to good, it was clear to me that in the past, I was a child walking around in the world with eyes but no vision. I was so out of touch with reality that I could not even clearly see the directional signals on my map. Yes, I was walking around in the world with life, but I was unable to enjoy any of the fruitful dividends it had to offer me.

Once I put on the superhero goggles Mrs. Johnson gave me, I was able to see things more clearly. Mrs. Johnson's involvement in my life gave me a greater appreciation for my own. Her sincere interest in me changing into a better person was genuine. She was not helping me in order to gain notoriety from other teachers or boost her own ego. When I realized she sincerely cared about my outcome in life, it motivated me to change my behavior from negative to positive. With Mrs. Johnson's help, I worked harder each day to revamp my dysfunctional life.

I must confess, even with the personal hardships I have encountered during my life—regardless of the storms, valleys, hills, or mountains—life has been good to me beyond my wildest imagination. I have no complaints about my struggles. Maybe it took the various trials, testing, and tribulation to get me to where I needed to be today.

* * *

I celebrate and enjoy the small piece of the American dream I have been allowed to achieve. Though bitter at times for the bigotry, hatred, racism, sexism, and disrespect, still America has a great reputation for promoting and giving opportunities to underdogs looking to excel as law-abiding and hardworking citizens. I encourage everyone reading this book not to become so distracted by the negative things in life.

Keep your eyes focused on the positive things you can get from every situation, whether good or bad. Having a good awareness is how you stay on top of most situations, regardless of the outcome. Remember, you do not ride a raging bull from the side or bottom of the bull. You have to stay on top of the bull regardless of how he bucks to throw you off his back.

If the bull bucks you off his back, you reassess the situation and ride it again until you conquer the moment. This is the same way you must ride your issues, situations, or problems in life. Don't give up—just keep on riding until you conquer.

It amazes me that I am still alive. I am grateful I have been given the opportunity to see my grandchildren. At a very early age, I was told I would never live to see twenty-one. I am amazed I graduated from high school. I became the first of my grandmother's and grandfather's offspring to attend and finish college and earn a master's degree, as well as a doctoral degree from a national accredited institution of higher learning (Oral Roberts University).

* * *

I am so thankful my mother allowed Rita Johnson and her husband, Jimmie Johnson (deceased), to work with me without any reservations or stipulations. My mother gave the Johnsons complete authority to do whatever it took to save my life from destruction. I am so glad she not only gave me over to them but cooperated with the plan they implemented. My mother saw the great need and did not get in the way of the surgical operation that was badly needed to save my life.

I am still baffled by the fact that a Caucasian man cared enough about a little unruly and disruptive African American boy to give him one last chance to clean up his life. This happened in the Deep South, where segregation and racial tensions were still running high. Keep in mind, during this era (early 1970s), mercy was not commonly shown to African American children living south of the Mason-Dixon Line. During the 1970s, racism was still a basic factor that continued to rear its ugly head throughout the South.

Who would have ever thought that a Caucasian man would see me drowning and go out of his way to give me a life vest? While many people in my community were talking about how terrible I was, here was a man who did something positive to help me. This visionary looked out upon his staff and asked the question, "Which teacher among the ranks can turn this child's life around?"

I believe that as Dr. Skinner was deciding where to put me until he could finish my school expulsion packet, fate showed up on the scene. A glimmer of wisdom popped into the mind of Dr. Skinner, and he said, "Mrs. Rita Johnson is the teacher!" Whatever procedure Dr. Skinner used to get me into Mrs. Johnson's class, it worked, and it was a great choice.

Although Dr. Nolan G. Skinner is deceased, I am most grateful he saved one life who continues to celebrate the legacy of his life. Thank you, Dr. Skinner, for giving me one last chance. You had every right to request my expulsion from the St. Lucie County public school system. Out of the kindness of your heart, you gave me one last chance.

I am grateful for the opportunity to live on the other side of trouble and destruction. Life only grants a few people the opportunity to make devastating blunders and then bounce back to recover their lives. America has a good track record of celebrating people who have proven themselves as overcomers, especially after failing and then bouncing back.

The willingness to give people opportunities to bounce back from their failures, pitfalls, or catastrophes is one of America's greatest trademarks.

Giving people second chances and abundant opportunities to excel is one of the many reasons America is the Land of Opportunity, where people crave to live. I am thankful I can share my testimony with others, especially the youth of this nation. It is my hope and desire that this manuscript becomes an instrument of inspiration for our youth and adults to help them overcome the hurdles and pitfalls in their lives.

As I reflect over my life as a disruptive juvenile, I am blown away by how Mrs. Johnson brought together educators, civic leaders, coaches, and ordinary people to support my efforts to become a productive citizen. Of course, it was not until Mrs. Johnson's efforts began to show signs of success that others began to initiate their own dance with me. By this time, the dance floor was nearly clean and ready to be waxed with the buffer. Yet I am glad and thankful that others joined me in the dance.

I am thankful I am no longer a liability to the community and society as I was when I was a delinquent juvenile. My drive today is to always live to be an asset to whatever community I reside in or around. Imagine the improvement that could occur if each person took the time to improve something within his or her community. The improvement does not have to be big—just a deliberate, devoted, and committed effort to improve your community.

* * *

I am very proud and honored to call Fort Pierce and St. Lucie County, Florida, my home. There were other people from Fort Pierce who tried to help me change my wayward ways. I rebelled against their help to the point where I refused to come to school.

When I did not go to school, the only persons who came looking for me were Truant Officer King Strong, a social worker named Ida Morgan, Truant Officer Jerry Black, and Deputy Sheriff Pat Duvall—to no avail. Mr. James A. McNeil, my elementary school principal, and my fifth-grade teacher, Mrs. Bertha Sullivan. I outright refused to go along with their corrective action plan. I guess timing is a key element to nearly everything we do in life.

I was too stubborn and would not listen to what was right and good for me. I did not live on the right side of the tracks and could not understand what good and wise counsel looked like. Maybe I was carrying too much baggage and did not have the maturity level to either check at the door or cast every dead weight overboard that was keeping me from rising to the top. The ship I was on was sinking. I was unaware the boat was on its way down, and I had no safety plan for survival.

In retrospect, I was like a runaway freight train headed for a great disaster if no one stepped in to helped me. I was fearless in my doings, and I had no vision or concept of a prosperous future. I thought I was on my way to making a name for myself as a gangster or thug.

Just think, if I had continued on that downward slope, what a tragedy it would have been—what a waste. What a foolish pattern of thinking I was living from day to day. What a sad ending and terrible example this would have been for my younger siblings to see my life wasted before their eyes.

The greatest tragedy of this story is that there are millions of Alvin Millers in the world today who will go unnoticed and without help. They will end up incarcerated, or become convicted felons, or serve on death row. They will become drug dealers, or drug users, or habitual law-breakers, or deadbeat dads and moms, or finally secure a permanent space in the grave, where all hope ceases. Once the grave comes into play, there is nothing anybody can do or say to help or defend you from its grip.

* * *

It was the spring semester of my seventh-grade year at Dan McCarty Middle School when my life changed. At this point, I was so out of control that my insubordinate and destructive actions forced the hand of those in power at the school board office. I had become such a public nuisance that the principal had no other choice but to act in order to preserve a positive learning environment for students, staff, and faculty.

The cold winter chill of life was breathing down my neck, and I had no covering to keep me warm. I could either change my ways or become a loser in life. The choice was mine to make. I had no one else to blame if I made the wrong decision about my destiny.

Yes, I had reached a crossroad that demanded a significant change for my own good. The issues and things going on in my life could not remain the same if I had any hopes of becoming a positive influence. I felt like the grim reaper was about to show up if I did not change my destructive and dangerous behavior.

There were other times during my young life when he showed up to collect but left empty-handed. Yet this time, I had a feeling that when he showed up, he would not take no for an answer. I was in no way ready for the grim reaper to spoil the party or stunt my growth in life.

It was evident by my report card, school suspension portfolio, and criminal activities that I needed a positive change. Even in a short time, I had become a public enemy and a threat to the safety and security of the community. In all reality, I desperately wanted to change for the betterment of society, and for the enhancement of my own life, security, and destiny. Yet saying it was always easier than actually doing it, at least for me at the time.

I had seen those dark and cold tunnels many times in my dreams and imagination as a little boy. During my dreams, in some kind a way, I knew the tunnels were death tunnels, and once a person was trapped inside, no one who went in was able to come out. It was a cold and frightening experience for anyone to get trapped inside the tunnels.

As the people passed through the tunnels, no one was smiling or excited about their travels. The weeping souls wanted out of the tunnels because they were being tormented and suffering from some type of excruciating pain. The tunnels were closing in on me, and I could feel the cold chill of darkness.

The sad thing about being trapped in the tunnels was that no matter how hard the people tried, they could not get out. From the look of things, there seemed to be only one way in and no way out. This particular tunnel in my vision was a constant reminder that I wanted no part of the journey that taunted me as a child. It was a reminder that if I did not shape up, eventually, I would be shipped out to the tunnels and into everlasting darkness. The sadness and tragedy about the tunnels is that they were chambers where overwhelming pain never ceases.

The dog that won't bark at you oftentimes will end up attacking you when you least expect it if you let your guard down.—Alvin E. Miller

A Change in the Making

When I was around thirteen years old, my middle school principal, Mr. Nolan G. Skinner, went to Mrs. Johnson and told her the story about this infamous kid who was a high risk and a liability to the order and safety of the school. Of course, I was that little tyrant he was referring to as he explained the situation to Mrs. Johnson. Without any inclination of the storm brewing over the horizon of my life, I was caught totally off guard when it surfaced at Dan McCarty Middle School during my last semester of seventh grade.

I had no idea that the game I thought I was playing was about to change, with a new set of rules. I did not know how long I would be able to ride the wave of out-of-control and disruption. I did know every wave rises and falls, like surfers who try to stay on top of them.

I did not know when, but I knew that sooner or later, something in my life needed to change drastically. I needed the change to come so it could force me to embrace the positive change that was occurring in my life.

Believe it or not, damages do not stay the same forever. Dirty dishes do not stay stained forever. Water and detergent shine dirty dishes and give them glowing beauty once the dirt and debris have been removed. As a child at Dan McCarty Middle School, I represented the dirty dishes that needed a thorough cleansing from the inside out.

I had not been aware that the principal of the school was in the process of recommending me for expulsion from the St. Lucie County public school district. During a meeting with Mrs. Johnson, Dr. Skinner told her why he was going to make the recommendation for expulsion: I was totally out of control. I was too unruly and a high risk to other students, faculty, staff, and the entire school district.

Dr. Skinner believed that I should not be allowed to remain in the public schools of St. Lucie County. Believe me, he was absolutely right about my attitude and disruptive influence. I never had any hard feeling toward Dr. Skinner for his action to rid the school district of me. He had warned me on several occasions about my behavior.

Dr. Skinner was well within his rights to tell Mrs. Johnson he was fed up with my disrespectful behavior and would no longer tolerate me disrupting teachers and classrooms, and fighting with other students. I had become a nemesis to the discipline and learning environment at Dan McCarty Middle School.

The time for tolerance was nearing its end. But the mere fact that Dr. Skinner approached Mrs. Johnson about me shows he was concerned about my fate. Yet he could not remain silent any longer or become complacent and allow me to terrorize his campus. As the school principal, Dr. Skinner was put in a position to serve as the overseer of curriculum and instruction, keeper of peace, and authority figure for the entire school.

I am so glad that hope, compassion, and understanding were on campus to help determine my destiny. Years later, I found out that a deal had been worked out between Dr. Skinner and Mrs. Johnson concerning my fate at Dan McCarty Middle School. In this agreement, Dr. Skinner would offer me one last chance to turn my life around with the help of Mrs. Johnson. I knew nothing about the deal or details concerning my future in the school district until some forty years, after the agreement had become a successful experiment for all involved.

I had to prove to Dr. Skinner that I could walk a straight line and stay out of trouble while on school property. It was told to me years later by Dr. Skinner that if I had slipped up just once or fallen back into a disorderly pattern during the process of turning my life around, I would have immediately been recommended for expulsion from middle school within the St. Lucie County public school district. I will be the first to admit that my actions had put my life and destiny between a rock and a hard place.

Keep in mind, I knew nothing about the agreement between Dr. Skinner and Mrs. Johnson until around forty years later. For forty years, Mrs. Johnson did not discuss her meeting with Dr. Skinner, until one Christmas when she was visiting my home in Nashville, Tennessee. She told me the entire story about how I really ended up in her seventh-grade English class.

As hopeful as Dr. Skinner was about giving me a final chance to get my life in order, he was also as adamant about expelling me from the St. Lucie County Public School District if I stepped out of line. Shortly after I left Dan McCarty Middle School and went on to ninth grade at Lincoln Park Academy Junior High School, Dr. Skinner campaigned for the top position (superintendent of schools) in St. Lucie County. He won the election in 1977 and became the superintendent of schools for the St. Lucie County Public School District.

* * *

Regardless of the obstacles you may encounter in life, someone will come from out of nowhere to help you overcome stumbling blocks. As long as you keep the faith and never give up, you too will make it to your dream world. Civil rights activist, Jesse Louis Jackson, used a phrase "Keep Hope Alive" in 1984 and 1988 when he ran for president of the United States. Jesse Jackson was telling his constituents that regardless of how hard the way may look or get, do not ever lose hope, because hope will help you overcome, excel, and accomplish great things in life.

It was a great act of compassion that Dr. Skinner demonstrated to me when he took the time to join me and Mrs. Johnson as teacher and student, with the hope of changing my life and destiny. The act of kindness by Dr. Skinner not only benefited my life but also the Fort Pierce community. Since this great man did so much to bring fulfillment into my life, it would be robbery for me not to return the favor to others.

The saving of one life can impact lives by the hundreds, or thousands, or possibly tens of thousands in need of guidance. You just never know the impact one life has on people across the nation and the world. Now, during the era of social media, there are no longer communication barriers that separate citizens across the globe.

The union that a middle school principal forged fifty years ago has become a lasting relationship. My relationship with Mrs. Johnson continues to transform my life with joy and the fulfillment of family. Mrs. Johnson was the advocate I needed to transform me into an asset for humanity rather than a liability.

Years ago, I could not make the claim that I am no longer a liability to the world but rather an asset. All I can say is, I am more than thankful for the actions of Dr. Skinner and Mrs. Johnson for creating the bond that helped save my life. Without the partnership of Dr. Nolan G. Skinner, Mrs. Rita M. Johnson, and Elizabeth Miller, there would be no Alvin E. Miller meeting and praying for the 44th President of the United States of America on May 1, 2011, at Fort Campbell, Kentucky.

In retrospect, I believe Dr. Skinner was aiming higher than just keeping order at school. All Dr. Skinner had to do was recommend me for expulsion. This in itself would have eliminated the threat or problem from the entire school district.

Think about it: since I was the common denominator for instigating trouble at the school, all Dr. Skinner had to do was make the recommendation to have me expelled. He had the support of the district administrators, because I had already established a disorderly track record. Or he could have kept me in some type of in-school suspension program/class.

I guess when Dr. Skinner put me into Mrs. Johnson's class, it *was* like an in-school suspension. Little did anyone know at the time that this would be the match that lit the candle of my rebirth. Mrs. Johnson would serve as the shock that jolted me into a world of correction.

It is easy to say my expulsion from middle school would have corrected a large portion of the school's disciplinary reports. It seems as though each day the disciplinary reports would go up to the district office, and guess whose name appeared on the list as a suspended party. As I look back, it is a sad thing to inform you that my name was the only name that appeared on the suspension list as a regular weekly occurrence. Some teachers had never met me, but they knew my name from the suspension list.

Over forty years later, as I reflect back on my life as a middle school student at Dan McCarty Middle School, I am of the opinion that Dr. Skinner's idea of pairing me up with Mrs. Johnson as a student and teacher team was not coincidental. I believe Dr. Skinner saw something within me that I could not see in myself. Yes, I was the little blind bird flying around in society without a clue of the things I was about to crash into, which could have caused my demise. I had wings, but no sight. I had eyes, but no vision. I had energy, but I was using it the wrong way.

Dr. Skinner took a big chance by extending the opportunity to help me find the way out of my personal trepidations as I maneuvered through the dark and cold tunnels of life. He helped light the way to the marvelous and exciting journey that awaited me in the future. I am most grateful for the gift Dr. Skinner offered me by allowing Mrs. Johnson to teach and supervise me.

The compassionate act of a generous man and an awesome woman allowed me to live long enough to share my story with you today. If either of these educators had been unwilling, the sharing of my life's story from tragedy to triumph would not be possible. All I needed was one last chance, and Dr. Skinner and Mrs. Johnson gave it to me. What a difference one last chance can make in the life of a person!

* * *

Years later, after I graduated from high school, I sometimes ran into Dr. Skinner during seasonal breaks while home from Eastern Kentucky University. Each time, I would thank him for giving me the chance to work with Mrs. Johnson and the opportunity to remain in school so I could turn my life around. I never fully understood the depth of what Dr. Skinner did for me until years after I graduated from high school. All I knew prior to graduating was that Dr. Skinner went out of his way to give a "rug rat" like me another chance to come clean with my life.

During my freshman year at Eastern Kentucky University, I felt an overwhelming sense of gratitude in my college dorm room for what Dr. Skinner and Mrs. Johnson did for me. The feeling was so powerful and overwhelming that I began to shed tears of joy. All I could think about was that if I had not accepted the opportunity from Dr. Skinner to change the course of my life, I would have probably ended up dead, or in prison, or a loser in life. I have seen each of those scenarios on numerous occasions. In my Florida neighborhood of Fort Pierce, the prior descriptions were like current daily news events.

Most importantly, I am grateful for the opportunity that was provided to me by someone who had no personal connection to me. Yet he offered me the help I needed in order to move from the valley of despair to the mountaintop of hope. Dr. Skinner and Mrs. Johnson both thought enough of me to give me the opportunity to rise from the dark and cold dungeons of poverty and destruction.

Dr. Skinner and Mrs. Johnson offered me something in a unique way that no one else had ever offered me. They presented my trip as a professional tourism company does for its clients. They offered me a journey of joy and excitement that I could internalize as the opportunity of prosperity in the right lane of life.

I was always grateful to Dr. Skinner for seeing something in me that I could not see in myself. When it dawned on me the extensive process Dr. Skinner went through to change my entire schedule to meet the demands of Mrs. Johnson's class schedule, I was even more grateful for his generosity. He even made sure my lunch period was changed so I could leave Mrs. Johnson's class and return to her afterward. This was done so Mrs. Johnson could monitor my behavior and separate me from my devious friends at school.

The strategy was to divide and conquer, and this tactic was being exercised in a very strategic way without me having any knowledge of it. The strategic plan of action from the very start of the experiment was formulated by Mrs. Johnson. She was systematic with her approach as she began the process of changing me.

Whatever you want to call it, it worked for my good. I am the finished product of psychologists, scientists, and educators putting their minds and hearts together to influence the destiny of a student against the odds. When educators look beyond the dark clouds of disparity and focus on the sunshine of hope in the lives of their students, they allow their own gifts and talents to create in young people a future full of realistic opportunities.

I remember when my alma mater, Eastern Kentucky University, won the NCAA I-AA (FCS) Football National Championship in December 1979 in Orlando, Florida. I was thrilled to return home during my winter break from college. After all the excitement from winning the national championship in football, the joy and excitement was still burning fresh in my soul.

I felt like I was living on top of the world, even though it was only for a little while. The accolades and joy that went along with winning the collegiate national championship in small-college football were a great inspiration for this country boy from Fort Pierce. Yes, I was the same kid who many people thought would not have the slightest chance at playing college football for a reputable institution of higher learning.

I was that same kid that many people said would not amount to anything that was worthwhile. I was the same person who people told Mrs. Johnson was wasting her time for trying to help create a better life for me. Now, this same person was in the spotlight before the entire world, and the critics were sitting in the stands in silence. All I can say to you reading this book is, "Keep hope alive!"

I will never forget, during my visit home in December 1979, that Dr. Skinner told me he was proud I had made the decision to allow Mrs. Johnson to help me. He mainly told me not to thank him, but to thank Mrs. Johnson; it was she who did all the work. He went on to tell me that I made the city of Fort Pierce and the citizens of St. Lucie County proud when I was selected as the NCAA-1AA national championship football game Most Valuable Player by ABC Television and the Chevrolet Corporation. I was lost for words with such an awesome compliment coming from the superintendent of the St. Lucie County Public School District, Dr. Nolan G. Skinner.

Just think—Dr. Skinner could have fed me to the wolves, or shall I say the gators, since we are telling this story near the Florida canals. Yet Dr. Skinner gave me another chance to walk away from my destructive past. At the time, my life was filled with broken dreams and left in a dark hole where most travelers do not return with good news.

When parents, community advocates, educators, and civic leaders unite for the preservation and the welfare of youth, many boys and girls can be saved. Educators have always worked to draw our youth away from gangs, drugs, illiteracy, incarceration, criminal activities, bad decisions, reckless living, and irresponsible actions that cause severe damage, pain, and suffering to others. Also, when adults intentionally include youth in their daily planning and activities as partners, it's like extending a survival pass to them. Having close relationships with children on a daily basis is a monitoring mechanism of accountability that many kids and adults may not consider.

As I look back on the success Mrs. Johnson had with mentoring me, it was her daily personal contact with me that allowed her to monitor and navigate my behavior each day. I was totally unaware that Mrs. Johnson was very deliberate and strategic in her process to bring about positive changes in my life. The daily contact was like a proactive way of mentoring, monitoring, and defending against mischievous acts destined to bring about destruction.

When parents and guardians do not monitor the behavior of their children, calamity is bound to happen. Youth cannot be left alone for long periods without the guidance and supervision of responsible adults. Wise adults will make the appropriate call.

All children need good examples and definitive road maps that allow them to easily navigate the difficult hurdles in life. Children need mentors who will teach and guide them as to how to avoid the dangers in their lives. They need adult leaders to teach them how to maneuver beyond the valleys, hills, mountains, tunnels, dungeons, and pitfalls they will encounter during their trip to adulthood.

Here is the bottom line: It was Dr. Skinner who forced me to either shape up or get shipped out. I knew Dr. Skinner was serious about the ultimatum he gave me through Mrs. Johnson and my other teachers, whom I had terrorized in their classrooms for nearly two years. A line in the sand had been drawn by Dr. Skinner, and I understood that I should not cross the line. At this particular time in my life, crossing the line would have meant the end of my time in the St. Lucie County Public School District.

* * *

I had always been under the impression that a committee or group of African American teachers was put together to help me come in line with school rules. Maybe I got this idea from some of the teachers who jumped on the bandwagon after they began to witness the success of the pilot program that Mrs. Johnson was engineering. Over the years, many have laid claim to all the wonderful things they did for me during my most turbulent times of life as a young kid growing up in Fort Pierce. The truth of the matter was, they did nothing!

It wasn't until years later, when I asked Mrs. Johnson to explain the entire process and decision to place me in her class, that I found this out. I remember the days when Mrs. Johnson would tell me, *"Some people are going to try to take credit for changing your life."* She told me not to dispute them about what they did not do for me; instead, I should thank them. And just as Mrs. Johnson had warned, there were people and teachers who would tell me what they did for me to help me make it out of the trenches of hardships in life—and even to this day, I thank them for what they did not do.

I often went to people to express my gratitude for their help. Many teachers and people across the community took credit for turning my life around. I am most grateful for all of the help I received in school, but three trees stood taller than all the other trees in the forest. I am very clear about the people in my hometown and across the nation who helped me achieve a small portion of the American dream.

Initially, it was an agreement between Dr. Skinner and Mrs. Johnson. Even my mother was not part of the conversation in the beginning. Mrs. Johnson was the only teacher Dr. Skinner confided in and trusted to undertake such a delicate mission. The reality of the matter was that some of the middle school teachers thought I would be a flop.

Can you imagine a teacher betting on a student to fail? Well, that particular teacher cannot ever bet against any more kids. Teachers are put on earth to teach, encourage, and mentor young people, not to discourage them by killing their dreams.

Once the Johnson/Miller Project started to bear a glimpse of success, it looked like a couple of the teachers became jealous and did not wish me well. Can you believe a teacher had the audacity to tell me to my face that I caused her to lose a bet? She said she had been convinced I would fail the test.

I am amazed at how the pieces of the puzzles fit together once I made up my mind that I wanted to live on the good side of life. A few years ago, Mrs. Johnson informed me of how she had the opportunity to work with Dr. Skinner at the predominately African American Lincoln Park High School in the 1960s. In around 1969, Dr. Skinner served as the dean of students and then assistant principal at LPA the following year.

As she was serving as a reading teacher in the school's after-school preparatory program, Dr. Skinner observed Mrs. Johnson's unique success for working with African American males. She could teach, influence, and mentor African American males who many teachers considered intimidating and threatening. Dr. Skinner was convinced Mrs. Johnson was an educator who had gifts like Harriet Tubman and Sojourner Truth that could bring out the best in any child, even if she was working with wayward children.

As I reminisce about my seventh-grade school year, I am captivated by the actions of both Dr. Skinner and Mrs. Johnson. I am equally as amazed by the actions of Dr. Skinner as I am with Mrs. Johnson even agreeing to receive me into her class. Mrs. Johnson not only taught me in her class, but she would go on to tutor me nearly every day for the next two years.

Neither the school district, nor me, nor anyone else gave Mrs. Johnson additional pay, or recognition, or accolades for the extra time she spent outside of the classroom tutoring me. She committed her own personal financial resources to help me and my family. The guidance she rendered to me as an adolescent kept me out of trouble and from relapsing back into the riotous life I learned as a boy street hustler while shining shoes up and down Avenue D.

With the networking of my mom; Mrs. Johnson and Jimmie Johnson (deceased); Mr. Curtis Johnson Sr. (deceased) and his wife, Ivy Johnson (deceased); the late Arthur T. Johnson; and Mrs. Beatrice Williams, an awesome and powerful force steered me away from failure and crime. Mrs. Johnson was the lead runner with the baton and the workhorse who made sure I stayed on task. She was adamant about me getting the things I needed in order to meet the requirements for graduation from high school.

Also, Mrs. Johnson was the catalyst who encouraged me to pursue a quality education from a credible college or university. The tireless effort and work Mrs. Johnson invested in my life could never be paid in full measure. All the gold in the world would not be enough for what Mrs. Johnson did for me in order to get me on the right side of life and the law.

* * *

I am more than thankful for the help and support I received from other people across the Fort Pierce community as well. I started my young years in life as an "ugly piece of a mess," but with the help of caring people, I passed the test. At the time, I was desperately in need of a genuine transformation that would help me change my life from bad to good.

I was given a heart transplant by two educators who first extended their hearts in compassion to me. As the old adage says, "It takes an entire village of compassion to nurture a child into a healthy and loving community." Because of the kind deeds Dr. Skinner and Mrs. Johnson rendered to me, I will continue to serve humanity, because I owe a debt to society that I will spend a lifetime trying to pay back—although I know I cannot ever pay in full what was freely given to me.

Without the help of a compassionate community, a person may reach adulthood in age and theory but not necessarily in actions that demand commitment and responsibility. This is part of the reason why we have people today who are adults in age and theory but act like irresponsible adolescents without responsibilities and accountability. If we expect citizens to become responsible adults, communities need to buy into the fact that they play significant roles in helping citizens become productive agents in the communities in which they reside.

Without the unity of the entire village, many children miss out on the essential developmental skills needed to grow into compassionate human beings. Such skills will help people become assets within communities rather than liabilities. Since one person does not know everything, it is important for us to work together for the good of everyone within the community. As we work together within a community by sharing and receiving pertinent information, we can enlighten each other about the evolving issues and techniques needed to show young people how to excel in life.

When iron sharpens iron, it is a great opportunity for people to learn from one another. When people share positive ideas in the lives of citizens, we all grow from the experience. The community as a whole benefits from the giving and receiving of beneficial information.

Paying it forward is the act of kindness that ensures everyone receives an opportunity to reap the harvest from a gift. Paying it forward is the passing of the baton to someone else in need. The unselfish act of passing a gift or talent on to someone else is the object of the entire aphorism. I encourage and challenge you to pay this book forward. I believe it will help a child or an adult to excel beyond the pitfalls and dangers he or she may encounter in life.

In all truthfulness, Dr. Skinner did not have to come to Mrs. Rita

Johnson to ask her if she would be willing to take me into her class as the last chance for me. The bottom line is, I was on my way out the door. Mrs. Johnson was my lifeline before I was thrown out of public school.

Some would call an unexplainable act of this nature a supernatural event that just happens to occur in life. Yet I know the conductor of the train on the particular tracks. Faith, hope, and perseverance have the ability to take you to your destiny regardless of your past failures.

My pairing with Mrs. Johnson was the last chance for me prior to Dr. Skinner recommending me for expulsion from public school in the county. This was not a coincidence or something that happened by chance. I am more than convinced that the actions of Dr. Skinner and Mrs. Johnson were orchestrated by a power greater than human relationships. I am overjoyed that I took my seat on the train of correction so I could enjoy the successes life had in store for me even while traveling on the train, and not only at my destination.

As I reflect over my infamous past, it had gotten to the point that my reputation and actions were so repugnant that all Dr. Skinner needed to do was submit my curriculum folder and school disciplinary records to the district office for expulsion. Once the board reviewed my packet, it would have given Dr. Skinner full support for my expulsion. Expulsion for an entire school year would have set the stage for me to become another statistic as a school dropout, and more than likely I would have ended up going to prison, at best.

The destructive path I was on as a delinquent juvenile had no good ending as far as I could see. I was too young and foolish to know there was a world with the sweet music of success and benefits awaiting my arrival. I was now willing to follow society's rules and guidelines in life that could move me from despair to success.

When I decided to cross over to the good side of life, I immediately became a productive student within the classroom. I began to experience a good feeling and enjoyed the life I could not have dreamt of without Mrs. Johnson coming into my life. Meeting Dr. Skinner and Mrs. Johnson was a life-changing experience for me that I will never forget.

After crossing over to the good side of life, I witnessed some of the splendor and beauty of what success looks like from the eyes of a champion. One of the first things that happened to me during my metamorphosis process is that my self-esteem went from low to high. Another thing that happened was my determination kicked in like the flames coming from a jet engine in full throttle and ready to take off.

I actually could see the shore after being lost at sea for so many days, months, and years. Over the years, I have come to the conclusion that many champions share something in common. They all seem to know the smell, feel, and taste, and hear the thrill of victory before it is actually accomplished. It is like when you are in an athletic game and the game's scoreboard has a few seconds on it, but you can taste, smell, see, feel, and hear the thrill of victory with assurance!

* * *

As a juvenile, I hardly had any respect for rules, especially school rules. I was so out of touch with the real world that I could not see beyond the devious street tactics that had me bound. I came to know the deeper side of the street life as a nine-year-old shoeshine boy on Avenue D.

On the weekends and some weekdays, I traveled up and down Avenue D shining shoes for twenty-five to thirty-five cents a pair, and fifty cents for a pair of boots. I would walk until shortly past midnight on weekends, marketing and promoting my shoeshine business from Eddie's Bar (a juke joint) on Avenue D and 20th Street all the way past the Chicken Shack (20th Street and Avenue D), Lincoln Theater (Douglas Court and Avenue D), Blue Front Night Club, and Granny's Kitchen (10th and Avenue D) to the Greyhound Bus Station on Avenue D and US Highway #1.

After the long haul down Avenue D, I would turn around and head back up Avenue D all the way westward to Angle Road Bar, which was located on the southeast corner of Angle Road and Avenue D. The liquor store had a covered outdoor dance floor patio and bar area that stayed crowded with people looking for a good time. Sometimes the people at Angle Road Bar would be so drunk they would tip me more than the cost of a regular shoeshine. Angle Road Bar was the outdoor hangout for nearly anyone looking for a party, a loud conversation, and alcoholic drinks to wash down their troubles and pains with the great sound of a jukebox.

Some of the customers were on their way to work, while others were getting off work, and their first stop was Angle Road Bar. The bar was the talk of the town. People would come from all over Fort Pierce just to hang out and look for a good time.

Many people who met up at Angle Road Bar ended up going home on a strange rendezvous. Some of the strangest relationships developed from the courtyard at Angle Road Bar. People from Okeechobee, Indian River (Gifford), and Martin County (Stuart) came to Fort Pierce to party. The African American community in Fort Pierce during my childhood had a rich culture that was full of African American businesses—stores, restaurants, juke joints, bars, barber shops, beauty parlors, churches, wealthy fruit contractors, a movie theater, motels, rooming houses, daycare centers, nurseries, the world-famous Florida Highwaymen Painters, and a host of other establishments.

To continue on with my experience as a shoeshine boy, I learned the game of street hustling with a homemade shoeshine box I made from scrap wood. It was a very small compact wooden box about the size of a large shoebox. I could only carry a limited number of items in my box, such as two shoeshine brushes and various colors of polish/paste in a tote and rags.

Believe it or not, I enjoyed being a shoeshine boy more than going to school. I was in my own world on the streets as a shoeshine boy. I had a severe stuttering problem, and out there, I did not have to stand before a classroom full of students who traumatized me simply because I was not a good reader. I did not have to worry about some teacher embarrassing me before the entire class. I did not have to worry about anyone making fun of my clothes. On the streets, I could just be Alvin, or "Hey, shoeshine boy!"

I still remember some of my customers, like brothers Amos and Paul Lundy. I remember Amos vividly because he rode a motorcycle and was a boxer. The Lundy brothers were always very kind to me and would allow me to shine their shoes even though sometimes their shoes did not need a shine. They just wanted to support my business. Fifty years later, I have never forgotten the generosity they extended to me.

* * *

Maybe the reason why school was not important to me as a lad was because I had never been properly prepared for the institution of learning. For some strange reason, as a child in elementary school, I oftentimes felt like a misfit in the classroom. To understand my reservation about education in the formal classroom setting, you probably need to have an understanding of the big picture about my upbringing as a child.

Moreover, once I realized I was so far behind my classmates and peers, I felt hopeless. I felt so incompetent and had no drive to try to catch up with the rest of the class. My lack of proper educational training made me feel that learning was not a fun process. At this particular point, learning in a classroom setting was the most difficult thing in my life. Each day I went to school, I was reminded of the fact that I'd had no prior training or learning prior to first grade, and it was not a good place for me.

Once you get a glimpse of my early childhood, you will begin to visualize and understand the issues I was dealing with as a six-year-old child attending first grade. In retrospect, I was put into the formal setting of a classroom with kids of my age group who had previously attended daycare and pre-K and had some type of kindergarten experience, unlike me. I felt very inferior and intimidated in a classroom setting.

Other kids would call me dumb because I lacked any knowledge of reading, writing, counting, and reciting my ABCs. I was unfamiliar with the nursery or Mother Goose rhymes because no one in my family had any educational experience prior to me going to the first grade. As kids, my siblings and I did not have anyone to read to us about Cinderella, Jack and the Beanstalk, Little Red Riding Hood, Jack and Jill, Humpty Dumpty, and Mother Hubbard.

Looking back over the years, I recognize that I was in no way prepared for first grade. It seemed like every student other than me had some type of advanced preparatory academic training prior to the first grade. I can remember some of the kids' parents coming into the classrooms volunteering their time to help students in the class. Yet most of the volunteer time spent by the parents was mainly to help their own children.

I would sit at my desk fantasizing about my mother volunteering her time to help me. Such dreams could be healthy for a child's self-esteem, especially if the child is battling or suffering from low self-esteem. I was not only suffering from low self-esteem, but I was suffering from being ill-equipped for first grade. I can remember sitting in class at Garden City Elementary School just dreaming my life away.

There's nothing wrong with dreaming, but you have to also know that reality is outside waiting on you to come out of your dreams. It would be unproductive for any person to attempt to dream forever. By attempting to dream forever, a person tries to avoid responsibilities and commitments.

As I stated, never having attended kindergarten, pre-K, or any other type of preparatory schooling or training prior to entering first grade had an impact on me and my educational progress from day one of school to this day. My first day of first grade, I felt as though I was in a foreign country trying to learn a different culture and language all at the same time. As I stated earlier, I was very intimidated and felt lost in a formal classroom setting.

Somehow, I knew I could not access the arena of higher learning from the ground I was walking on. It was like sending me to a soup kitchen to eat soup without a soup bowl. As I looked around the kitchen, I noticed all the other kids had soup bowls but me. Prior to entering first grade, I had never heard of the alphabet or arithmetic. They were like a foreign language to me.

Needless to say, I became frustrated with education at a very early age, and with the many rules and regulations I had to abide by. I was lost, and the teacher did not make things any better for me. The teacher would spank me on my bottom, on the palms of my hands, and on my knuckles in front of the entire class simply because I did not know the answers to the questions that were asked of me.

No one ever stopped to ask me if I had attended nursery school or any type of kindergarten. I was punished for not knowing things that had never been taught to me. I acquired a pain and hurt that the rain could not wash away from my little mind and heart. I don't think school is supposed to be this evil to a child.

As a first-grader, I did not know my alphabet, colors, or how to count past ten or twenty. I did not know how to stay in the lines while coloring. I could not stand still in lunch lines without trying to act out as the class clown, which was how I tried to fit in with the other students in the classroom. It's like my attitude was making a vindictive statement: "You either allow me to fit in, or I will become a disruptive influence during your daily learning process."

I became a constant disruption in the classroom by talking when I was not allowed to talk. I would make noise, push other students, get out of my seat, and a host of other annoying things aimed at setting the teacher on edge. I constantly complained to the teacher on every assignment because I did not know how to start or complete it.

I was too hyperactive and aggressive with other children in the classroom, at lunch, and during recess. I had no home training on how to behave in school. I was clueless about the school environment. If it had been left up to me, I would have eaten lunch and left for the day.

If I had been the offspring of reputable persons within the community, I would have automatically received the utmost respect the minute I set foot on the grounds of the school, not to mention the classroom. When I was in school, especially in elementary school, if your parent or parents were teachers, or educators, or doctors or lawyers, or people with credibility in the community, you received attention, opportunities, and breaks at school and across the community.

But I was only the son of an unmarried female who was classified as a migrant worker. I'd like to point out that during the 1970s, 1960s, and prior, the term *migrant worker* was something people frowned upon. It was not a badge of honor within the community. My grandfather, my grandmother, my mother, and her twelve siblings were all classified as migrant workers, moving and living between Georgia and Florida in the 1940s, 1950s, and 1960s.

During my entire childhood, my mother's income was below the poverty line, which entitled us to state and federal aid programs. I can vividly remember my mother receiving welfare to help her care for her five children, including me. This was a time in my life when there was no Mrs. Johnson to come to my aid and rescue me from the degradation of poverty and crime.

Although the US government provided us with some things while we were in a state of economic and social depression, my mother was a very hard and dedicated worker, even though her earnings were very limited. I can remember my mother getting up very early in the morning, and then waking up everyone in the house with her daily instructions. Still to this day, the memory of my mommy waking up everyone in the house in the wee hours rings in my mind like the music and words of a sweet love song I just cannot let go. I guess some memories have a way of hypnotizing people with the hope that we could relive those moments again.

As I got older, I began to realize that my mother was not totally dependent on the welfare system to take care of her and her children. Unlike many of the mothers I knew from the government housing projects where I grew up, my mom worked every day in the tomato fields or the orange and grapefruit groves of Florida. I can visualize the scenes of her knocking off from work and walking through the door as a tired and broken-down African American woman looking for rest, but she knew she had to get ready for her night gig at Eddy's Juke Joint.

During the early and mid-1960s, my mother was the sole breadwinner in the house. I cannot ever remember a time my mother did not work when I was growing up. Even until around 2013, my mother continued to work at a fruit packing house in St. Lucie County, Florida.

For many years during my boyhood until my ninth or tenth grade year in high school, my mother worked as a laborer in Vero Beach, Florida. She was an employee at a tropical fish farm that was located in the southern section of Indian River County. She became the in-house expert on the various types of tropical fish and how to feed and nurture them. She even became an expert on species of tropical fish coming from South America and other places around the world.

Bad Turns in Life Produce Bad
Results, No Matter Who You Are

I t is sad that as a young boy, I knew more about the rules concerning breaking and entering than I did about making good grades in school. At the age of six, getting a good education was the furthest thing from my mind. It was interesting for me to live life as a renegade. The things I needed to know the most, I knew the least. The things I needed to know the least, I knew the most.

There was something gravely wrong with this picture. How was it possible for a little elementary-school child, under the age of ten, to know more about doing wrong than doing right? I lived for the rush of skipping school and breaking into things.

The unbalanced knowledge I possessed would haunt me for the next nine to ten years of my life. Even to this day, I believe my adolescent educational and learning deficiencies are the primary reasons I have difficulties with taking standardized examinations. I have a handicap when it comes to taking standardized tests that I cannot overcome even with tutoring sessions, my military training, my educational learning, and the advanced education I have pursued and received in non-military institutions and schooling.

There is a great disconnect between the knowledge and information I missed as a child and the skills and knowledge I've needed to pass standardized examinations as an adult. There is a skill set and knowledge I missed while committing acts of truancy in elementary and middle school. The important things I missed in my life as a child I liken to a father who has never done anything for you but all of a sudden, one day, falls out of the sky by chance and shows up in the picture trying to connect with you, simply because the word was out on the streets that you might one day go to the NFL.

It was as though the interference in the line was so bad that it would not allow me to connect with my dad in order to establish a relationship. Everything was null and void, because I had no feelings or experiences that would allow me to connect the dots for emotional attachment. Even though I tried my best to be a cordial person toward the man who was my dad, the feeling of camaraderie was not in me to embrace him with adoration.

Although I did my best to draw something from the bank of compassion toward my dad, I was bankrupted when it came to feelings. Just like my absenteeism from school negatively impacted and affected my ability to pass standardized tests, so did an absent father in my life affect my ability to connect and have a relationship with my dad. He may have felt the same way about me. I will never know, because he never expressed himself to me.

The majority of times we were in each other's presence, it was like two strangers meeting for the first time. Or, shall I say, two enemies meeting and trying their best to be cordial to one another. For the first seven and a half years of my school life, it was a roller coaster ride with me and my dad's relationship. I did not see him much, and then only in passing.

* * *

It is imperative to understand that I never earned promotion to any grade prior to the end of my seventh-grade school year in 1973. The truth of the matter is, I was socially promoted to the second, third, fourth, fifth, sixth, and seventh grade in order to rush me through the school system right into the penal system. The term *social promotion* is defined as "the practice of promoting a child to the next grade level regardless of skill mastery in the belief that it will promote self-esteem and keep the student with his or her peers."

As juveniles, my two brothers, Gary and James (or "Stewbeef"), and I picked up some bad habits during our youthful escapades in a world of darkness. I was around seven years old when we started breaking community rules. It was during this time that I started fighting in school and began to resist any type of structured discipline and administrative authority.

My disrespect toward teachers, students, and citizens in the community was setting the tone for a devastating ending if a change did not occur in my life sooner rather than later. The reward for my rebellious behavior was a permanent place on the school's suspension list. Nearly every week during the majority of my middle school experience, I was suspended because I failed to follow the school's rules.

Even to this day, I am amazed how I was granted a safety-pass or badge of hope out of the hood that read, "One last opportunity for success!" My pass of hope was given to me during a time when very few guys from my neighborhood were being issued a pass to excel and succeed after messing up so badly. As I look back over my life, sad to say it, but not many of my neighborhood friends and playmates were as fortunate.

Maybe some of them were given the same opportunities but did not take advantage of the road less traveled. I am glad I took that road, because it gave me one last chance to win in life. I am so grateful for Mrs. Rita Johnson, Dr. Nolan Skinner, and my mother, Elizabeth Miller, who unified their forces to help save a wretch like me from destruction.

Grace and mercy allowed me to escape the doom of prison and death. Some guys I once knew are in prison even as I write this book. Some of my boyhood playmates and friends are on death row in the Florida State Penitentiary, and at least two of my friends and neighbors have been executed in Florida's electric chair or by lethal injection.

During my fortieth class reunion in Fort Pierce, we counted over thirty classmates who had died. These were the classmates we believed had died prior to our fortieth class reunion. Just like the time had come and gone so quickly, our beloved and deceased classmates had also come and gone in life in the same way, with the swift transition of time.

On Monday, January 4, 2021, I called one of my classmates who is the fact-checker for our class. Emily Davis Quarterman probably had more information on the people in the Class of 1977 than anyone I knew. Even to this day, if you mention a classmate's name, Emily could tell you the exact spot where that student lived while growing up in Fort Pierce. She knew the family members, the momma's or daddy's name, and how many siblings lived in the house. Whenever I forgot the name of a classmate, I called the Thesaurus of Emily Davis Quarterman. Many of our classmates relied on Emily for current information about classmates and their families.

During my conversation with Emily, she informed me that she had counted over fifty of our classmates who had died since we graduated. These were only the African American students. We did not have information on our Caucasian classmates who had died. The great tragedy about this data is that there are probably a lot more of our classmates on the deceased list, but we were totally unaware of who they were.

With help from other people, I understand now that life is a very precious jewel and should never be taken lightly or thrown away. Please take my advice and always strive to do positive things with your life. Give life your very best to make your parents, family, teachers, and community proud of you. In the end, you will be glad you did.

Always work to become an asset and not a burden or liability to your family members, friends, and the community. The exception to this rule is that in the event of some catastrophe, accident, or injury, you may become limited in controlling your destiny, and others will have to care for you. This expression of love is the sincere compassion of family members, loved ones, and friends.

* * *

My story is not uncommon for many African Americans growing up in single-parent dwellings within the public housing we called the Projects. There was no community support system in place to give us guidance and educational training beyond school hours—unlike today, when there are so many different social and community-based organizations in place to keep kids and families from failing. America is investing in the lives of children, families, and communities like never before.

Keep in mind that I grew up in the Deep South during the 1960s and 1970s under the dark shadow of racial segregation (racism). Resources were very limited across the canal in "colored town," and our neighborhoods, schools, and supplies were constant reminders that we were the outcasts of a segregated society. Yet our elders did their best to make good with the little they had.

For me and many kids like me, it was a struggle just to find our way on a daily basis to the shores of safety without being eaten by the various sharks of life. In an environment where depression and oppression were at high tide, opportunities were rare to none. In order for young people to survive the vices and detriments the world has to offer them, then a community must be united to become radical and innovative with its efforts to save youth from destruction. A progressive community must be willing to expose its youth to positive and productive activities and educational ventures that allow them see a vision of a bright future and a safety network for the present moment.

Sometimes it takes our young people longer to see outside the box. We have to learn how to encourage our youth with patience and lots of compassion if we intend to influence their lives in a positive direction. If our youth will survive the evil vices of life that are aimed to make them go astray, we must provide them with love and a nurturing environment, where opportunities for them to excel are readily available.

When I was a child growing up in Fort Pierce, my immediate community looked like many small inner-city communities across America. When you look at these communities, it is easy to conclude that the future for the youth seems dim and not very fruitful beyond the box in which they live. Communities that invest financial and community support, moral support, and other resources in their youth, along with personal time supporting and promoting strong mentorship programs, expose youth to a wide variety of enrichments such as arts and crafts, music, business, economics, money management, entrepreneurship, and a chance to excel in life. These are communities where youth and community residents are thriving.

It does not take a rocket scientist to know that whatever you put into a person, institution, or community is what you will get in return. When we deliberately or unknowingly create unfair living environments, working conditions, learning conditions, and practices for people, we then are training and teaching them to duplicate the behavior we would like to see them emulate. This is why it is imperative to give our youth the very best we have to offer. If we have to sacrifice things to ensure the success of our youth, that is a worthy investment with guaranteed dividends.

For people living in the trenches of despair, a better future looks almost unattainable. Yet you have to keep hoping and trying, with the desire to never give up on finding your dreams. If you cannot dream big, then I recommend you create a story in your mind with a happy ending. If you can dream for positive things to occur in your life, more than likely, it will happen with your positive input and actions.

To the people caught in the struggles and traps of poverty, it seems like everywhere you turn, babies are having babies, people are hooked on drugs, and murders are as common as the common cold. There seems to be no cure for the never-ending deprivation. I often ask myself, when one lives a life of poverty, how does one survive in a world where there seems to be very little help and almost no hope?

Once help came my way, I never gave up, regardless of any difficulties. I kept fighting for success. I encourage you reading this manuscript to do the same. Don't ever give up! Even if you have to pick yourself up from the ground, don't give up!

My advice to you is to keep believing and striving for success, because there is an opposite side to the coin of life in the valley of poverty. I am a living example that when you work hard and believe in doing positive things in life, you can achieve nearly any dream you have. When the coin of life is flipped to heads, you can get ahead and put your deficiencies behind you. People and especially kids have to grab on to hope and never allow it to get away from them, regardless of the dangers they may face in life.

Life's journey has a tragic ending for criminals who refuse to conform to the rules of society. Young people have to create a successful vision in their minds, hearts, souls, and hands. They must keep their eyes on the awesome prize that awaits them at the finish line. Distractors will come and do their best to shift your focus away from the prize, but you must pursue your goal or dreams as if your life depends on it—and it does!

Hopefully, such positive visions will encourage and motivate youth to work hard with patience and excel in making their vision or dream a reality. You have to be willing to look and feel beyond your present situation and condition. I had a dream, and regardless of whatever happened in my life, I kept dreaming and refused to let the dream die along with the personal tragedies I had experienced during my life as a child.

* * *

Many people in America are oblivious to the different kinds of things kids are exposed to on a day-to-day basis while growing up in government housing, the hood (ghetto), or on the streets, or while living in poverty or just a regular family environment. Life on the streets forces a child to grow up and survive by any means necessary; become a victim of the streets; or, worse, perish trying to survive. Many people would not believe that a little nine- or ten-year-old child could run away from home and stay gone for over a year and survive during the late 1960s.

Yes, I ran away from home, but I was able to survive by living with strangers and families I did not know. I lived in abandoned buildings, churches that were left unlocked, cars, and unlocked new construction buildings and sites when workers were not around. Just think, at any time I could have lost my life or been overtaken by some adult.

I lived the great falsehood that I could take care of myself even against grown men or women. I believe today's world would have presented impossible challenges for me to survive as a ten- or eleven-year-old child today in America. The youth of today seem to have too many snares lurking to engulf them, whether it is cyber crooks, video games, toxic uncensored television shows, and the internet's hidden and dark webs that are very contagious and lethal to the mind and the lives of our youth.

For some reason, it seemed like fear never entered my mind during my foolish escapade as a runaway youth. I was more concerned about surviving the day with a meal and acquiring a safe place to sleep at night than I was with being attacked or even killed. Although the threat was more than likely in the atmosphere, eating was more on my mind than someone hurting me.

It is interesting that my classmates did not know any of this information prior to the writing of this book. Some may know I was very bad in elementary and middle school until I met Mrs. Johnson. Others know I spent a great deal of my life in middle school life on the weekly suspension

Alvin Miller Sr., D. Min.

list. Some may even know I had various brushes with the law and was put in juvenile detention for a brief period as a youth.

Yet as I look back over my life during such a vulnerable time, all I can say is that I was at the mercy of fate. I was shown kindness and compassion by fate at an early age. I am glad I was allowed to grow up and live to a point where I am able to share my story with you. I hope my life story helps save someone else from taking the wrong turn down the path of destruction that I was once on as a youth.

Just as a schoolteacher helped me and my mother turn my life around, I am hoping my life's story will encourage and motivate someone in the same way. I am especially motivated about helping to turn our youth from the same lethal road of destruction I was traveling.

My homelessness experience was a daring quest I wish no child would attempt to pursue unless it is a life-or-death situation. Sometimes even as a youth, you have to do what needs to be done in order to survive in life. Many people will not understand this statement, but most people are not put in the situation I am talking about here.

Just think of a little nine- or ten-year-old child attempting to live on the streets where the code of conduct is "It's a dog-eat-dog world!" It is only by the kindness of others and the protection of hope that I survived. I thought I could defend myself, but how could a little child defend himself against some of the most vicious situations that have consumed strong and healthy adults? I was only kidding myself, but I didn't know it.

* * *

Back in the 1960s, a migrant labor camp was no place for a child unless the parent was there to protect the child's interest. A child growing up in a migrant labor camp had to constantly be under the stalwart supervision of a loving adult due to serious safety concerns. Life in a migrant labor camp for a child without strict adult supervision was vicious to say the least. Regardless of the camp or contractor, each camp had its share of criminal activities.

To change the environment without changing the mindset and the conditions of the people, the rules of engagement must remain the same. Although the people, buildings, and streets may change, the hearts of the people will forever remain the same without the presence of a true transformational paradigm shift. There must be a tested and proven track record of positive change in the lives of people seeking and searching for liberation in life. Some people will talk a good and great game, but always remember, actions speak louder than empty words.

I am more than convinced that people, including children, look for avenues to change their lives from bad to good; from misery to contentment; from doubt to hope and faith; from sadness to happiness; and from war to peace. I believe nearly everyone in America wants to live free, enjoy the wonderful things in life, and have the financial resources to live above poverty with great joy. When people feel good about themselves, their environment, and the things they do in life, they are more eager to help others achieve the same status.

One of the greatest beauties of life is the investment in relationships rather than the selfish isolation of individualism. People need each other in order to survive the various struggles in life. We have communities and neighbors because we believe life offers more and greater joy with other people rather than by ourselves. We believe family and friends are the greatest nucleus we have on this earth.

With today's Department of Children's Services, it is nearly impossible for DCS not to be involved in cases of my magnitude. Today, hardly anyone would believe that a ten-year-old child could run away from home and become integrated into the homeless population by living in and out of local churches, cars, and abandoned homes and buildings. I slept in churches, buildings, and places within the Lincoln Park community (African American community) that are still standing today.

More than likely, many people would not believe or fathom that a youth under the age of eleven could think about running away from home and living on the streets. One reason why is because many people cannot visualize the pain and shame of poverty. If poverty is not in your worldview, then it will probably be difficult to make a personal connection to a severely poverty-stricken environment unless compassion steps in and overwhelming a person with the burning desire or motivation to help in some form or fashion.

Growing up in a family of migrant workers, I was too young to know the full extent of negativity that was associated with migrant work. The fruit contractors and their families were immune from the virus of poverty that haunted the laborers in their fields and groves. Fruit contractors and their families were considered wealthy across the African American community. Some of the African American fruit contractors were on the boards of local banks. Holding such a prestigious position when the banks were always under the control of whites was a great accomplishment in the African American community.

When you grow up living in a tiny box, you only know the things you have seen and have been taught to you from within the box. In order to experience a paradigm shift and grow beyond the status quo, a person has to step outside of the box and see things in a world that is larger than the tiny box. Then one has to be willing to accept a more diverse experience than the little box that isolates one's mind to the small world in which one resides.

I was blown away with excitement and disbelief when I realized the beauty of the world beyond my own. To this day, I am still amazed. Probably one of the hardest missions in life is to get people to come outside of their boxes. Just think with me on this: if you cannot come outside of your box, you definitely cannot see outside of your box.

I embraced the feeling of being overwhelmed when I began to understand the many choices people make when they are on the right track. When I decided to step outside of my box and experience the beauty of the world beyond my box, only then could I realize and see the rewards that come to people who make good choices in life. It was then that I made up my mind to pursue some of those rewards.

All I had to do was make good decisions and work hard, and opportunities throughout life would be in my reach. In reality, this was the life I desired when I was a little boy growing up on 18th Street and Avenue D, and as a youth living on 23rd Street in government housing. After meeting Mrs. Johnson, I made up my mind that I did not want any longer the life that brought me failure, punishment, and embarrassment.

I often tell Mrs. Johnson that our meeting and the cooperation of my mother allowing the Johnsons to help mentor me was orchestrated by some great order of destiny for my life. I am so thankful that my mother had the wisdom, compassion, and vision to recognize I needed help that she could not give me. I thank my mother for not being a stumbling block when fate sent Mrs. Johnson into our lives to help me succeed.

Mrs. Johnson and I often talked about how my mother could have sabotaged the entire experiment or effort, but she never fought the process or the progress. I know of many mothers who would have stood in the way of the opportunity for their child to excel. Yet my mother stood back and allowed destiny to take over and give me the opportunity I needed in life to change my direction. I love my mother for not allowing her pride to stand in the way of a great opportunity for one of her children.

Frankly, it was a big deal that my mother was not selfish or threatened by the Johnson family's relationship with me. Throughout the entire time Mrs. Johnson taught and mentored me, my mother showed a heart of compassion. I can remember some of the grueling days and nights of boot camp while on the grind during the years Mrs. Johnson was tutoring and mentoring me. She was hard on me and did not cut me any slack; but I knew she loved me and had my best interest in her heart.

Mrs. Johnson would work overtime by helping me in classes and subjects that I had missed during my early years in grade school and middle school. I was a serious victim of school truancy and had weekly appointments on the Dan McCarty Middle School suspension list. I am still amazed by the enormous amount of time Mrs. Johnson invested in tutoring and mentoring me. She received no extra pay or reward for her sacrifice and selfless service to improve my academic standing in school and help me avoid the crime-riddled behavior in the local community.

As much as she could, she helped close the gap of my deficiency in education. The need for help had always been there. Yet no one else had been willing and compassionate enough to step up to the plate and take the time to train the troubled kid who people said was hopeless. When Mrs. Johnson hit the home run, other spectators tried to take credit for the win when they had never come onto the field. They stayed in the bleachers or stands as spectators.

* * *

Whenever I share part of my childhood story with others, including some of my classmates, schoolmates, and people I run into, they cannot believe I was not promoted to the second grade during my first year in school. Believe me, by no means was I ever promoted to the second grade because of the stellar schoolwork I had done in class. The very first time I ever

Alvin Miller Sr., D. Min.

earned a promotion in school was during my seventh-grade school year. Even then, I think I had help from a strong wind that helped me cross the finish line in the good old fashion that I did.

Today, there is almost no way a child can be promoted who misses a total of three months from first grade unless there is some type of special situation with health issues or learning disabilities. I missed nearly ninety days of school as a first-grader. I was not sick. Neither was I diagnosed with a learning disability that prevented me from learning. I was just a plain old deviant and destructive little boy without any fear of the consequences or harm I was causing to people in my community.

Over the years, I have learned that persons without conviction or respect for the boundaries of others are some of the most dangerous people you will ever meet. At all costs, do everything within your power to avoid these insensitive monsters who have no feelings or respect for other people. The reason I know a little about this subject is because I lived in the neighborhood as a delinquent during my adolescent years.

With the laws as they are today, most people cannot fathom a six- or seven-year-old child playing '*hooky*' from school. Living in America today, with all of the sophisticated technology, it is nearly impossible for a child to get away with what I was able to do in the 1960s and early 1970s. Today, if a child attempted what I was able to do in the years 1965–1972, a mother or father would be given a citation and hauled off to family court or jail.

I was able to escape the system for a long time before the school truant officers, policemen, and social workers began to hunt me down like a fugitive running from the law. During the chase, I experienced a range of emotions—fear, excitement, and anger. I was angry because of the meanness I encountered from both teachers and students. I am well aware I may have brought a lot of the negative reactions upon myself because I was bad, poor, and unkempt.

Some years ago, I went to the district office of the St. Lucie County school board and acquired a copy of my curriculum records, mainly from elementary school. There were two things I noticed right off the bat: most of the information was faded, and the records reflected eighty-nine days absent from school during the first grade. As the older generation in my family would often say, "The proof is in the pudding." My elementary and middle school curriculum folders showed evidence that truancy was my daily habit while in elementary and middle school.

I was a very misguided child in life. I was so thrown off as a youth that I was summoned to juvenile court. As I stood before Judge Jack Rogers, the St. Lucie County Juvenile Judge, he decided to expel me from Chester A. Moore Elementary School during my second-grade year. The judge said I was a disruption to the educational progress of students, teachers, and staff.

C. A. Moore Elementary School is still located on the outskirts of the 29th Street Projects somewhere between Avenue G and Avenue I. I loved my time at C. A. Moore. I met some loving teachers and some good boyhood friends (David Washington, Stanley Blackshear, Reginald Marshall) during the two years I attended the school in the second and third grade.

As a second-grade student at C. A. Moore, I either stayed on the absentee list or in the principal's office because of some disciplinary infraction. I remember this one time in second grade when my principal, Mr. Broxton (deceased), made me do the duck walk (for corrective action) for about an hour in front of the school building so everyone could see me. Mr. Broxton was a very good man, but he was a stickler for discipline and structure at his school. As I was doing the duck walk, I had to recite, "I will keep my hands to myself!" Let's just say after that episode, I never had to do it again during my brief time at C. A. Moore.

Pride is designed to boast about itself, and not to apologize to you! Even if it attempts to apologize to you, it does not mean it, because it will boast again as soon as the opportunity presents itself. —Alvin E. Miller

Judge Jack Lee Rogers

When I was around eleven or twelve years old, Judge Jack L. Rogers (deceased) threatened to send me to reformatory school—not the one in Okeechobee, Florida, but the one in Marianna. He sat up in his chair and said to me, "If you ever come back into my courtroom as a juvenile, I promise I will send you away to Marianna until you become an adult. Do you understand me?"

My elder brother Gary was already serving time at the Okeechobee Reformatory School. As you read this section, I want to remind you it was Judge Rogers who expelled me from school while I was in the second grade at Chester A. Moore Elementary School.

Judge Rogers said he was not just expelling me from school due to my disciplinary infractions, he was expelling me because of my consistent truancy record and the disruption I was causing within the school. Judge Rogers confirmed what teachers and administrators had already stated about my unwilling attitude toward learning and order.

Judge Rogers made the decision to expel me for the remainder of the school year as a second-grader in Mrs. Simpson's class. Judge Rogers believed I had no respect for teachers, administrators, and other students and staff at the school. He believed that whenever I showed up for school, I was a troublemaker and a tyrant. On one occasion, he referred to me as a little bandit!

On another occasion, Judge Rogers told me he was sick and tired of me dodging truancy officers and police officers. He said I needed to understand the consequences for breaking rules. So, after his verbal thrashing, he made the decision to expel me for the remainder of my second-grade school year. I was only around nine years old at the time. I believe this was probably the third out of several times I had come into Judge Rogers' courtroom.

In Judge Rogers' courtroom, you never knew what you would see or hear coming from the bench. Depending on the day or situation, it was rumored amongst some of the criminals facing Judge Rogers that he had a temperament somewhat like a Dr. Jekyll and Mr. Hyde. You did not want to catch Judge Rogers on a bad day or after a case where someone before you had upset him, because it seemed like he would take some of the punishment out on everyone who came after.

* * *

I will never forget the day Judge Rogers told me he was tired of seeing me in his courtroom. He said if I continued to show up in his courtroom, he would throw the book at me! I knew exactly what he meant when he used that particular phrase. I knew he was threatening me with a harsh punishment to the maximum extent of the law.

He was going to incarcerate me by assigning me to a youth prison, also known as boys' reformatory school. Judge Rogers told me that he would not send me to Okeechobee Boys School, which was within a 40-mile radius of my hometown of Fort Pierce. He stated he was going to send me far away to the roughest and toughest reformatory school in the State of Florida.

I can vividly remember the conversation and him saying how he would make good on his promise if I decided to come back into his courtroom. Just think—I had not committed murder or been found guilty of robbery or some other felony crime. Yes, I had a problem with going to school, which I'd felt extremely unprepared for from the very first day I showed up in the classroom and attempted to state my name. I was overtaken with nervous fear when I was instructed by the teacher to recite something like the ABCs that I knew nothing about. My first day of school, I felt great joy, fear, and intimidation all at the same time.

Judge Jack Rogers was known throughout the state of Florida for being a very strict and tough juvenile judge. He had a low tolerance for disrespectful and disobedient children, and whenever he promised to do something, he delivered on his promises. I remember this one day when I had to report to juvenile court with my mother. I watched Judge Rogers send nearly every young man who stood before him either to jail or to the reformatory school. He would rule his chamber like a roaring lion, and you knew when he was roaring. This particular day, Judge Rogers was roaring very loudly so the entire jungle could hear him.

Sad as it may sound, my older brother, Gary J. Miller Sr. (deceased), was in the group of young boys Judge Rogers sent off to reformatory school as he was roaring in the jungle. Gary was only around twelve years old at the time. Those of us who were living as criminals back in the 1960s and early 1970s knew Judge Rogers. He had a reputation that preceded him.

* * *

Judge Jack Rogers' courtroom was the helm of justice for the juvenile court system in St. Lucie County. No one had the guts to question his authority or the decisions he made. He was like Marshall Matt Dillion in the 1960s and 1970s weekly Western television show *Gunsmoke*.

Word on the streets about Judge Rogers was that he had a heart of stone and would throw the gavel at a person quicker than one could flinch or wink. He was known to give defendants time in reformatory school or jail before the accused had time to think about it. I watched mothers cry and plead for their sons, because he showed no mercy on them.

I believe Judge Rogers was on a mission to clean up the juvenile problem across the Treasure Coast of Florida. Over the years, I found out that Judge Rogers had connections with judges, lawyers, and governmental officials throughout the state and across the nation. I have heard other adults say Judge Rogers was the most powerful man in St. Lucie County.

We heard rumors that Judge Rogers sentenced two juveniles to adult prison. There was a rumor floating around that Judge Rogers got very angry in a court case and threw the book at some white boys for stealing chickens. This decision by the judge circulated on the streets like wildfire. In all reality, there was a lot more to the story than what was being circulated on the streets among us small-town hoodlums.

Nevertheless, as we rallied on the basketball courts, playgrounds, and streets, we could not believe Judge Rogers sentenced the boys with such harsh sentences for stealing chickens. We were not talking about rustling cattle or stealing sheep. We were talking about very young teenagers who stole some chickens. I am still of the opinion that the crime did not fit the punishment. To this day, I often ask myself, where was the mercy in this case?

Judge Rogers' legend struck fear and terror in the hearts of many who were preparing to stand before his bench. He was a powerful force to reckon with. He was a man who demanded respect, or else, by the time he finished with you, you would reap a more terrible thing than you think you sowed.

You could tell that Judge Rogers was a man of great integrity just from being in his courtroom. He did not care about your gender, skin color, or ethnicity. All he seemed to care about was making sure juveniles followed the laws and rules in society. Once Judge Rogers gave you his instructions or an ultimatum, if you failed to follow through according to his order, he would charge you with contempt of his court, and justice would be served like bolts of lightning striking from the sky. You never wanted to double-cross Judge Rogers.

As I said earlier, I have witnessed mothers come into Judge Rogers' court and break down crying and wailing for his mercy on their sons. The judge never blinked or batted an eye. One thing I knew about Judge Rogers, before he gave you the hammer, he always would give you a very stern and defined warning. He was very clear about making sure the offender and parents understood his instructions.

Sometimes Judge Rogers would ask the person to repeat the instructions back to him just to make sure the youth and parent understood what was expected. However, during my nearly five years standing before Judge Rogers, I never saw a girl getting any kind of time in jail. It may have happened when I was not in the courtroom, but I personally never witnessed it.

Nearly everyone who entered Judge Rogers' courtroom would leave with an unbelievable story to tell. He was a fascinating man, to say the least.

* * *

Alvin Miller Sr., D. Min.

Over forty-five years later, I decided to research the youth chicken-stealing case that made Judge Rogers's name stick out as a hammer-crushing legend. A headline on page 24 of the *Tuscaloosa News* for Thursday, November 13, 1969, reads "Florida Officials Fear for Two Boy Convicts." The story goes on to say: "St. Lucie County Juvenile Judge Jack Rogers sentenced two boys to be committed to Florida's Adult Prison System, leaving state officials fearing for the youths' safety among harden hoods and homosexuals."

The article goes on to give a more detailed description of the boys from St. Lucie County. Donald Douglas was an 84-pound fourteen-year-old boy who looked ten, and he was sentenced along with fifteen-year-old Richard Copas to serve three-year terms for breaking and entering with the intent to commit a misdemeanor. Judge Rogers' response to turning the youths over to circuit court for trial was, "When you've got a bad apple, why keep it?"

Judge Rogers went on to say that the youths continued to commit offenses and break probation, and he felt the juvenile court facilities could not rehabilitate them. All I know is that nearly one and a half years before Judge Rogers left the helm of the juvenile court system in St. Lucie County, he promised me that if I ever came back to his courtroom, he would send me to Marianna Reformatory School for a long time.

Come to find out, a large number of boys did not return to their families after going to Marianna Reformatory School. They were murdered by some of the officers while doing time. During the 1960s and 1970s, my brother Gary was afraid that I would end up going to Marianna. He and other older guys in the community (including Terry Miller and Bob Washington) used to talk about the rumors of how evil and wicked Marianna Boys School was to its young criminals.

While I was standing in front of Judge Rogers, I was always terrified of the idea of being sent to the reformatory school. Yet the minute I left his courtroom and got with my neighborhood partners in crime, it was back to business as usual. It was like the Dr. Jekyll and Mr. Hyde syndrome all over again for me. I wanted to do the right thing, but there was this great pull from within me that seemed to drive me in the wrong direction each time I said to myself that I was going to do better.

Within the depths of my heart, I had every intention of staying out of trouble. Each time I would stand before Judge Rogers, I promised him

I would do better with my school attendance and obeying the law. Each time I came back to the judge, I was worse off than the time before.

I somehow knew my life was in shambles, but I did not know how to straighten it out. One thing I knew for sure about my life was that time was running out for me. I needed to do something to find a better way of living, because what I was doing at the time was not working for me. I dreaded the thought of the judge's wrath coming down on me or any of my relatives or friends.

* * *

Whenever I tried to do good in school or in the community, peer pressure always showed up to influence me to do the wrong things. Peer pressure celebrated me in my wrongness, and I did not have the maturity or intelligence to know it was only a setup for a downfall. Peer pressure among kids probably works its greatest magic of influence simply because young people are going through a state of developmental transition. To say the least, the psychological and physical changes that come along with puberty or adolescence makes our youth particularly vulnerable.

Kids are easily influenced to do right or wrong, and oftentimes they rebel against adult leadership and parental guidance. The greatest challenge is not to get our youth to do wrong but to encourage them to do the right things in life. A person's greatest struggle in life probably will be an inability to do the right thing and not focus on doing wrong.

For some strange reason, even at a very early age, it is more difficult for children to do right than to do wrong. It seems like doing wrong comes naturally but we have to work at doing the right things in life. There is so much negativity pulling at our youth that we have to plan and organize our resources, talents, and gifts to shelter and protect them.

We have to create an overwhelmingly positive environment with appealing activities that will keep youth focused on the positive things and not on the negative things in life. I have learned over the course of my life that people do not have to go looking for trouble; it has a way of finding them wherever they may reside. We have to purposely create positive activities so our youth will not have time or room to second-guess us and look for things on the bad side of life.

Kids really want to be like other kids, probably more than they want to be like adults. Kids enjoy being around and playing with other kids more than they do adults. Children will tolerate adults, but their hearts' desire is to mingle and play with other youth.

When I was a child, my friends and I wanted to be like our teenage role models. We considered those guys to be the toughest and strongest in the neighborhood. They were the leaders of the pack in our world—or shall I say *box*.

We thought adults were too boring and not hip enough to understand things that were happening in our youthful world. If we thought you were too old, we classified you as old-fashioned and old news. We thought we were the new generation with new ways of doing things better than the old ways. This is the philosophy of youth in every generation that comes along.

Our role models were bad guys and thugs. They were the ones who had all the money, women, cars, jewelry, fame, friends, and influence. So we thought we could do the same with our lives. As youngsters, we thought we knew what was best for us. We later realized we were the most ignorant kids of all. We found out it was just our imagination running away with us. We spent most of our young lives living in a fantasy world where dreams turn into nightmares.

* * *

One of the saddest things about my neighborhood is that I personally watched lots of people—including the elderly, teenagers, and young adults—living in a world of deception and false promises. When they finally came to the truth, it was too late for them to recover from the lie or deception. Adults may have all the knowledge and sophisticated machinery in the world, but they do not have a monopoly on the world of youth. Nature has a way of forcing adults out of the world of youth when they reach a certain age.

No matter how much a person desires to stay in the land of youth, no one is allowed to stay beyond checkout time. Neither can the person request a late checkout with the hope of staying forever. Some people attempt to move the hands of time in their favor by rolling them back. Yet with some things, nature remains faithful to the process of time.

It is a terrible thing when a ship loaded with people is sinking in shark-infested waters but the passengers on board are arguing about who are the best swimmers. How soon we forget that we are all in the same boat. There is a thin line between triumph and disaster. Disaster has a slow and sneaky way of approaching the scene without detection until it is too late, while triumph has a boisterous way of coming on the scene with all the bells and whistles.

Within a split second, there can be peace and then suddenly war. A person can be up one second and down the next. It is important to remember to never put ourselves above other people regardless of their circumstances or situations. Compassion for humanity is the golden rule that leaves no person behind.

Growing up as a child, I had bad examples of what a productive citizen looked like. From home to the migrant camps and then to the neighborhoods, I had observed people gambling and getting shot, stabbed, and cut with knives. I observed people "shacking up" with limited or no future. I stood in the same room with people smoking cigarettes and marijuana like smokestacks, and drinking liquor, wine, beer, gin, and moonshine (white lightning) like water.

I watched men and women fighting, and men abusing women like savage beasts. I saw grown men and women having sex before I was ten years old, in labor camps and within my community. How is a child to remain a child after witnessing such events? How are children to remain children when they have to take over the role of mother or father before their tenth birthday?

I saw things as a child under the age of twelve that the majority of people living in America will never see during an entire lifetime. Yet somehow, I was able to keep my sanity when it seemed like everything around me and within me was going wrong. Some things in life are just destined to turn out the way they do. I believe I was chosen to undergo hardships at a very early age so I could one day help others overcome obstacles, hardships, and dramas.

The simple philosophy that has helped me to succeed in life is to believe there is no problem so hard you cannot conquer it. There is no situation so big you cannot defeat it. There is no mountain so high or valley so low that you cannot overcome it with faith and perseverance. There is no trial or test so big that you cannot pass through with the help of good guidance, especially from loving family members and true friends.

I did not have time to look around and discuss the sadness of being exposed to such dehumanizing conditions as a child. As bad as it was for me, I thank life itself for giving me the opportunity to learn from my experiences. I am convinced my experiences from childhood pole-vaulted me over the many obstacles I faced in my life while growing up and as an adult.

At times, the road may have been hard and rough, but I was determined not to give up, and I continued until I crossed the finish line, where vast opportunities awaited. If I had complained and paraded my feelings in bitter sorrow, I would have become just another statistic. I did not make it through the obstacles and the various barriers in life by feeling sorry for myself.

I did not want to be like those people who spend a large portion of their lives complaining and blaming others for their downfall. I believe it is a tragedy to spend unproductive time complaining about one's situations rather than doing something positive to change it. People should not allow failures or mishaps in life to dictate their journey to happiness.

If a frog just sits on a log and make lots of noise, eventually it will get eaten by a predator. It's better to move anywhere good than to stay in the same spot with the same old complaint. I realized that the very first person who could help me change my situation from bad to good was me. I needed to take the necessary steps in the right direction to rewrite my life's story so it would have a good ending.

My childhood experiences became the anchor that kept me afloat when I went through many storms in life as an adult. My childhood experiences are constant motivators that feed my drive to succeed in life even to this day. My childhood experiences are the teachers that continue to stand before me, reminding me of the bad and horrible examples I used to exemplify when I was an unfulfilled little boy and young adult.

* * *

It was my experience of not having a father that showed me the type of father I wanted to be to my children. I never wanted to be an absent father without any type of support, responsibilities, or legacy to leave for my children and grandchildren to follow. I may not have been a perfect example or the world's best father; but I did my part to the best of my ability.

By no means was I going to be a deadbeat dad. For me, it was a torturous experience growing up without a father in my life. Why should I have to make up lies about my father taking me fishing or playing sports with me in order to hide the fact that I had no father actively involved in my life? It was all a façade. There was no father in my life as I grew up as a child—or when I became an adult. No Christmas toys, no birthdays, no vacations, no field trips, and no after-school activities. My father never showed up, participated, or attended.

As a misguided lad, my life was in shambles. For the most part of my young life, I was lost in the wilderness without a compass to give me direction. To this day, I am amazed that I found my way out of the dark forest that has consumed so many young lives. I recognize over the course of my life that there has been so much mercy extended to me by other people, both African Americans and Caucasians.

When people see and feel your heart's desire to succeed, they will be willing to reach out and give you a hand regardless of your skin color or sex. People love fighters and overcomers who play by the following rule: "Good things come to those who are willing to succeed through hard work." When people see you step in, they will step up to help you achieve great things in life. In America, if you make the decision to be honest, work hard, and exemplify compassion for humanity, I guarantee someone will come to your aid and help you succeed in life.

I would be remiss not to give back to others when so many have given so much to help me find my way off the road of destruction. I am constantly reminded that I should not be here writing this book. I know this is one of the main reasons I am compelled to give back to the community, especially to people who are as poverty-stricken as I once was. If goodhearted people can step into my life and help me to excel, then I can do the same for someone else.

If you truly want to experience success in life, you can have it on your doorstep if you put forth the effort with integrity. If life is willing to give you such great opportunities, you have to be willing to take advantage of every one that comes your way. If a person or child wants to succeed in life, there are people in your village who will give you a helping hand to become a productive citizen. I know this to be true because it happened to me.

No person walks in another person's shoes. Each person walks in his or her own shoes in life, regardless of how much the person attempts to imitate another. Here is the bottom line: each person is responsible for his or her own actions. I guarantee that if you follow the rules that produce productive citizens in our society, you will succeed in life.

Believe it or not, there are people in your world who will help once they know you are sincere and want to make a positive change. Find your Mrs. Rita M. Johnson, Mrs. Bertha Sullivan, Mr. Larry Lee Jr., Mr. Raymond Gordon, Mr. Arthur T. Johnson Jr., Mr. Curtis Johnson Sr., Mrs. Ivy Johnson, and Mr. Scott Van Duzer who will help you achieve your life's goal. There are community safe-havens standing by to help you excel and succeed in nearly any endeavor. You just have to believe in yourself, trust in others, and take advantage of every opportunity that comes your way.

I am grateful for the many heroes who passed my way in life. These heroes and heroines helped to shape and mold my life into what it is today. Their kind deeds motivated me to emulate that same compassion toward others along my path in life.

* * *

Each day I rise in the morning to greet new life, it is my greatest desire to become a beacon of hope for our youth as well as adults. I look to pass on the deeds of kindness to others I may know or may not know. I feel obligated to help shape and mold the lives of young people for the good of humanity. As the late great radio commentator Paul Harvey would often say, "Now, you know the rest of the story!"

In 2005, the Rapper T. I. released a song called "U Don't Know Me." It climbed to number 23 on the US Billboard Hot 100. In the song, T. I. says, "Yeah, you know they call me T. I., but you don't know me." I echo the words of T. I. to people who think they know me just because they grew up with me or remember me during my silly adolescent days in Fort Pierce.

The great African American spiritual singer Mahalia Jackson would sing, "Nobody Knows the Trouble I've Seen." Always remember that every storm has its own story, and even though the storms may be similar in nature and destruction, no two storms are identical. Yet you can survive nearly any storm with the help of devoted friends and loved ones.

Whenever I share portions of my story with family members or close friends, they seem taken aback by some of the things I had to endure as a child. These people often say, "I did not know that," or "Why didn't you let us or someone know what you were going through?" Then I say to myself, *Just because you know my name, it doesn't mean you know me*, even if we are bloodline kin. If you knew me from elementary through middle school, prior to my meeting Mrs. Johnson, you would have more than likely classified me as "most likely not to succeed in life."

No matter how well you do in life, there will always be people from your past who will make attempts to destroy your character. Such enemies will hate your success based on their hidden jealousy that surfaces as lethal shots of destruction. Keep in mind that a coral snake cannot change its stripes. It will always be one of the deadliest snakes on earth. Your enemies will never love you, for if they did, they will no longer be your enemies!

Sometimes as a small kid, your maturity level and mind may not process things the same as teenagers or adults. You may not even know the procedures of how to file a complaint or how to handle your fear about certain issues taking place in your life at the time. As a child, you are still learning who you can trust.

As you mature in life from childhood to adulthood, you will learn how to differentiate between trustworthy and untrustworthy human beings. So, at best, you have to do whatever you can to shield and protect yourself from enemies wishing you harm. Keep in mind, it is a great undertaking to protect yourself from enemies; you must ensure you do not allow yourself to become your enemy as well.

Many of the things I went through and endured as a child resonate in my mind like vivid scenes, as if they happened yesterday. All I can say is, the proof is in the pudding. Longevity has allowed special people to remain alive who can corroborate and support what I have written here today. Just because you know my name, and you may even know a portion of my story, does not mean you truly know me or my full story.

* * *

Within the pages of this book, I hope you will see I am willing to share my life story with the hope of helping to change the lives of children and adults so they may experience the best things life has to offer. I do not want any child to endure the hardship like I brought upon myself. Working together as a village, I believe we can make life more enjoyable and easier

Alvin Miller Sr., D. Min.

for our young people. I am committed to this sacred task where no kid is left behind. What is your vote on this important matter?

Most people who know me do not have any inclination of the various tunnels of despair that I came through as a child as well as an adult. Nearly all of my friends and acquaintances today have come to know me after I came through life's fiery refinery. During my adolescent years, I could not stand myself, and it was difficult for others to accept me as well.

On one particular day, I saw my mother with water in her eyes, and I felt the pain of hurt when my actions and those of my brother Gary forced her down to juvenile court to stand before Judge Rogers. Believe it or not, it was a long time before my mother found out that we had missed so many days in school. We would beat her to the mailbox and hide or destroy any mail that we suspected came from the school board or Children's Protective Services.

We knew how to play the game, but not well enough. Criminal losers, whether small or big, young or old, Black or white, Hispanic, or any other ethnic group, always get caught by the law. The best thing is to do the right things in life and save yourself, your family members, and your friends from great pain, embarrassment, and shame. You and your loved ones deserve better than to be given the mantle of disgrace.

Regardless of how things may sound or look to you concerning my life's story, it is what it is, and no one can change it or take it away. Many things that happened to me as a child I brought upon myself. I earned scars, stripes, and experiences on the battlefield of life. I am not proud of how I lived life as a juvenile, but I am very thankful for the people I met during the novice years of my journey in life. I am not proud of some of the things I did as an adult, but I am happy to grow up and live in a nation where second chances are foundational gifts to all.

Just think, from the age of six to thirteen, I was a runaway suicidal cannonball waiting to explode in society. I am thankful that I never landed on a target. I am thankful that I was defused by some arsenal experts before I could ignite into an explosion. I was like an airplane in free fall and headed to the ground for a crash due to the loss of power. I was a disaster as a juvenile.

I am amazed by how I was protected by a very powerful veil while walking in a state of total darkness. Only by the mercy of goodhearted people was I able to overcome great hurdles and give back to society. I am keenly aware that if it were not for the mercy of a middle school principal, the compassion of a seventh-grade teacher, and the unselfish attitude of a mother in need, I probably would have made prison my home or a cold grave my resting place as a wayward juvenile. This is my story, and I find it an honor to share it with you.

Happy to Be Alive

I t is amazing that I am still alive to make contributions to society by helping people to get on or stay on the right road in life. It is my greatest desire to help others overcome their own daily trials and tribulations. I truly believe my story as a boy could serve as an encouraging key to release boys and girls from the destructive dungeons of life. Given the reckless life I lived as a delinquent juvenile, it is amazing to me that I am still alive to share my story in this book.

I have made a vow that I will spend my life working for the betterment of humanity. I feel like I owe my life to the service of helping others achieve the American dream, like others helped me. For this reason, I am willing to share my story and testimony with the world.

I believe I can help others rise out of their dungeons to make positive changes in their lives, like others have done for me. Some kids may only need an encouraging word or boost from an adult to put them on the path to a positive change. It is a very delicate process when helping youth make the transition to deliberately travel the right road in life.

In retrospect, my life story is like a puzzle with many pieces that I will put together to some degree, for you in this book. There are so many pieces to the puzzle that I have forgotten some of the things that have happened to me during my lifetime. Even some of my dearest friends and closest relatives do not know the full story of my life.

Some people may know a quarter, or half, or three fourths of the puzzle as it relates to my upbringing and my life. Although I have forgotten much, only life knows all of the pieces to the puzzle I was given. There are personal tragedies and things that happened to me during my youth that I probably will never talk about.

When I was a little boy, I used to hear the old folks say, "There are some things that need to be buried and never brought up again." Another saying amongst some of my seniors was, "Some things are not meant to be told." Here is another saying by the old folks when I was growing up: "No one would know your business if you did not tell it. Stop the gossip!" The moral to the story was to limit your information flow in order to keep people from knowing your business.

The less people know about your personal life, the more information you can keep to yourself. During the age of social media, it is pertinent that you keep your personal information sealed in a vault as much as you can. You have to do everything within your power to protect your information so hackers do not retrieve it and spread it throughout the world. Keep in mind, some pieces of information are public records, such as birth certificates, marriage licenses, your address, vehicle registrations, and other pertinent information.

If you were born after 1966, you probably would not be old enough to know the depths of my personal struggles in life. I am not proud of the fact that I probably broke more laws and school rules by the time I was ten or eleven years old than most people break during their entire lifetime. This is nothing to brag about by any means.

I share this information so you will know the calamity I encountered as a juvenile, and to encourage you not to make the same mistake. Believe me on this: nothing is impossible when people put their minds and actions together to accomplish a desired result or goal. Unity breeds success when everyone works together for the good and well-being of our young people.

By the time I reached middle school, I was considered the most notorious juvenile in the St. Lucie County Public School District. Dr. Skinner, other school administrators, and teachers within the district were sick and tired of my shenanigans. When I was in sixth grade, I probably set a record for the most days on the suspension list, which caught the eye of my principal and the superintendent of schools.

Some people who lived at the 23rd Street Projects housing development with me—and around Avenue D and 18th Street, where I spent a large portion of my adolescent years—can attest to my brushes with the law as a juvenile. During some of my youthful years, I spent a large amount of time with my grandmother and some of my aunts (Aunt Betty, Aunt Carrie, Aunt Vera, and Aunt Ethel). They know of the turbulent times I had as a child.

I spent a lot of my time in and out of the juvenile court system, to include various suspension lists while in middle school. I was known as an elementary school truant while attending Garden City and Chester A. Moore elementary schools and Dan McCarty Middle School. As a young boy, I felt as though school was not a friendly environment for me, so I did not attend.

Of course, if you are in generations X or Y, or a Millennial, you probably cannot begin to fathom my story and some of the things I went through as a child. Before one can begin to understand the picture, one needs to research the era and culture I grew up in during the 1960s. My upbringing centers around being a fatherless child with a single mother who spent a lot of her time absent from the house because of her work schedule.

At an early age, I found myself having very little respect for authority figures. I spent the majority of my juvenile years living in government housing projects, working in tomato fields, and picking oranges and grapefruits in the fruit groves as a migrant worker. I was a dissident from education and school because there was no connection between me and education. This was the bleak story of my childhood prior to my thirteenth birthday.

* * *

My journey through life is something I have just begun to talk about in detail with the writing of this manuscript. I was of the opinion that my disgraceful past was too personal and private to let other people in on it. With the encouragement of Mrs. Johnson and my wife, I have begun to open up and share my story with the world, with the hope that I will be able to help others overcome struggles in their own lives.

Through much pondering and very careful consideration, I decided to write this book. I came to the conclusion that if my story can help others overcome their life issues, I am obligated to help them avoid some of the pitfalls that hindered me. I believe I have an obligation to help others as others helped me overcome my battles and personal struggles during my journey through life as a boy.

As I open up and share my story, I do not need to make up anything fictitious in order to inflate a story for book sales. My goal is to share my testimony in the hope that people around the world will be helped. One of the most important things to remember about life is that it is not always about what you get out of life for yourself; it is more about what we put into life so others can benefit from our positive actions.

When we give a helping hand to others who are in need of our support, we have given the best gift of all. Being our brother's or sister's keeper is one of the most noble honors we can achieve in life. Imagine living your entire life and leaving a legacy of never helping anyone but yourself. What a tragedy that would be!

There is one thing I know for sure: During my earlier years, I lived in a box that encouraged me to shape my world on the dark side of life. My world was one of poverty, shaped by the sounds of misery and destruction. Growing up in poverty and having kids and adults making fun of me sparked an internal rage that could not be medicated away.

I did not come from some middle- or upper-class family that had it going on in the community. We were classified as so low on the poverty spectrum that even poor families would pick at me and my brothers. Many mothers and parents we knew growing up did not want their children to hang around us or play with us.

I can't blame the parents for their insecurities, especially when it came to me and my brothers. Protective parents considered me a terrible influence as a child growing up in Fort Pierce. In retrospect, I was a danger to the community and a bad influence on other children.

When one of my aunts saw me and my brothers coming toward her house, she would call her son inside the house and tell us to go home. We were living too rough for the lifestyle my cousin was accustomed to. He was a good boy and knew nothing of the streets.

All we wanted as kids was to play with our cousin. But my aunt would tell us, "He cannot come out and play with y'all today." This was pretty much the script every time we tried to play with him. We had no intention of inviting our cousin to become a part of the life we were living. As kids, we could not understand the fear that was going on in the mind of our aunt and uncle. You see, they were married, with two loving and well-behaved children.

My cousin grew up as a good child without any blemishes on his childhood track record. But as an adult, he sadly became the thing his mother tried her best to shield him from. It is amazing to me how some people's lives consist of two halves: night and day. As for me, my night was the first half, and now, I am living the second half of my life in the daylight. As I reflect on the darkness of my juvenile years, I can cherish the beautiful sunshine of my adult years regardless of the weather forecast. I have walked through the shadow of darkness and know the devastation of living in the dark world of defeat.

* * *

I vividly remember my mother as a very hard worker in the tomato fields, fruit groves, and the fish farms of South Florida. I have reflections on the times I spent as a migrant worker with my aunts, and the nearly three years I spent with Mr. Raymond Gordon Sr. (deceased) and family while working in the following states as a migrant worker: South Carolina, Virginia, Pennsylvania, Maryland, and New York. Keep in mind, I was a migrant worker in each of these states as a boy between the age of eight and thirteen. I went "up the road" or "on the season" with Luke Sandlin (deceased) at least three times and with Raymond Gordon Sr. at least three times when I was a child in elementary and middle school.

Many migrant labor camps looked like pictures of rundown slum slave plantation camps, which were familiar to neighborhoods in the south where I had either lived or visited. The other amazing thing about each migrant camp was the outhouses for all your restroom needs. The popular pool halls, jukeboxes, juke joints, bars, dance halls, bootlegging houses, and living quarters gave tenants some type of accommodating pleasure or thrill for the moment.

The living quarters would sometimes look like a plantation big house or section of slave huts. I kid you not, during the 1960s and 1970s, the places where migrant workers lived resembled slave huts to say the least. Nearly all of the migrant labor camps were very dirty, unkempt, and infested with bedbugs. The iron-framed twin beds had mattresses that were dry-rotted, with urine stains from previous years. You bathed in your own purchased tin tub because the camps did not have community showers.

Another thing that was unique to nearly every migrant labor camp was the fact that there were big shade trees located on the properties where old-school crews hung out. The guys and ladies who hung out under the trees were known for giving history lessons about things in life that they themselves could not follow. These people had all the answers about life, gambling, drinking wine, and liquor, and a host of war stories to share.

The old-school men and women hanging around the shade trees stood ready to give streetwise lessons about life. Some had taught in public schools somewhere across the United States but had fallen on hard times somewhere along the line. I was familiar with the process, because it was similar to my growing up in Fort Pierce. Some of these places and hangouts in Fort Pierce are still in existence today, as they were when I was growing up.

My return home is like going to a family reunion, where you feel honored and appreciated by a group of people who still remember your name. Such hometown recognition by people you grew up with is an honor to have in your vault of appreciations. I find great joy in returning home just to see how far faith, hope, and the help of others have brought me.

During my short visits back to Fort Pierce, I get a chance to see what's left of the neighborhood and community I once knew. It thrills my heart to see some of my old neighborhood friends and to witness the old-school gangsters teaching and training the new school youth for their patrol and survival training sessions on the streets of life. Many of the names and faces in the crowd, I can still recognize. Yet some of the new names and faces I did not know. Although there are new faces in the crowd, you can almost tell their family bloodline or roots by their physical characteristics or names.

Oddly enough, growing up in poverty-stricken Fort Pierce was an awesome experience for me. I enjoyed the camaraderie that families demonstrated even though they were not physically related. We would go in and out of the little hut houses as though we lived with the family. We knew the names of all the siblings and everyone living in the shack, hut, or house.

When my grandmother would be cooking her evening dinner and needed a little flour, lard, eggs, or butter, she would tell me to go down the street and get it from Mrs. Fannie or Ms. Margret or go to Mother Price. I would return to my grandmother with the items she sent me to pick up. None of the people seem bothered by me coming and asking for the items. This was in an era when neighbors truly lived out the creed of "good neighbors."

People had a heart of giving to their neighbors when the need arose. To this day, I am still fascinated by how people looked out for each other on a daily basis. I yearn for those wonderful days to return when you could leave your doors unlocked without some intruder coming in to do you or your family bodily harm.

During my childhood days, community members took the responsibility to help mentor and care for each other as though they were blood-related family members. Adults watched out for children as well as other adults within our poor neighborhoods. We may have been in poverty when it came to monetary wealth, but we were rich when it came to community support, compassion, and communication. If Mrs. Daisey knew about it, Ms. Susie knew about it as well, and so on. Then the pertinent information would pass throughout the community like wildfire.

* * *

Let me share a piece of very important information with you. I was not enrolled into the public-school system by my mother or any of my blood relatives. It was a very dear friend of the family who enrolled me in first grade. After she had enrolled her son in school, she made sure I was enrolled as well.

Yes indeed, it was Ms. Lessie Mae Cook who registered me for elementary school. This was the very first time I'd had any interaction with formal education in my young life. Ms. Lessie Mae Cook was the mother of Bob Washington, Jerry "Tip" Cook, and my childhood friend, the late Michael Lee Cook. I can still remember her taking information from my cousin, Terry Roosevelt Miller, and marching right into the school office at 21st Street and Avenue Q.

My mother could not take off from work as a migrant worker in the tomato fields to register me for school. So, the responsibility was left up to my big "brother-cousin," Terry R. Miller. Terry was to enter the sixth grade this particular year. My mommy asked Terry to take me to school and register me. I was six years old at the time, and Terry was around thirteen.

When we arrived at the main office of Garden City Elementary School, I was initially denied enrollment because there was no adult on hand to vouch for me and sign me in. Terry could not enroll me into school because he was not an adult, according to the office secretary.

Keep in mind that Terry was only around seven years old—ten months older than me. School district policy prohibited a child from enrolling another child in school. Terry should have been an adult family member or guardian, according to district policy.

Believe it or not, Ms. Lessie Mae Cook registered me as one of her children. You may call it whatever you wish, but I call it a "ram in the bush"! I call it enrollment or registration completed. Yes, it really does take a village to raise a child and to have compassionate morals for self, family, and humanity.

Alvin Miller, 14 years old, (right) at Southern University in Baton Rouge, LA with Fort Pierce native Arthur Lee Boatright (left). A summer trip with Jimmie and Rita Johnson

Mr. Boatright (deceased)
Alvin Miller in middle school at thirteen years old.

PART TWO

The True Confession
of My Testimony

Lost Boys

I received a telephone call from one of my younger brothers, James *'Stewbeef'* Miller. *Stewbeef* told me that one of our boyhood heroes had been put to death by lethal injection in Florida on Tuesday night (January 7, 2014). Thomas Knight was his birth name, but while in prison, he changed his name to Askari Abdullah Muhammad. At the time when my brother informed me about the execution of Thomas Knight, he had very little information about it.

During our brief telephone conversation, *Stewbeef* said he'd heard the news about the execution on the streets of Fort Pierce. According to the families of the people Thomas Knight had supposedly killed, including a Florida prison guard, his execution was long overdue. The execution of Thomas Knight was the subject of conversation all over the city of Fort Pierce.

For years, the Thomas Knight story was one of the top stories in the Northwest section of Fort Pierce, Florida. Fort Pierce has seen its share of characters over the course of the past sixty years, but the Thomas Knight story may have been the biggest one of them all.

On January 29, 1989, the *News Tribune* newspaper of Fort Pierce published an article entitled "Treasure Coast Killers Still Years from Execution" by Janie Gould. The news article highlighted Fort Pierce as one of the smallest cities in the state of Florida population-wise. Yet it was the number-one city per capita for highest number of persons on death row in comparison to other cities across Florida. According to the 1988 Florida Statistical Abstract in the *Tribune* on February 1, 1989 (pg. A-12), Fort Pierce had one of the highest per capita murder rates in the nation with 29 murders, with 74 murders per 100,000 people and a population of only 39,188.

Thomas Knight, aka Askari Abdullah Muhammad, was put to death for fatally stabbing a prison guard, Richard Burke, with a sharpened spoon. According to news reports, Thomas was originally sentenced to die for the 1974 kidnapping and killing of Sydney and Lilian Gans of Miami. Thomas Knight had spent nearly forty years on death row due to various appeals.

Finally, at the age of sixty-two, on Tuesday, January 7, 2014, at 6:45 p.m., Thomas Knight was pronounced dead by a Florida State Prison spokesperson. When I learned of the news, I immediately called my boyhood friend of over fifty years, Jerome Rhyant, and shared the news with him. We'd both had a sense that Thomas's execution was inevitable, but we were both shocked that it had actually happened. For nearly forty years, Thomas Knight had used loopholes in the law to escape the death penalty—until 6:45 p.m. on January 7, 2014.

Fate has its own time and way of keeping its appointment. Death has a way of chasing us down no matter how hard or fast we run, especially when we have a scheduled date with justice. I am still amazed that Thomas was able to dodge the Florida electric chair and death row for so long, even after killing a prison guard during a breakout from prison.

When my brother told me that Thomas Knight had been executed, all I could do was reflect on our family and reminisce about the times when we were kids playing at the Knights' house in the 23rd Street Projects. I thought about his mother, his brothers and his sisters, and the pain and shame they probably felt for a large portion of their lives due to the crimes Thomas had committed. I also thought about the years of pain and suffering he'd caused innocent people and families. When men and women take the lives of innocent people, there is no honor or fame attached to their name, only shame.

As I think about the life of Thomas Knight, I reflect that many people believed I was headed in the same diabolical direction. Due to our ignorance and youthful innocence, Thomas Knight was one of the heroes from the 23rd Street Projects, along with other leaders like Bob Washington, Eugene "Bee" Dixon, John Cobbs, and Terry "T. R." Miller. The greater tragedy about this situation is that a young man grew up thinking and believing he could take innocent lives simply because he felt disrespected or entitled to something that did not belong to him.

During my childhood, I played and hung out with Thomas's younger brothers, Tony and John. Although I knew Dewitt and Allen Knight, I hung out with the two older brothers. We were kids living inside a box where poverty is choking you so severely that you have no sense or knowledge of its crippling effects and shrewdness.

* * *

Most people growing up poor become desensitized to the constant pains of poverty that strike them at every turn. I once knew this feeling, and believe me, it is very dehumanizing and bitter. Being poor is a like a terrible bee or wasp sting that continues to cripple and affect your immune system for life or until you receive the proper medication to treat your injury.

Poverty is a lethal weapon. Its venom spreads over a community like a cancer. Poverty penetrates down to the souls of men and women, boys and girls, and surgically removes its victims' hopes and vision, replacing them with blindness and numbness about their condition. Once poverty has performed its mission, it leads the injured to destructive graves.

The victims of poverty must wake up and fight for their lives with the acceleration of success and prosperity through hard work. Poverty is like a flash of darkness that people must battle with everything in them, never succumbing to defeat. I know poverty so very well because it lived with me as my most dominant family member for all of my childhood, as well as some of my adult years.

When your reality is so depressing, in order to just cope in life, a person sometimes has to create a make-believe world that offers hope even if it is a sense of false hope. I can vouch that this is sometimes the case with children when nothing else is working for them. This is how many children learn to cope, especially if their lives are filled with chaos, confusion, abuse, and other deficiencies or uncertainties.

Alvin Miller Sr., D. Min.

Although I was traveling and swimming in the waterways of deception, I continued to dream about finding a place of opportunity where I could feel the warmth of love and appreciation. I did not want to continue floating in the waterways of deception and end up drowning in the trenches of lost hope. I am thankful for the Miller, Johnson, and Skinner partnership that saved the day for me. I sincerely believe I would not be the same without the intervention of concerned and loving people like Mrs. Johnson, Dr. Skinner, and my mother. I would not be here writing this book if this trinity had not worked on my behalf.

As foolish boys growing up, we began to talk and act like some of the older boys we idolized in the neighborhood. We were totally oblivious to the danger and criminal path we were taking in our lives. We had no idea of the monsters we were demanding to be employed just for false perception of material things, fame, and fortune. This roller coaster ride would turn out to be a rough and dangerous one for all of us.

Keep in mind, we were only a group of kids, not knowing much about the reality of the various vices that were connected to the bigger picture and the bigger world. We did not know that a wicked world awaited us if we decided to live our lives on the wrong side of the road. We had no idea that if we took the road that leads to nothing, we would definitely end up at a dead-end like some of the guys we once knew.

We were clueless about the trouble and destruction that awaited us if our decisions kept taking us on wrong turns. Remember, the people traveling on the left side of the road in life have to travel on this wide and winding road that leads to trouble, embarrassment, and eventually destruction. They all made up their minds to serve their own personal desires regardless of the people they end up hurting along the way.

* * *

I can remember this one kid and his family when they first moved into the projects. He was a good kid until he started hanging around with me and my brother *Stewbeef.* This young kid's name was John Earl Bush (deceased), and prior to meeting me and the clan, I don't believe he had any devious intent in his mind. I know for a fact he did not have a troubled record within the community of Fort Pierce prior to us talking him down off the front porch this particular day.

I cannot remember a time when John Earl had ever left his house to play on the playground with the other kids living in the projects. He was not allowed to leave the house to play with us, because we were considered the bad kids. I still remember the day when we were walking by the apartment where John Earl lived. It was a day that would change his life forever.

The Bushes lived next door to the Phillips family. We taunted John Earl Bush by calling him all sorts of derogatory names like *coward*, *chump*, and *mommy's boy*. We angered him so badly that he forgot the rules his parents had given him. He became determined to prove to us that he was none of the things we were calling him.

So, on that particular day, John Earl left the porch and followed us. The sad thing is that from this day forward, he never returned to the porch. John Earl made one of the biggest mistakes of his young life by coming off the porch and following the wrong crowd in life. I would like to encourage you to realize that it is always better to listen to your parents who sincerely love you over some so-called friends who may or may not even like you. I believe if John had it to do all over again, he would have listened to his parents and stayed on the porch.

At first glance, when you looked at John Earl, you would have said to yourself this small guy seems harmless or he can't harm a mosquito. You may not associate him with being a deadly killing machine. John Earl Bush was a small-framed, thin-built young man. He was not a loudmouth like me, Tony, or *Stewbeef*. You would not have known he was in the crowd until he opened his mouth, and then it was on and popping with vulgar words.

Even for project kids, John Earl and another friend could make up language you've probably never heard before. You did not want either of these guys to start joking on you with their fresh jokes. They would slice you up so smoothly with their jokes, and then turn around and look at you with a smile.

When I first met John Earl around 1969, he was a very quiet and timid kid. He did not like us pushing him to the limit by challenging his boldness, manhood, or authenticity as a real gangster. The sadness to John Earl Bush's story is that once he got a taste of the so-called street life, he was out to prove his point of being a real genuine street thug by any means necessary. All of this occurred during the early 1970s, when we were mostly around ten or twelve.

These events with John Earl Bush took place in the early 1970s. I remember that because hair braids, Afros, and platform shoes were in style within the African American culture. John Earl Bush had this huge Afro that covered nearly his entire face. Sometimes John wore his hair loose (free of plats or unbraided), and we would tease him about looking like Michael Jackson due to the look of his afro and his wide eyes like MJ.

Keep in mind that to be identified as looking like any of the Jackson 5 guys was a great honor! And looking like Michael Jackson meant you had hit the jackpot with all of the girls. Back in the early 1970s, to be identified with the Jacksons was the ultimate compliment for an African American young male.

When I was a child in elementary and middle school, the Jackson 5 sensational singing group was probably the most famous teenage group in America. Within the African American culture during the 1970s, the Jackson 5 was the dream of every youth across America, both male and female. Their awesome music wasn't the only thing that was on beat to the ears and hearts of Americans. Their rise to stardom gave hope to so many African Americans who were coming out of the racial turmoil of the Civil Rights Movement.

The Jackson 5 was a very unique group with their big globe-like Afros, their attire, and their smooth dance moves that memorized crowds by the millions. The Jackson 5 gave a beat and dance to a generation of people who needed something good to dance about after years of turbulence and disruption.

I am not trying to take anything away from the fabulous super-phenomenon from Liverpool, England. The dynamic Beatles were in a class of their own. However, it was the famous Motown Sound of the Jackson 5 that melted the hearts of African Americans. We all seemed to fall in love with this teenage fad that changed the sound of music in our hearts.

They showed off their synchronized moves on *Soul Train*, *The Ed Sullivan Show*, and *American Bandstand*. John Earl Bush loved it when we called him Michael Jackson. It gave him a great sense of recognition to be associated with the Jackson 5, even though it was just an imagination gone wild.

For some strange reason, I always felt like John Earl Bush believed he had to prove himself in order to be recognized as a real gangster. He made us think he was out to prove something to the world. He constantly thought people were trying to intimidate him and bully him simply because of his small stature. He had a complex about people not giving him the respect he thought he deserved. He was very paranoid about people trying to walk over him.

John Earl was bent on the idea of proving that he had the tools and power to be a real hard-nosed gangster from the hood. It was like he had something to prove to the guys and girls he would encounter while doing our devious deeds, trying to survive in the ghetto.

It probably was this chip about demanding respect from others that lead to John Earl Bush's demise. He was very adamant about people respecting him as a real gangster. It looks like John Earl pushed for the recognition to be intimidating and strong and not weak or timid.

* * *

In 1996, while teaching at my alma mater, Fort Pierce Central High School, I received a telephone call from a news reporter asking me about the young man who had just been executed in Florida's electric chair. At first, the news reporter called Mrs. Gloria Johnson, the principal of Fort Pierce Central High School at the time, but she referred him to me. This particular morning as teachers, staff, students, and employees arrived at school, the word had surfaced that John Earl Bush would be executed sometime during the day. I was clueless as to the exact time.

As a result, people from Fort Pierce were waiting on the report, simply because of the last-minute stays of executions we had witnessed over the years in the Florida court system. The entire last-minute stay of execution process was a seesaw and a whirlwind of a ride for victims' families and death row inmates. It seemed like the dreaded long wait was about to be over, especially for families awaiting justice in the aftermath of criminals murdering their loved ones.

At my high school, you could feel the tension in the atmosphere as we waited for the news about the execution of John Earl Bush. In many of the classrooms, you could hear a pin drop on the floor. It seemed like a quietness came over Fort Pierce Central High School. Students were being quiet and mild-tempered while awaiting news about the execution.

Finally, after I regained my composure from the initial shock of the news that my childhood friend was dead, I began talking to the reporter. He wanted to get my thoughts on the execution. I was in a state of shock, because it could have been me, my brothers, or any of the boys who hung out in the group with us. Eventually, I sat down at my desk and talked about growing up on 23rd Street in the government housing project with John Earl Bush.

I was somewhat baffled as to how the reporter knew about my relationship with John Earl. I wanted to know how he had connected the dots all the way from the Florida State Prison in Bradford County to my childhood, and then from my childhood all the way to my classroom in Fort Pierce. I was thankful the call came during my planning period, because I did not want any of the students to hear the conversation between me and the reporter.

I often tell my children, church members, family, and friends, as well as other people and especially kids, that there are some things in life that will form your reputation. One of those things is your integrity. Also, there are things we do in life that will follow us to and beyond our graves. The echoes associated with our actions will live long beyond our natural lives.

The longevity of our reputation is why it is so important to leave a worthy legacy for those who will come and walk in your footprints. For this reason alone, it is important to plant good seeds and leave a good reputation of helping and loving people beyond their faults and personal limitations. The greatest gift we can give to each other is compassion that uplifts lives without limitations or demands for some type of attachment in return.

As I reflect on my life, I can see that growing up without certain things taught me a very valuable lesson about materialism. I have learned not to gloat over things that do not have the power to love me back. When we really think about the material world that many people chase during their lives, in all actuality, it is just a bunch of stuff they are running behind. If you lose it all, just remember that friends and loved ones are more important than all the stuff in the world.

My life in poverty taught me not to be selfish or stingy. I know what it's like to not have any toys on your birthday or for Christmas. I know what it's like to not have a father in your life to bring you dignity and self-worth along with a host of other things that are important to building a child's self-esteem. I know what it's like to endure embarrassment simply because you are poor. I also know how to overcome pitfalls that others have planned for my downfall.

The reporter asked me how it made me feel to grow up with someone who had just been executed. How was I able to overcome so many obstacles and pitfalls while some of my classmates and childhood friends were not? The reporter was amazed that two boys who came from the same housing project and hung out together and committed some of the same devious acts could end up on two different roads later in life.

"What made things so different?" the reporter asked me. He was intrigued by our family dynamic and backgrounds. One boy grew up with a mother and father in the home, while one boy was without a father and had a mother who was hardly ever in the home because of her work schedule. Yet the boys took two totally different roads in life.

The news reporter could not put his finger on the scenario of my life and Bush's life, especially after finding out that I was the ringleader of the group. He said he had heard rumors about my dysfunctional childhood, and it seems like I was expected to be the person who would be sitting on death row or in the electric chair, and not John Earl Bush.

I became very quiet and agreed with his statement that I was the one projected to end up in the electric chair. I probably should have been the one executed instead of John Earl Bush, but that is not the way things turned out. I reminded the reporter that one the beauties of America is that so many people have been given multiple chances to excel in life even after serious mistakes. I am one of those persons.

I explained to the news reporter that one day in seventh grade, I came to a fork in the road. When I turned to the left, the wrong direction, I saw myself walking on the road to destruction, but I did not know what to do or how to get off the road. Everywhere I turned, I ended up right back on the same path. Then, out of nowhere, a hand reached out and turned me from the wrong direction to the right direction. Just think—if I had not changed my directional travel in life when I was in the seventh grade, I too would be facing a disaster in the making.

For some reason, I could not get myself to do the right thing without a strong support system giving me wise guidance. It took the combination of my mother, my seventh-grade teacher, and my school principal to give me the opportunity of a lifetime. I desperately needed and desired to go the right way, but I did not know how to get on the right road. I was lost in a world without any kind of road map or GPS to get me to a productive destination in life.

* * *

As of January 2014, out of the eighty-two persons who have been executed in the state of Florida since 1979, two of them were from my hometown of Fort Pierce. Both men came from the same project housing area and street where I grew up. Neither of these guys was a stranger to me. I knew both of them. I knew them to the point that we impacted each other's lives in some way.

As you peruse the Florida's Department of Corrections execution list of inmates who have been executed since 1979, numbers #37 and #82 are products of my hometown. The number does not include the inmates from Port St. Lucie and St. Lucie County who continue to await their fate on death row. From the initial writing of this book, there are still some of my boyhood friends waiting for their appointment with death.

As I reflect on my poverty-stricken beginnings, I will never forget what love has done for me and where its kindness has brought me. I will tell my story every time I get the chance. I will never become ashamed of my ghetto past, or my illiterate educational woes, or my fatherless childhood, or the painful and hurtful deck of cards that embarrassment dealt me as a child. There is this Awesome Man who brought peace to me in the midst of my many defeats and struggles.

Although my upbringing brought me lots of shame and pain as a child, I was never too ashamed to take the blame for my destructive actions. I am a living example of what we can become if we stop blaming others for our failures or misfortunes in life. Believe me, if you start doing something positive to correct the situation or environment, help will greet you on the trail. Remember, the buck starts and stops with you being willing to chart your own path with positive steps and constructive leaps as you go through life.

The Legacy of a Hard-Working Mom

From the time I was about seven years old all the way through middle school, my mother worked in the tomato fields and orange groves of Florida. I can see her struggling with those heavy fruit sacks of oranges and grapefruits, dumping the sacks in the fruit bins.

My momma would return to the fruit trees only to repeat the same action over and over again as a fruit picker attempting to do her best. I can see large veins popping out of her arm when she would pick up her tomato basket to move down the row in the tomato field. She was a hardworking woman doing her best to make ends meet for her fatherless children.

Yes, Mommy was a very hardworking woman, and if you know my family, you will know this to be a true statement. During my entire life, my mother has had a job or two and has been a very committed and loyal hard worker. Growing up in a citrus county and being surrounded by counties that produced vegetables and fruits like cabbage, oranges, grapefruits, lemons, tangerines, watermelons, and tomatoes meant guaranteed work for my mother's kids. On the weekend, she would make us go to the citrus groves and tomato fields and help her make extra income for the household.

Even at the ripe age of seventy-four, my mother was still working in the Florida fruit industry as a fruit packer and grader from time to time. She also loves working in her yard, planting and nurturing her vegetable garden, or packing fruit in a packing house factory. She gets great joy and satisfaction out of what she does at work, even now, at eighty-one years old.

As I reflect over my past, it seems like work for my mother was her way of clearing her mind from the degrading conditions associated with poverty. Somewhere in life, my mother found herself stuck in a life of poverty with her children having to endure the hardship each day they would awake. I remember my mother trying to change her situation by coming home from work and then going to night school at Lincoln Park Academy (LPA) in the late 1960s, but life's stumbling blocks kept disrupting her from reaching her goal of gaining a high school diploma (GED).

After several attempts at LPA's Night School for Adult Learners and Indian River Junior College Adult Education Program, my mother's dream of receiving her high school diploma seemed to slip further away. What can a single mother do for her children (ten by that point) when she has no husband or formal education beyond the eighth grade? Her only hope in life was to trust in fate to intervene for a miracle to save some of her children from the traps and pitfalls of life while living in the ghetto or hood.

Sadly, over the years, I have seen too many mothers in similar situations lose too many of their babies to some of the many misfortunes of poverty, crime, and the lack of a higher education. If you are reading this book and are thinking about quitting school, please don't do it! The greatest hope a child or adult has to beat the odds of poverty is a good education.

A quality education is the bargaining power you will need in order to lift yourself out of poverty. Your education is the key that will open the door to an ocean of opportunities beyond your wildest dreams. Try it and see for yourself. It worked for me, and it will work for you if you are willing to put in hard work with faith and hope.

My mother never complained about her situation or tried to shift the blame onto her parents or our useless and despicable fathers, who refused to help her with child support. She always attempted to do something positive to change her situation for the betterment of herself and her children. Fate would meet her with another pitfall that would push her back, but she never gave up her hope of coming out of poverty and the housing projects.

Although most of my siblings' fathers did nothing to help my mother support us, she never said a negative word against any of them. Growing up in public housing, it was common to hear a single mother fussing or cursing about some deadbeat dad, usually the father of one or more of her children. There are some things in the projects that never change.

My mother continues to fascinate me. Like the Energizer Bunny, she just keeps going and going. Over the years, my mother took her share of lickings from us because of our delinquent behaviors. She just kept on ticking even after each hard licking that life dealt to her.

It seemed like my mother stayed in and out of juvenile court with me and my brothers, Gary and *Stewbeef*, during our growing-up years. She also spent her share of time at various reformatory schools across the state of Florida because of my older brother's misfortunes. Like an old soldier, she tried her best to fulfill her mission as a mother; but she was fighting against negative forces that were beyond her control. Gary, *Stewbeef*, and I gave my mother so much trouble coming up that it is a wonder she is still alive and in her right mind.

Big Trouble at the Migrant Labor Camp

As a lad growing up in poverty, being subsidized by the United States welfare system and state governmental support and assistance systems (governmental housing development and rental properties) from birth to eleven years old, I had lived in about ten different locations across the city of Fort Pierce. This number does not include the twelve to fifteen different migrant camps across the eastern part of the United States (South Carolina, Virginia, Maryland, Pennsylvania, and New York) in which I lived. As a child, I enjoyed every migrant camp we lived in regardless of the bedbugs, outhouses, and terrible sleeping arrangements.

As a child, I can remember going on the Migrant Trail with my mother and my aunts Carrie (deceased) and Betty. The names of the contractors we went up north with were Luke Sandlin Sr., Mack Harper, and Mr. Raymond Gordon Sr. and family. Mr. Raymond Gordon Sr. was a very honest and prominent fruit contractor in Fort Pierce during the 1960s and early 1970s. I was fortunate to be closely connected with the Gordons as a drafted family member.

As a child resident of the various migrant labor camps, I experienced some things beyond the years of a typical child under the age of twelve. Many of the things I witnessed cannot be included in this book, because they are too graphic. In all honesty, the migrant camp was no place for children who were not under the strict supervision of a parent or adult guardian. There were too many things about life that were too open for kids under the age of eighteen. Nothing that could be seen or heard in the labor camp was off-limits for children.

There was very little or no discretion in migrant labor camps as it related to youth. Many of the labor camps were lawless pits of ghetto activities. For example, no one at the migrant labor camp had a liquor license, but some of the camps sold liquor, beer, wine, gin, and whiskey. Very rarely did you hear of a migrant camp being raided for selling alcoholic beverages without a liquor license. No one at the camp had a license to operate a restaurant and a certificate or inspection score from the health department, yet every camp had a kitchen where dinners were prepared, cooked, and sold to tenants living in the camp as well as visitors.

Can you imagine the culture and living arrangement in a migrant labor camp for a child under the age of twelve? It was like growing up in a Third World nation where invisible posters read "Survive at your own risk!" I had to learn to hustle and to understand the street life and its vices if I did not want to become a victim. I had to learn to communicate in the language of survival with people who had no problem hurting a child. Some of these camps were similar to a slave plantation with the presence of the fruit contractor and his foremen.

I had to learn to play the role of an innocent child in order to keep my throat from getting slashed by a switchblade or hawk beard knife. One of the migrant workers threatened to kill me because I refused to supply his gambling habit. He had told some of the other guys in the camp that he was going to get me by cutting my throat. Trust me, he was not joking! He meant every word he spoke. My life's story of survival is one of amazing grace.

Some of the workers in the migrant camps were men who had just been released from jail or prison for heinous crimes. Some of the workers were homeless guys who we picked up along the way to various camp sites. I had to learn how to fit in and survive with some of the best street gangsters, thugs, and counterfeiters who had fallen from their thrones only to find themselves confined to a migrant labor camp.

Imagine the side effects of an elementary-school-age child mingling and conducting business with some of the most treacherous people in society. As I hinted earlier, some of the men in the migrant labor camp were ex-convicts, dope addicts, drug dealers, murderers, thieves, pedophiles, liars, and killers. You could almost deduce where they had lived and worked from their conversations and the company they kept. Looking at some of them, you would have thought they were just innocent lambs, but in actuality, many of them were cold hard killers. It seemed like some of the misfits in life would end up in a migrant labor camp.

I rode the same migrant buses that the adults rode. I heard the same debates and conversations that the adults shared with other adults. I not only listened but also intervened and gave my input in the same adult conversations on the buses, in the trucks, in the fields, and at the labor camps as well. I would argue and debate with these adults in the potato, cucumber, and tomato fields while working alongside them.

* * *

On one occasion, while in the town of Melfa, Virginia, right off of Highway 13 in Accomack County, I sold alcoholic beverages to adult migrant workers as though I was a business owner with a liquor license. I worked in the '*juke joint*' with my Aunt Carrie. The juke joint was also the general store for the migrant camp, where we sold items such as beer, wine, liquor, cigarettes, and food to the workers. The money made at the *juke joint* was profit for the fruit contractor.

Also, the juke joint served as the main cafeteria for the entire migrant camp. Many of the labor camp workers could eat on credit by running a tab, where all proceeds went to the camp boss or contractor. The juke joint was located in the biggest building on the site in order to handle the dancing crowd, drinking regulars, and people coming for dinner after a long and hard day's work.

Speaking of the juke joint, it was no lavish building. It was just a big hut that allowed people to congregate for fun and mischievous activities. A lot of unscrupulous things went on at the juke joint! I witnessed things that are not feasible to talk about in this book.

My Aunt Carrie was the main cook for the camp. She prepared daily meals for purchase by the people who did not cook in their rooms.

Another important role for the juke joint was serving as the central command post for the entire camp. If there was any information or anything you needed to know, all you had to do was come to the juke joint. All the mail that came in and went out of the camp was processed through the juke joint.

I watched many romantic relationships start and die at the juke joint. The relationships would begin at the bar or the gambling table or on the dance floor. The one thing I liked most about the juke joint was that the liquor store, grocery store, restaurant, night club, party hall, gambling casino, meeting hall, and all the camp's gossip were all conducted in the same room.

It was the most fascinating multipurpose building on the entire migrant trail. Yet there was no restroom in the entire building. People had to step outside of the building and go to the outhouse. Running fresh water and toilets in restrooms were somewhere in the future, because the camps I lived in did not have them.

Sometimes the labor camps were so large that two to three different crews would live in the same camp, with the possibility of each having its own juke joint. There was nothing unusual for a larger camp to have anywhere from two hundred to three hundred people on the site. When it was time to work in the fields, the camps were cleared out by the foreman and his henchmen.

Everyone living on the camp grounds had to go to work except those too young to work in the fields or orchards, the few people designated to cook, or those too feeble to work. Whenever the crews left for work, the camp looked like an empty ghost town on the Western frontier. On the other hand, when the crews returned to the camp in the evening, the party would get started at the juke joint and in the tenants' boxed-shaped bed rooms. Upon the arrival of the crew or crews to camp, things became noisy, loud, fun-filled, and dangerous due to alcohol and drug intake among many of the persons living on the campsite.

One of the things that saddened me about migrant camp protocol was that even people who were sick had to leave the camp and go to work to make the fruit contractor some money. Some of the migrant contractors were known for treating their workers worse than people mistreating stray street dogs. I watched one particular boss man make people go to work in the fields even when they were very sick. The migrant contractor showed no mercy for the wounded or any compassion for his employees.

Migrant labor camps in the 1960s and early 1970s were no gravy-train rides. Migrant labor camps back then did not have the strict government oversight like we have today. Working and living on migrant camps in the 1960s and early 1970s was brutal in every aspect—unless you were the contractor or foreman, or one of the contractor's lead men, or a family member, or the owner of the plantation.

* * *

Before I was eleven years old, I had witnessed and experienced things I wish no child would encounter in life. For example, when I was around nine or ten years old, while we were living in the migrant camp located in Melfa, Virginia (Accomack County), right off of Highway 13, a man not only threatened but attempted to cut my throat with a knife. My aunt had to defend my life by shooting the man as he attempted to retrieve his pocket knife to slice my throat. The horrific scene took place in the juke joint.

As the man reached into his pocket for either a knife or a gun, my aunt beat him to the draw. It seemed like from out of nowhere, Aunt Carrie drew a pistol and began firing a volley of rounds in the man's direction. I began to see blood dripping from the man's face around his cheeks as he staggered backward after each shot my Aunt Carrie fired.

I believe she shot the man at least four to five times in his face to keep him off of me and her. Can you believe all of this happened during an argument while at the juke joint bar counter? It seemed like the juke joint was the arena for fights on a daily basis. Nearly every weekend there would be at least one or more fights over various issues, from cheating relationships to cheating during a gambling game.

This particular man was known throughout the migrant labor camp for killing several people. He went around camp telling others that he was going to slice my throat because I talked too much. He was feared by many of the workers in the camp. Some of them knew of his dangerous past.

I witnessed the entire incident in slow motion. I was in the ring as the shots were fired. Everything happened so quickly that I did not have time to duck or run for cover. All I have to say is there had to have been a shield of protection covering me, because I was in arm's reach of the man with the weapon.

As my Aunt Carrie pulled the trigger of her pistol, I saw her hand and arm move up and down like a waving motion because of the kickback from the firing of the pistol. I am amazed that the man did not still attempt to cut me. He walked away from the scene of the shooting. I guess every time he was hit by a bullet from the gun, the force of the round caused the man to step backward and stagger.

As a young boy, I had no idea the force of the pistol being fired was causing the up and down motion of my aunt's arm each time she pulled the trigger. For years, until I fired my first pistol, I thought that a person firing a pistol had to make an up and down waving motion similar to what my Aunt Carrie did while shooting the man. I was totally wrong about that.

I was also very wrong about life when I attempted to live in the fast lane as a delinquent juvenile. People used to tell me to slow down, but for a long while I would not listen to anyone. My lack of life experience obscured my ability to see things correctly. When people have not been exposed to the good things in life, they do not know such things exist. A large part of my youthful years, I walked around with blurred vision and an uncertain future. I lived in a small dark box; there was no light in the people and things that were shaping my world.

As a result of the shooting, the entire camp was put on lockdown by the local sheriff and state police authorities. The work crew had to remain at the site even though the vegetable picking season was over in Melfa, Virginia. We did not move on to the state of Pennsylvania until the shooting case involving my Aunt Carrie went to trial and got resolved. I personally overheard the local police authority telling the fruit contractor that he could not move his crew from the site until my Aunt Carrie went to trial.

My Aunt Carrie spent four to six weeks in jail for saving my life as well as her own life. She was the guardian angel who watched over my life that day and during the time we were up the road. I will never forget her motherly instinct for protecting me even though she never gave birth to a child. Her calm reaction saved my life that day, and I am still baffled some fifty years later.

Can you believe the argument and confrontation started over the man calling me a "signifying monkey"? He was angry with me because I refused to loan him money so he could gamble by shooting dice. The man was a heavy gambler, and he could either lose or win hundreds over a weekend at the migrant camp. Sometimes he would win, but most of the time he would end up losing.

Nearly every week, this particular man would come to me and borrow money. Yet he oftentimes ended up digging himself deeper into debt. You may be asking yourself, how in the world would a little boy have enough money to loan to a man with a gambling addiction? I am glad you asked the question, because I'm going to answer it for you in the following paragraph. Keep in mind, back in the day, you heard and saw some of the strangest things on a migrant labor camp.

From time to time, I would help my Aunt Carrie run the migrant camp canteen store or goodie store whenever the state inspectors were not snooping around. The goodie store was located in the juke joint, and lots of tax-free money came through those doors. The juke joint was one of the largest undercover operations in the area whenever a labor camp was fully operational. All kinds of deals were conducted at the juke joint.

As a young entrepreneur, I would often help myself to some of the cash from the goodie store sales, especially since I was working and was not getting paid for my hard work. One thing I knew for sure in my devious mind was that I was not a slave, nor was I rendering free labor for this particular fruit contractor. Many of the winos would seek me out for small loans so they could purchase their bottle of wine. I used to sell them wines like White Polk, Thunderbird, and Boone's Farm, as well as gin and malt liquor, just to name a few.

I knew no one was going to pay me for my hard work that caused me to stay up late hours on weekdays and weekends. Also, I knew no one was going to take responsibility for illegally working a minor child, especially when it came to selling alcohol. As the old folks used to say, *"An even swap ain't no swindle!"*

I paid myself like the contractor paid himself from his juke joint. Even back then, I understood the basic fact that no entrepreneur or boss would work and earn dividends without compensating him or herself. In essence, why should I work for any person without getting compensated? I did not think this was fair to me! If you are going to take advantage of me, then pay me for abusing me!

I would work in the fields picking and loading nearly hundred-pound potatoes sacks and picking cucumbers in the sweltering heat of the eastern shores of Virginia. Do you think I was not supposed to get paid for my labor? Not only was I working harder than some of the adults, but some wise genius decided not to pay me for my work! Even to this day, I feel like I was taken advantage of by the adult in charge of pay. I received not one penny for my labor.

* * *

With some injustices, we cannot wait for the law to intervene, because the law might be too slow coming to our aide, or the law may even overlook our plight. We learned this valuable lesson from Dr. Martin Luther King Jr., and the Civil Rights Movement. Prior to the Civil Rights Movement, African Americans begged for social justice and pleaded for equality and freedom. Yet the cries of African Americans fell on the deaf ears of the American government and the ruling class of American society. Old Lady Liberty and Ole Glory refused to show the same compassion and respect for African Americans, the no-class citizens, as it did for white first-class citizens.

We learned a very valuable lesson about how sometimes you can't wait for a broken or crippled government to liberate you from the segregated dungeons of unfair laws. Just think, even the Founding Fathers of America were determined to gain their freedom from King George III of England. They refused to wait any longer in the dark dungeons of taxation without proper representation. The colonists decided to fight for their freedom rather than continue sitting under the rule of a tyrant.

So, as the story goes, these same Founding Fathers of America signed the Declaration of Independence in Philadelphia, Pennsylvania on July 4, 1776. Yes, it was during the time the newly formed colonies were separating from Great Britain. Such formation ignited the birth of one of the greatest countries in the history of the world, America. The birth of America came about because a group of people got tired of waiting for justice and freedom. The colonies knew they had to take positive actions in order to secure their destiny in life as a nation.

In America over the years, we have observed lots of positive and beneficial changes come about through peaceful protest. During the 1960s, when it was against the law to eat at segregated lunch counters, we saw peaceful protests and demonstrations usher in justice. Before the national government accepted the social justice changes across America, there was a group of people who were crying out for social justice and basic human respect.

Let us not forget it was through peaceful protest that the women's suffrage movement gained rights for women from about 1848 to 1920. It was under the leadership of Elizabeth Cady Stanton and Susan B. Anthony, who reignited the "fire of freedom for women's rights" in America in 1869 after the Civil War. No longer would women have to take a back seat and be ignored in mainstream American life. Although total freedom did not come overnight for white women, they at least were able to "breath without a knee on their necks!"

* * *

After the shooting incident at the Melfa, Virginia, migrant labor camp, reality began to set in for the first time as to how precious life was, in the sense that once it was gone, it was gone forever. I wondered how life could be taken away from a person in an instant. Can you imagine a child of about nine or ten years old caught between a rock and a hard place in this way?

I was faced with testifying at an attempted murder trial when I was around nine or ten years old. It was not just any attempted murder trial. It was a trial where my primary caregiver was arrested and sitting in jail for saving my life as a vicious criminal attempted to kill me. In this situation, even though she was incarcerated, my aunt was not the criminal. We just had to prove she shot her attacker in self-defense and protection of her child nephew, for whom she was totally responsible.

Not only was I slated to testify in my aunt's case, I was the key witness in her defense. The defense attorney had made it clear to me that my testimony and information could determine whether my aunt went home with me or to state prison in Virginia for a very long time. I knew I had to come face to face with the same monster who attempted to slice my throat with a knife. But I had no fear. It was time to save my aunt's life against a lie. After all, she was the one who stepped up and saved my life during the altercation at the juke joint.

The plaintiff had three witnesses on his side—his girlfriend and her two children, ages seven and thirteen. But just because you are outnumbered doesn't mean you can't win. The truth will always defeat a lie no matter how long it takes. Faith and hope always shine brighter than doubt and hopelessness. Whatever the predicament you find yourself facing, there is a river of hope waiting for you to cross. I guarantee you, there is a good and right way out of any situation. You just have to be willing to take the right and high road to peace and hope.

Of course, the man who was shot denied to the prosecutor and the court that he owned a gun or a knife. He denied such ownership because he was a convicted felon who was not entitled to carry or own a weapon. The reason children and adults need to make right decisions in life is because the decisions you make now will more than likely have an everlasting impact on your life.

All of the decisions we make in life are like a conjunction of roads that eventually leads us to the same freeway, junction, or destination. Our decisions are like an inescapable network of communication lines that affect everything we do in life. Some of the decisions you make today will reach out and touch you forty, fifty, sixty, even seventy years later. Every decision you make is connected to some kind of action, whether good or bad.

Foolish decisions I made as a child haunt me to this day. I hear them calling my name every day that I live. Some decisions you cannot erase; you just have to live with them as best you can. This is why it is very important to make good and positive decisions that will allow you to reap great dividends in the present moment and the future. Whenever you make a bad decision, you must shake the dust off and move in the right direction, because bad decisions have the potential to produce winners and overcomers if a person is willing to fight for what is right and turn in a positive direction.

I can remember the defense attorney interviewing me about the shooting incident in the juke joint while my Aunt Carrie was still in jail. The defense attorney interviewed me and prepped me for what to expect during the trial. He explained to me that the white man in the long black robe was the judge, and the other white people in a box were the jury that would decide my aunt's fate. I never mentioned to him that I was somewhat familiar with a judge and jury in a courtroom.

The defense attorney told me not to be afraid of the people in the courtroom—neither the judge nor the jury. He told me that a man would ask me some hard questions, and I should answer based on what I had witnessed and knew for sure, not what I thought. He made sure to tell me not to speculate on the questions or answers.

He reiterated to me that I should listen to the questions very carefully before I answered. He went on to tell me that if I was not sure about a particular question or questions, I needed to ask the person asking the questions to explain it to me, or ask it again in a way I could understand. I told the defense attorney I understood his instructions. I was ready to sit on the witness stand and tell the truth based on what I witnessed during the shooting incident at the juke joint.

The defense team won the court case with my testimony and the facts I gave to the court, including some information that others did not know. I had been in the man's room and knew where he kept certain things. He had forgotten that he had shown me things when he was drunk as well as when he was sober.

Remember, when you show a child something, do not leave it in the same place if you do not want the child to double back and finish investigating the scene. Of course I was very intrigued by things I should not have had access to. I was a very nosy and inquisitive little child growing up. A child will watch the habits of adults when you think they are not watching.

* * *

Shortly after the trial ended, my Aunt Carrie was back with us at the migrant labor camp and ready to leave the state of Virginia for New York State. We were ready to move on with our lives and leave Virginia behind us. I can remember us having a big welcome home party for Aunt Carrie at the same juke joint where the shooting took place.

A few days after my aunt's release from jail, we moved on to the state of New York to pick apples and plums. Everyone in the camp was ready to go and started shouting, singing, and clapping when we left the migrant labor camp in Virginia. I will never forget that when we crossed over the Maryland state line heading toward New York State, everybody on the bus broke out with great jubilation.

The migrant bus I was riding on gave a great big shout of celebration and dancing like I had never seen or heard before. Some of the people who never danced on the dance floor in the juke joint were standing up and dancing on the moving bus. It was a scene that left a lasting impact in my mind even to this day. Some of the people were singing the song "Mr. Big Stuff" by Jean Knight, recorded by Malaco Records Studio of Jackson, Mississippi.

The Hiding of the Winchester

One of the ironic things about the shooting incident involving my Aunt Carrie was that just one year prior, I'd had to hide a Winchester rifle that belonged to my aunt's friend. I hid the rifle with the hope of keeping him from hurting my Aunt Carrie. One day early in the evening, I heard the two of them arguing and fussing at each other like a serious thunderstorm on the horizon.

I was used to them arguing and fussing at each other, but I'd never heard it to the degree that it rose to on this particular night. I knew something was slowly brewing on the stove, but I could not figure out what was cooking or why it was cooking. Sometimes it would take days before the brewing turned into a full boil.

This particular day, I felt in my heart the pot was going to boil over before daybreak. I had learned their fight habits from my months and years of living with them. Kids have a good habit of learning from the actions of adults, even when adults think they are not watching. Many things children acquire and carry into adulthood with them, they learn from adults.

The choice of words being used, the loudness and deep tones in their voices, and the aggressive anger toward one another sounded like destructive winds from a hurricane or tornado. They were really going at each other this particular time. In my opinion, someone was going to end up getting hurt if they did not stop fighting with vicious words. I became nervous and very afraid for my aunt.

I made up in my little boyish mind to stay out of the conflict—until I heard my aunt's boyfriend threaten her with his shotgun. When I heard this threat, I no longer felt the need to stay neutral. After hearing the deadly threat on my aunt's life, I could not go to sleep that night. I can remember being awake and thinking about how I was going to get to the weapon, which I planned to bury offsite so he could never find it.

I lived in the room right next to their room. My living quarter was designed this way so my aunt could keep a watchful eye over me as best she could. There was only a thin piece of sheetrock or drywall and a few two-by-fours that separated the two rooms. Some of the rooms only had one open-faced piece of board on one side of the room, and the other side of the room was open, where you could see the backside of the drywall and the two-by-fours.

During the night, all I could do was think about this man hurting my mommy's younger sister. I felt like I had to do something to keep my aunt safe from this man's rage. After hearing the ordeal go on for hours and throughout part of the night, I felt like I needed to keep a watchful eye over my Aunt Carrie as best I could as a child.

The language was so harsh that I thought they were physically fighting each other. Again, in my childish mind, I was not going to stand back and let him hit or beat on my aunt. I was prepared to get hurt in the midst of the fight if that is what it took for me to protect my aunt. I was terrified, yet not afraid.

I had made up my mind that he needed to hurt me that night if he was going to attempt to beat on my aunt. I knew he would kill me if I intervened and thought nothing about it. As I sat up and monitored the conversation, it became very ugly. I heard words I will not attempt to write in this book. The language was not new to me, but I did not remember any of their arguments ever escalating to this level.

I became very angry, concerned, and fearful that my aunt was with a crazy, abusive, controlling, and violent man. I felt like I needed to protect her. I did not know the exact time of the night or morning the argument started, but I knew I could not go back to sleep. I was not sure what I could do to help, but I knew I had to do something to keep her from getting hurt.

* * *

The next morning, when the work crew went out into the fields, I was left behind at the camp by myself with a few other people who normally stayed back. The gossip around some of the other labor camps was that the government was checking the fields to see if minors were working. Somehow, the state or federal inspectors from the Department of Labor had gotten information that young children were working in the fields.

Fruit contractors in the area and their henchmen were always on the lookout for inspectors. So, all minor children under a certain age were forced to remain at the labor camps until the inspectors were no longer around or a threat. Our particular camp was not the only one under observation or surveillance. A couple of the other migrant labor camps in the region were being watched as well, according to camp gossip.

Since I had to stay at the labor camp, this seemed like the opportunity I needed to keep my aunt from getting hurt or getting in trouble with the law. I had heard the stories about how people lost their lives in migrant labor camps due to violence, especially domestic violence. I did not feel that the argument and fight was over between my aunt and her boyfriend.

The only times I'd ever seen him back down were in the presence of law enforcement or while dealing with white people. He would sometimes become nervous and would even change his speaking tone and dialect when he had to explain something to the Caucasian farmers he was working for during his migrant escapade. He would go above and beyond the call of duty to submit to the people who were making sure he had revenue coming to him.

On this particular day, when my aunt and her boyfriend left the camp to go work in the fields, I lifted myself up to the ceiling on a wooden box and crawled over the rafters in the open loft, which had no sheetrock or drywall. It was an open ceiling with only trusses, a strip of white electrical wire, and a host of spider webs. I was nervous and afraid someone would come in early and catch me.

Once I dropped down into their room, I began searching for his rifle and pistol. I was convinced he had the pistol on him. He always carried his pistol on him even if he was stepping out for a second. He seemed to feel a need for protection everywhere he went for some reason.

During the search of the room, somehow, I located his beautiful Winchester rifle behind a makeshift locker cabinet next to the door, or underneath the bed on the floor, I cannot remember exactly, because I came across two other guns in my crusade for the rifle. I don't believe I was aware that he had so many weapons. I should have suspected that he came with adequate firepower.

During my search of the room, I confiscated another 38-caliber handgun and the rifle. I was determined not only to get rid of the rifle but all of the lethal weapons, for the safety of my aunt. Once I had the weapons in my possession, I took them into the woods with the intent of hiding or destroying them. The weapons were used as tools to bully people rather than instruments of protection.

It felt like I had to travel miles into the woods in order to go far enough so no one would be able to find the weapons. When it seemed like I was at a safe location to get rid of the weapons, I dug a hole with my walking stick and the rifle. I then buried the rifle in the ground and threw the handgun into a body of water, which seemed to be a pond or small lake.

I was very nervous and hoped no one had seen me going into the woods with the rifle and the pistol that was bulging out from my pocket. I was a nervous wreck for several weeks after the ordeal of burying the weapons. I even had nightmares about someone finding the rifle or the pistol washing back up on the shore. Even to this day, I consider this undercover operation one of the most foolish and daring things I've ever done.

* * *

Several days later, my aunt came to me asking about the rifle, as though she knew I was involved in its disappearance. I believe she had a hunch that I might have overheard them arguing. She first asked me if by any chance I had seen the rifle. I told her I had not, but I asked her to describe the weapon to me, hoping this would throw her off the trail. I must say, my aunt was a lot smarter than I expected her to be when it came to her detective work.

Several days later, just when I thought I was off the hook, she came back to me and pleaded with me to return the rifle. She started telling me her boyfriend was only playing with her, and he would not hurt her. She tried to convince me that he was only "mouthing off." Within my spirit or soul, I knew there was more to it than just running off at the mouth.

I believe she knew I'd heard the argument between the two of them. I believe she was more than sure I had taken the rifle. My aunt tried her best to convince me that her boyfriend would never hurt her. She thought that giving me this information would encourage me to surrender the rifle. I was more concerned about saving a life than giving the location of a Winchester. I may have been young, but I was no fool. There was no way on this earth I was going to tell my aunt I had seen the weapon. I knew the fox had sent my aunt to question me. I stood my ground for her protection.

All I could hear and see in my mind was him acting out his threats on my aunt's life. She begged and pleaded with me to return the weapon, but I made sure my aunt's boyfriend would never see the rifle or the pistol again. I knew he had the resources to get more weapons, but he would never see or use those two lethal weapons against anyone.

Several times afterward, my aunt told me she knew I'd heard them arguing. Yet each time, I acted like I was fast asleep and did not hear their argument. Sometimes a boy has to do what a boy has to do in order to protect his family from danger or harm. I could recognize an untruthful and diabolical plot when I saw one, regardless of what my aunt said.

I have this saying that I often share with close friends and family members that goes something like this: "Nobody gets away! No matter how long it takes, nobody gets away!" The best life to live is one where you do the right things and demonstrate an overwhelming compassion for humanity.

* * *

During my childhood years, I never admitted to my aunt that I had taken the rifle, but I felt like she knew I was the one who had taken it. Years later, when I became an adult, someone in my family brought up the incident. I believe it was one of my other aunts who brought up the conversation "out of the blue," as we often say back home in Fort Pierce.

One of my instigating and agitating aunts asked, "I just want to know, what ever happened to the rifle, Alvin? Did they ever find it? Who took it? They say Alvin went into the room and took the rifle!" By this time in my life, I had told my brother Gary and first cousin/brother Terry that I had taken the rifle. But I'd never said anything about the pistol until the writing of this book.

Although many years had passed, and my aunt was no longer in a relationship with this particular man, she turned to me and asked, "Alvin, where did you bury the rifle, and how did you get into the room?"

I told my aunt Carrie where I hid the rifle and the technique I had used to get into their room. I told my aunt I had to do it for the safety of her life and my life as well. I shared with her that one of the worst things a person can do is put a lethal weapon into the hands of an angry man or woman. I had to disarm the threat, bottom line.

I shared with my aunt that when she begged me for the weapon, there was no way in my right mind I was going to turn the weapon over to her. I knew that as soon as I returned the weapon to her, she would return it to the man who was threatening her life, and he possibly would have ended up hurting her and me. I believe the preservation of life is one of the greatest callings we have on this earth, whether of our own family members or someone else's family. As human beings, we are tasked by nature to save lives and not destroy lives. Giving my aunt the rifle would have been like me helping to plan her execution and funeral all at the same time.

* * *

During my tenure as a migrant worker, I endured life's hardships as a bitter soldier, and definitely not as a good soldier. I experienced some painful things on the various migrant labor camps that have shaped my thinking and zeal about providing for the poor. My experiences in the various migrant labor camps have given me an overwhelming compassion for people, especially hurting and poor people who have fallen on hard times in life.

As a child growing up in migrant labor camps, I gained a great deal of love and respect for people who are considered by many in society as downtrodden, losers, hopeless, and failures in life. I was considered one of these as a young boy while growing up with my family. Some of these same people who others called losers or downtrodden were the ones who took me in and treated me as their own.

I will never forget some of these very special people because they took care of me. I can remember some of the names like it was yesterday: Saul and Gaycilla, or Red and Ms. Juanita, or Dennis Clark Sr., who was the main bus and truck driver for this particular fruit contractor. All of you are gone, but I salute you for the kindness, love, and help you extended to me at a very vulnerable time in my life.

My life experiences on migrant labor camps, along with growing up in government housing projects and working on the streets as a shoeshine boy, have shaped and molded me into the person I am today. Although my childhood was rough, it has impacted my life in so many positive ways that I cannot begin to attempt to list them. Although most of those days were very hard, with the help of other people, I was able to put past disappointments behind me and embrace a brighter future in middle school.

In retrospect, when I look over my blunders in life, I am more convinced than ever that an honest day's work is worth its weight in gold. Hard work has an innocence that cannot be purchased with all the money in the world. Once one puts in an honest day's work, one has a sense of pride about life, even in the midst of being poor. Honest dealings and good behavior with integrity open all kinds of doors for opportunity if a person has the desire to achieve success in life.

Living in migrant labor camps has shaped my life and the way I live today. One thing for sure about my camp experience is that it is not the kind of life I desire to live as an adult. Back in the 1960s and 1970s, living and working in migrant labor camps was a very hard and demanding lifestyle. You woke up on the grind, and you went to bed preparing for the grind that was just around the corner at the break of dawn. Rest did not come easy in the migrant camps because someone was always moving and grooving in some way or manner. This was the bottom line for life in the migrant labor camps.

I paid my dues to the world of poverty as a child and young adult, and I do not want to stand in that line again. I am doing whatever I can to liberate myself from a life of poverty. It has not been an easy battle, but I strive each day not to return to my old life of being poor, being miserable, and living in total disappointment. There is no fame to being poor and ashamed. I know—I lived it for over twenty-two years of my life.

* * *

I am not embarrassed about my upbringing on welfare as a poverty-stricken youth. Neither do I try to hide or downplay the fact I grew up mainly off of 18th Street and Avenue D and 23rd and Avenue I in Fort Pierce. It is what it is, and it has played a major role in shaping me to be who I am today. I love my city and the people of Fort Pierce and St. Lucie County, Florida.

All of my past experiences have brought me to the place I am today. Hard work, personal determination, and opportunities given to me by others have allowed me to excel in life. Growing up in poverty may have helped mold me, but good-hearted people and the drive to want a better life are what kept me focused. I come from a city where the drive to build champions in life is evident on the gridiron of the local high schools.

My humble beginnings are partially why I am so passionate about helping the poor, the needy, and those who are considered underdogs. I have experienced firsthand what it feels like to have people make fun of you simply because you have very little to eat or received no toys for Christmas or do not have clothes to wear to school beyond three days in a week without wearing them again before they are washed. There were many days in my childhood where I ended up wearing oversized clothes that belonged to my brother Gary or my cousin/brother Terry.

When you wear clothes to school that are too big for you, it is very noticeable to the other students, teachers, and staff. I became the target of laughter, jokes, and belittling. I know firsthand what it feels like to be asked to go home just before a family sits down at the dinner table, and your stomach is telling you that it is hungry too. These were some of the most turbulent times in my life, and I never want to see those days again.

I know firsthand what it is like to run away from home at the age of nine. In 1968, I ran away from home, and I stayed gone for two or three months. I bounced around abandoned cars, buildings, churches, and construction sites until I ran into a dear friend named Michael Campbell who took care of me like I was his little brother. He was willing to get in trouble with his parents just so I could have a warm bed and a decent meal. He was a true brother and friend to me, and I will never forget his compassion. It's good-hearted brothers like Michael Campbell that make the world go around.

I remember one occasion when I had been expelled from school for the rest of my second-grade year by Judge Rogers, who said he was expelling me from school because of my disciplinary and truancy records. Even with Judge Rogers, I salute him because he gave me adequate chances to get it right before he warned me that if I ever came back into his courtroom, he was going to send me away to the Dozier Boys School in Marianna, Florida.

I was told I had the worst truancy record in the entire St. Lucie County School District. During this time in my life, I was walking on the road to total destruction. There seemed to be no way out of the trouble I had gotten myself into while living life as a delinquent juvenile. When children determine there is no way out, they will accept whatever lifestyle is presented to them at that moment.

* * *

As I mentioned earlier, when I first ran away from home, I stayed in abandoned cars, vacant buildings, businesses, and churches on some days. Back in the 1960s, many people did not lock the doors to their cars, or vacant buildings, or buildings on new construction sites like we do today. There was no need to lock up churches or businesses like laundromats (wash-houses is what we called them back in the 1960s and 1970s).

Back then, who would dare to think of breaking into a church building? The doors to most houses of worship in the African American community of Fort Pierce during the 1960s were unlocked. I would enter these sacred buildings looking for food and a place to sleep just for the night. Always I would find a safe haven of refuge.

During my runaway escapades, I sometimes stayed with families and people I did not know. I would meet some kids playing on the streets, and eventually they would sneak me into their houses and hide me from their parents. The children would save me food and give it to me during the night. I ate from various places such as churches, homes, and gardens. I had a covert operation, because I did not want to be detected by the police or truant officers (Mr. King Strong, Mr. Jerry Black, and Mrs. Ida D. Morgan).

I will never forget my dearest surrogate family: Mr. Raymond and Mrs. Dora Gordon. I lived with the Gordon family for about two years as if I was one of their own children. At first, Mr. Raymond Gordon Sr. and his wife had no idea their son, Earl Gordon, had been hiding me on the back porch and other places within the house for several weeks. Earl and the Gordon family were a lifesaver for me during such a crucial time in my young life.

Prior to meeting the Gordons, I stayed with whomever would allow me to stay with them, and I ate whatever I could find to eat. When you are a runaway, you cannot be particular about what you eat or where you get your meal. I found myself eating off of the ground or from garbage cans. I had no shame to answer the important call whenever my stomach started painfully crying out to me to feed it.

When I ran away from home, I quickly realized I had to transition to survival mode in order to make it in a world where some looked at me as bait instead of a child in need of help. Out of my own disobedience and rebellion, I had put myself in a very vulnerable situation. I had become very disrespectful toward my mother. I refused to allow my mother to whip me with a belt, so I decided to run away from home, where I would be in charge of my life, or so I thought! The most important thing in my little mind was to survive by any means necessary.

* * *

My disdainful attitude toward school and the educational system started when I entered the first grade. Keep in mind that from the start of my academic pilgrimage, it seemed like I was a couple of years behind my peers. When I was in the first grade, and in the years prior to the first grade, my mother and relatives knew nothing about the requirements for early childhood education. Many parents and people I know today are in the same boat.

Today's society is more advanced with the basic knowledge about educational information. Computers, tablets, cellphones, and access to the internet, social media, informational hotlines, and other educational tools represent a great advancement for humanity. In my day, there were no such things as taking classes online or virtual learning, other than by television, and even then, many of the poor people I knew growing up did not have televisions in their places, huts, or rentals.

During the 1960s and '70s, we did not have this privilege of tapping into a computerized web network from anywhere in the world, like people and students do today. In my day, families and kids suffered or got the short end of the stick if they did not have the appropriate information to share with their children or the community. Even as African American people living in the same community, middle-class African Americans received information before the lower-class African American people could get it.

The lower-class African American people lived in government housing or the rundown houses on nearly all of the streets. One of the ways to definitely tell if a person or family was lower-class was to find out if they were recipients of government welfare. If you went to the grocery store and saw someone in line with a book of food stamps, you need not wonder or question the person. This was before EBT cards replaced the various lively colors of the government food stamps.

It was amazing how many people, including me, had to stand in line to pay for their order with overwhelming embarrassment. Yet whenever we returned to our project housing hut, we enjoyed the products we had purchased with our food stamps, like little kids enjoying the toys at a birthday party.

It was a tragedy for me and my brothers that none of my family members knew anything about early childhood education. Part of my struggle to advance was that I never grasped the basic instructions from the pre-K and kindergarten world. You can probably guess what happened to my opportunity to receive any type of early childhood education. The lack of good information has always proven to be a detriment in my world. Good or positive information has always added to my life and success rather than detracted from it.

When I was under the age of six years old, although I existed, I was not being tracked by the local Department of Children's Services. We moved about three times that particular year, and maybe that is why it was hard to keep track of me and my truancy. Back in the 1960s, homeschooling was not a big topic of discussion, to my knowledge.

I believe the practice of homeschooling did not exist in Fort Pierce and St. Lucie County, Florida, on a large scale like it does today. I believe the push for homeschooling probably occurred as a result of the **1954 US Supreme Court decision in *Brown v. Board of Education.*** It was the first time in the history of America that the US Supreme Court ruled that segregating on the basis of skin color was unconstitutional.

Because of this ruling, many white families in the South started pulling their children from public schools, because they refused to buy into the concept of desegregation. Prior to this monumental 1954 ruling, homeschooling may have taken place in some of the strict religious sects like the Mennonites, Quakers, or Mormons, and in some places across the country. But the 1954 Supreme Court ruling gave many families an incentive to hide behind the veil of "protecting religious freedom and rights" over loving and treating their African American brothers and sisters with compassion and dignity. Even to this day, some continue to hide behind the dark and black magical veil of religious freedom.

It was not until I became an adult that the Department of Children's Services or the Department of Education required children to have an early childhood educational curriculum by a certain age. Most states within the US require children around the age of five years old to be in some sort of formalized curriculum-based educational program, whether homeschooling, private, or public education. If they violate the Department of Children's Services rules, parents have to make a choice as to whether to suffer legal consequences or put the child in school.

Today's children have greater protection under the law than when I was growing up. Child abuse was not considered a reoccurring event in communities where I grew up, as it is today. Although child abuse probably happened on a daily basis, it was not reported.

I guess back in my day, people had a different definition of child abuse. It seems as though the rules changed during the outbreak of a desegregated society, within the classrooms and halls of our schools. As I observed our schools and community during desegregation, I came to the conclusion that desegregation was a double-edged sword for many African American students, teachers, parents, families, employees, and administrators.

Back in the 1960s and early 1970s, when we got whippings or beatings with extension cords, sticks, broom handles, switches, or whatever the hands could find, it was not labeled as child abuse. It was called "you got your behind tore up!" Whatever method is used by a parent or adult for disciplining children, abuse should never be an option. However, with all of the whippings I may have gotten as a child growing up, I am convinced my mother or grandmother never abused us.

People are entitled to their opinion on this. I know many of you may not agree with the method or way of discipline people used back in the day. But neither can you overlook how the practice of "not sparing the rod" helped save the nation from overflowing prison systems and jail cells, and overflowing graveyards and funeral processions, plus the confused and unfilled role of the African American father and mother to the African American child.

Chastising back when I was a child may not have been the best correction in the neighborhood, yet it seemed to work at the time. As I look at the murder rate, crimes, and children's disrespect toward mothers, fathers, grandparents, siblings, neighbors, teachers, and school staff, I am deeply saddened. The depravity I witness in the news across our country and local communities has never been seen in my sixty-plus years of living.

The need for children to go to Head Start or a pre-K program back then did not seem as urgent or as necessary as it does today. No letters came in the mail, and no social workers came to our place of record and told my mother she was in violation by not having me in a pre-K program. It seems like it was not against the law for a five-year old African American child not to be enrolled in a pre-K curriculum or kindergarten. Who cared?

At any rate, pre-K and kindergarten attendance was not enforced in my neighborhood. My mother, aunts, grandmother, uncles, and neighbors did not get the memo that a child could enroll in a government-sponsored (free) pre-K program when the child reached the age of six. We never knew about the program named Head Start that was started in 1965, by President L. B. Johnson's administration, as the first publicly funded preschool program.

In small country towns across the South, being the last to get the news seemed to be the general rule for poor African American kids whose parents, grandparents, and great-grandparents had been deprived of an education for some reason or another. I grew up in a migrant town where African Americans were segregated into a very small section of the city. After nightfall, we were not allowed to cross over the canal into "White Town."

Canals and streets separated the white people from the African Americans. Nearly all the streets in the African American section of town were dirt roads, while many of the streets in the white section of town were paved or gravel roads. We had no streetlights in our section of town when it turned dark. Some of us had no running water or a modern indoor toilet system or tub to wash our clothes or bathe our bodies. Outdoor pumps that needed priming before use, and outhouses right on 80th Street, were our labor of love for survival.

All the major stores like Rosslow's, W. V. Grant, J. C. Penney, Sears, Woolworth, and Swiss Jewelry, just to name a few, were located in the section of Fort Pierce called downtown or "White Town." We had our African American family-owned stores that were located in the African American community, like Williams Department Store, Russ Department Store, and Williams Clothing Store. This was the little box I grew up in. Yet it seemed so large to me back in the 1960s and early '70s.

Let your life be an inspiration to others and not a desecration.—Alvin E. Miller

My Elementary School Experience

In 1965, when I entered Garden City Elementary School for the first grade, I was totally unprepared for what was ahead of me. I knew nothing about the ABCs or how to count to one hundred. I was totally oblivious to the learning spectrum within an academic environment. I was antagonized and picked on by the other students simply because I did not have the basic information a first-grader should. At the time, it was the most humiliating experience I had ever encountered in my short life.

Even worse, some of my teachers would embarrass me simply because I did not know the things that were expected of a student entering first grade. I also had a severe stammering/stuttering problem that made me the laughingstock of the class and a target for ridicule. First grade was a very tough experience for me.

Yet my first-grade school year did prepare me for what was to come later down the road. It prepared me to handle rejection, and to keep my focus on the prize of success in life. My first-grade year was the groundwork that prepared me to encounter hate, jealousy, and ill-treatment, and trained me to look at the positive side of life regardless of the negativity that came my way.

My first-grade year of school was so disappointing to me that I began to do all sorts of unthinkable things as a six-year-old, or a seven-year-old, or an eight-year-old to avoid going to school. My actions were unacceptable regardless of the era. It was in 1965 that I developed the dislike for school. Over the next eight years, school would become a great struggle for me.

I became enraged about going to school and made a vow not to return except to eat, not as a student seeking to learn. My goal switched from attempting to learn to obtaining a well-balanced meal for the day. I made up in my mind that I was too far behind to catch up with the other students. Somewhere along the journey, fear and doubt got the best of me, and my downward slide in life began.

Just the thought of standing in front of a crowd or being singled out exacerbated my stammering/stuttering problem. Inwardly, I felt like I wanted to go and hide in a hole. Yet there was nowhere to hide. My problem with stuttering was probably the most humiliating time of my life at such an early age. I found it nearly impossible to hide when the spotlight was shining directly on me, patiently waiting for me to speak. I could not even utter the words.

I felt so embarrassed and ashamed that I would sit at my desk and think of ways not to come to school. I did not want to get into trouble with my mommy, but going to school was not my cup of tea. I had already been eaten alive by my teacher and the other kids because of my stuttering problem and not knowing the information a first-grader should have known.

One thing I knew for sure was that I could not take being badgered on a daily basis by my classmates and teachers. I had to come up with a school rejection plan real soon so I could survive the pain and shame of being picked on and laughed at by the other children and the teachers. Each day I attended school, I looked for a hiding place, but I found none. In desperation, I made a terrible decision by refusing to go to school.

My severe speech impediment continued to show its head on a constant basis until around my seventh-grade year. No matter how hard I tried to talk or explain something, I just could not get the words out when I needed them. To make matters worse, whenever I was put before a class or crowd of people, I would totally freeze up, as if I had seen a ghost.

I became so overcome with fear that I could not articulate one word clearly. Even during times when I was one-on-one with a person, I would become very nervous and start stuttering. The spirit of fear did not want me to speak, and it did everything to prevent me from speaking. My method of dealing with my stuttering problem was to start a pattern of truancy and delinquency that would last for nearly eight years.

* * *

Not only did I become a master at playing hooky from school, I also started a life of deviant behavior. This shaky road I was traveling was about to lead me on a path to destruction if I did not take a detour. I began to hang out in the streets with older guys from the neighborhood. I felt accepted as long as I was with those guys.

It is fascinating to me how I would feel accepted on the streets but rejected in school or the classroom. There is something terribly wrong with this picture for a six-year-old boy in the first grade. It seems like a child should receive more protection and acceptance in a school environment than on the streets.

Rejection is a terrible blow to the self-esteem of any person, especially a child. Just imagine the detrimental impact rejection can have on the psychological developmental of a child, especially during such critical developmental stages. The thought of being rejected by my schoolmates and teachers was a big letdown for me. It crushed the fun-filled perception that I had about school.

My first time in first grade was a no-win situation. In my small world, I thought I was winning in the game of life. I was more wrong than I was right to believe such an untruth. I disliked going to school so much that I developed this delusional idea that I did not need an education to make it in life. This was one of the biggest deceptions I bought into as a vulnerable misguided child.

I was fed up with feeling like a loser while in elementary school. I wanted to become a winner but did not know how to climb this mountain. I wanted to be smart like some of the other kids but did not know where to begin. I so desperately wanted to know the answers to the questions when the teacher asked the class, but I fell short.

It seemed like every student in my first-grade class was so far ahead of me academically. I did not even know my colors when I entered first grade. I felt like I was the dumbest child in the classroom. I thought this was the sentiment of the entire elementary school, so I used misbehaving as a tactic to deflect attention away from my learning deficiency.

It seemed like every other student could count to one hundred, or say the alphabet, or recite their vowels, or do addition and subtraction. Some of my classmates could even read with precision, like a well-educated adult learner. I was amazed at how smart and articulate some of my classmates were in first grade. Looking back, I believe I was at least two or three years academically behind my peers.

Yes, I know I was a terrible little kid in first grade. Not only was I unprepared for first grade, but my severe stammering and stuttering problem made things worse for me. As I stated earlier, my stuttering problem caused some of the students to pick on me. I do not blame the children, because kids will be kids, especially when they do not know the seriousness of the situation.

My inability to communicate smoothly with elementary and middle school teachers and students only added fuel to the fire of my school resentment. To me, it was like being caught in the wilderness without any knowledge of how to survive this new environment you are totally unfamiliar with. I was one of those kids who could not keep my seat regardless of threats or punishments from the teacher or principal.

* * *

Seven years later, there was finally a teacher who rescued me from the dungeons of destruction. She gave me the extra time I needed to ensure I understood and learned. Instead of bringing tears to my eyes, she brought joy to my heart! She enriched my ability to dream beyond my personal scars, pains, and disappointments. She brought hope to my life that I was unaware I had in me.

After meeting and receiving help from Mrs. Rita Johnson, I am of the opinion that no one should ever work in a profession where they dislike or hate the clients or customers that they serve. No one who dislikes children should ever be in the field of education. If a person is in the field of education and cannot be patient with children, then I recommend the person leave the field as soon as possible—like yesterday! Trust me, such people have chosen the wrong profession.

No one who is not willing to help children excel in life, so they can overcome their pitfalls, challenges, and fears, should be in the field of education. No one who thinks it is all right to humiliate, belittle, and prey on children's self-esteem should be in the field of education. No teacher has the right to talk condescendingly to students and other adults.

Teachers and educators must always remember that they are servants of the system and not dictators giving commands from their ivory towers in the sky. It takes a servant's heart to be a teacher or educator. I love and admire teachers and educators, because they saved my life. I was a teacher and educator in the public schools of St. Lucie County, Florida, for nearly ten years. I enjoyed every minute of serving students, parents, and the community.

No teacher or educator has the right to make students and parents feel less than human. No teacher or educator should ever dehumanize another human being simply because the student or parent is not educated or does not have the same or equal educational level as the teacher or educator. No teacher or educator should ever think that all rights, power, and control belong to the teacher or educator regardless of the situation or conversation.

My experience with teachers who treated me not so kindly is a lesson learned for my good to pay it forward. A person can acquire the best education and become one of the smartest people on earth but can be void of wisdom and gentleness. Some people can wear the latest fashions and most beautiful clothing but have no class. Some people can afford to live in fancy and beautiful homes, yet there is no love in the rooms. People who behave like this particular teacher are like this little poem I wrote:

You can paint a house beautifully on the outside;
But if compassion is not visible on the inside,
Then the paint job is just a smoke screen
like your false dreams!
—Alvin E. Miller

I am amazed how some adults and children think they can say disrespectful things to people and then believe their disrespect is acceptable behavior. I need to know when such behavior became the standard for a civilized society. The same principle applies to children speaking to other children as well as adults. I have learned kindness and respect can bring you more favor than all the money, fame, and notoriety in the world. Respect for everyone should always be the golden rule in life.

My personal story about my year in first grade is an example of how cruel some adults with power and authority can be to children. I challenge you to never allow disrespect to become one of your trademarks in life. We have to always keep in mind that there are things and people who will come into your life with the intention of destroying your dreams, killing your hope, and making you miserable. Never allow their insults to cause your world to crumble. Never allow people with zero ambitions to disrupt your flow to a successful journey in life.

Positive energy will always supersede a negative force if you can only believe and do the right things in life. Negative people will enter our lives, but we cannot allow them to succeed with the mission to bring disruption. Stay strong and focused. Reach your goals in life regardless of the attacks that may come your way. Remember, you are the victor and not the victim. Remove the debris from your path and keep moving on your successful journey in life.

* * *

As I stated earlier, it seemed like every student in my first-grade class during the 1965–1966 school year was way ahead of me academically. In actuality, they were *way* ahead of me academically. It was this negative thinking, along with peer pressure from other students, that encouraged me to become a truant. I felt like I was out of my league when it came to school.

I did not know anyone in the class to ask for help, especially after I had earned the reputation for being a class disruption. I had no one in my class from my neighborhood except my Boyhood friend, Michael Lee Cook, (deceased 2017). Some of my classmates knew each other from kindergarten or pre-K and remained friends from the first grade until this day. I just felt out of place in the first grade, not knowing any of the other children in the class and not being familiar with the information that was put in front of me to learn.

It did not take me long to realize that I had jumped in water where I couldn't swim, and neither did I have a life vest to save myself. I was struggling so badly that I felt like I was drowning in a sea of ignorance. I felt like I was a lost stranger in a world all by myself, with no one to turn to for help. As I look back, I believe my first-grade year was probably the worst of my educational life. I was failing in the classroom, community, with my own self-esteem, and in life.

I take full responsibility for all of my failures and the bad decisions I made as a six, seven, eight, nine, ten, eleven, twelve, and partially as a thirteen-year-old. As a young kid, I was a ticking time bomb just building the momentum to explode one day. Believe me on this truth: in my heart, I did not want to have hate or anger toward anyone. I just wanted to learn and have fun like the rest of the kids in my class. I only wanted to be a normal six-year-old child in the first-grade. I just wanted to learn, play, and be loved like the rest of my class. It just never seem to happen for all the pieces to come together like it did in middle school when I met Mrs. Johnson.

Again, as I stated earlier, I am to blame for all the shame I brought on myself down through the years. I've noticed that some people who continue to play the blame game do not ever pull themselves out of the self-pity webs and dungeons in life. These people tend to spend too much time and energy blaming other persons for all of their mistakes and failures.

Also, there are people who spend lots of quality time accusing and blaming others for their defeats in life. They tend to blame everyone but themselves for all of their wrong turns in life. If you see some of the same people years later, many are still living in misery. If you are not careful, they will make every attempt and effort to force their misery onto you.

Then you have those people who will make every attempt to take credit for the good things you have accomplished. Yet they have no idea about the lumps and bumps, sorry, hurt, blood, tears, disappointments, and trouble you endured to cross the finish line successfully. They fail to understand that many runners take off from the starting line but fail to cross the finish line because somewhere during the race, life's journey became too difficult for them. Or, they may have made the wrong turn in life, which allowed them to get way off track or altogether leave the course, never to return to the race of life.

* * *

Life is sometimes like a running back on a football team. The running back is given the ball of life to carry across the goal line, where great jubilation, celebration, and joy is expected. Once the ball is given to the running back, there is an expectation of excitement in the minds of the home team for the running back to either score or move the ball as close to the goal line as possible without fumbling. There is always the expectation for the home team running back to make good with every handoff.

Yet after receiving the ball, the running back may be stopped in the backfield for a loss of yardage, or stopped at the line of scrimmage for no gain. Or the running back may fumble the ball while running, or break the line of scrimmage for a big downfield yardage gain.

As a result of good coaching, hard work, and teammates working together, sometimes the running back does cross the goal line for a touchdown. Life for me has included some fumbles, some loss of yardage, some short gains, some big gains, and some touchdowns. Over the years, my life has been like a running back who works hard, and the success is revealed on the field during the game of life.

This is how life has played out for me. As in football, if you work hard, learn the playbook, prepare yourself physically and mentally, and stay a team player, you will excel in the game as well as in life. Everything in life is a technique, and if you master the technique, you will enjoy the rewards and all of the benefits the game has to offer.

Keep in mind that just because the running back gets thrown down for a loss, gets stopped at the line of scrimmage, or fumbles the ball, that player does not quit or give up because things did not go as planned. After each play, whether yards are gained or lost, the running back returns to the huddle to get the next call from the quarterback. Then the running back returns to the play formation with the hope of crossing the goal line or helping a teammate to do so.

Usually, one bad play does not determine the entire game or season for a team. Hopefully, one bad decision will not determine the outcome for your entire life. I made lots of bad plays in life, especially when I was a young kid. I made some bad calls and plays as an adult as well, but I kept fighting for yardage.

I challenge you not to live your life as a miserable person. Always look for ways to do positive things with your life, regardless of your failures. As you know by now, I made many mistakes during my life, but one thing I did not do: I never gave up, regardless of my pain, shame, embarrassment, or pitfalls.

A wise old man, Mr. Curtis Johnson Sr., once said to me: *"Alvin, midnight does not last forever!"* I have never forgotten those wise and life-sustaining words. I live with the hope that midnight does not last forever. I encourage and challenge you to never forget that midnight does not last forever if you do not give up.

Whatever has gone wrong in your life, it does not have to be that way forever. The bad experience does not have to destroy your joy and opportunity for a better life. Happiness can be found even in the midst and after the experience of great tragedy, depressions, rejection, and disasters. You must be willing to keep hope alive, because someone believes in you somewhere. Believing in yourself is one of the most powerful pieces of equipment you have to rescue yourself from your failures in life.

* * *

Sometime during my first-grade year, I went from caring about things and people to caring less about things and people. I went from the excitement of anticipating my first day at school to wishing it was my last day of school. My negative emotions and attitude about school and the field of education during my elementary school days were due to a relationship gone wrong between me and a teacher. It's like I was on an emotional roller coaster, and I just did not know where or when to get off it.

Later, of course, it was the relationship between me and my seventh-grade teacher that would reshape my life in a very positive way. At one time in my life, I declared I would never become a teacher. Yet Mrs. Johnson had a great impact on me, changing my opinion of teaching in a classroom. One day, out of the blue, I realized that as an educator, Mrs. Johnson had influenced my life in a way I was totally unaware of.

It was not until years later, after graduating from college at Eastern Kentucky University, that I went back to school to receive certification as a teacher. I taught high school for about seven and half years. Teaching full-time at my high school alma mater gave me a different view from inside the tower rather than a ground view. I later received a promotion to serve in a district-level supervisor's position. I became the coordinator of transportation for the St. Lucie County Public School District. As I said, I have a different feeling and attitude about teaching and the education profession after serving on the battlefield of the classroom.

In retrospect, the terrible experience I had as a young boy did not damper my overall hopes and opportunity. Neither did the bad experience force me to give up on all teachers and educators. Yet my disdain for some educators was rough and rocky for nearly the next seven years of my life after my introduction in the first grade. After my initial experience in first grade, I was finished with the idea of being a student learner. I had made up my mind that school only brought me shame, pain, and rebuke. I wanted neither of them on my journey.

The Community
Truancy Gang

My eldest brother Gary and I decided school was not for us at a very early age. We discussed the issue and felt like we needed to abandon the educational ship, simply because the ride was too rocky for us. In our naïve minds, we felt like school was a waste of our time.

Oh boy, were we so wrong! Education was the salvation that we desperately needed to save our lives. Years later, I was overhauled and revamped into a new person via the devoted work of a dedicated teacher, Mrs. Johnson.

Instead of going to school, Gary and I started hanging out in various neighborhoods across the Lincoln Park community, and in some undeveloped areas that were under construction. One of our favorite areas to hang out in was the Dr. Benton Quarters housing development. Dr. Benton Quarters was a low-income housing complex in the heart of Northwest Fort Pierce called the Lincoln Park community. Most of the houses were torn down after the Benton family sold the property to make room for the expansion of the northern portion of Lincoln Park Academy High School.

Keep in mind, when my brothers and I roamed the Lincoln Park community, we were some of the real genuine street rats. It was during the era of 1965, 1966, 1967, 1968, and 1969, and Fort Pierce was a segregated community. This was a time when nearly all African American people were forced to live within or near the Lincoln Park community. Initially, the street rats operated undercover near 18th Street and Avenue D. Then we moved into the Lincoln Park Area on Avenue M and 22nd Street, and then to 21st Street and Avenue M right across from Lincoln Park Academy gymnasium.

When Gary said he was not going back to school anymore, the two of us made an agreement that we would never go back. For me, school was not an exciting place to camp out. The thrill of education had died, and for the next seven and a half years, I became a youth on the run from education. It's called truancy.

Consequently, we became the neighborhood street rats, like the character in the Disney movie *Aladdin*. We were a group of troublesome youths who did things according to our own deviant childish minds. We deduced in our limited minds that we had to do whatever was necessary to survive the harsh street as elementary-school dropouts. We were just a misguided bunch of young people who needed good direction in our lives. We did not have good supervision and became misguided missiles of destruction.

I must say, we never did anything violent or malicious to bring bodily harm against humanity. We were mainly driven by the appetite to break into buildings and homes to steal food and any money we found to buy us food. We got the biggest thrill of the day when from time to time, we made ourselves uninvited guests at other people's dinner tables when they were not home. Even to this day, sometimes I tell people that I have eaten at their homes, and they look at me in disbelief and denial.

During this time, Gary and I were not on the state free or reduced lunch program while in school. I am amazed that each school day, my mother would remember to give us our lunch money to purchase our school lunch. I am not sure about the exact cost of a school lunch in 1965, but I know it was less than fifty cents. My mother thought she was buying our lunch for school, but we were buying our lunch at our daily rendezvous.

I believe that kids on reduced lunch paid around 15 cents and received a red or yellow ticket in the classroom to give to the lady receiving the money in the lunch line. I must admit, the best meal of the day for me was during the school lunch hour. For a while, my brothers and I would attend school only to eat a balanced meal for the day. I was just following in Gary's footsteps.

* * *

For some reason, I just could not get things together between the ages of six through thirteen. I seemed to have fallen into a pit that I could not pull myself out of. I always said I was going to do better by making good decisions, yet the more I intended to do right, the more negative choices I made. It was like I was traveling on an out-of-control roller coaster ride that was headed for a destructive crash.

My attitude became worse as time went on. When I tried to do better with my behavior, it seemed like temptation came my way to do bad. From my young perspective, it appeared to me that doing the wrong things in life always painted a glamorous picture of deception just to attract me to continue doing wrong. Whenever I tried to do the right thing, wrong appeared on the scene and offered me more incentives to do wrong.

Inwardly, I kept telling myself I must do better. Yet outwardly, it seemed like the pressure to do wrong with my childhood friends was too overwhelming for me to resist. It's like doing wrong was in my veins, controlling my every move, even against my will. I was living such a deceived life. Even though I knew it was bad for me, I just did not want to let it go.

My elementary school days were filled with an overwhelming truancy experience. I can remember when I attended Garden City Elementary and Chester A. Moore Elementary, located on 21st Street and 29th Street, respectively. I stayed on the run from the police and truant officers like an outlaw running from law-enforcement officers on the Western frontier. Mr. James A. McNeil was the principal when I attended Garden City Elementary in the first grade (twice) as well as the fourth and fifth grades.

When I attended Chester A. Moore Elementary School for second and third grades only, Mr. Herman Broxton was the principal. Even though I continued to have a severe truancy issue, I was never mistreated by any of the teachers (Mrs. Simpson and Mrs. McGehee), the administration, or the staff. The two teachers at C. A. Moore rekindled my love for education, as did Mrs. Bertha Sullivan and Mrs. Harper (Simmons), my fourth- and fifth-grade teachers.

Some of my boyhood friends were from the 29th Street Housing Project area: Reginald Marshall, Stanley Blackshear, Rodney "Bae-Bae" Jones, Lester Graham, and a few fellows who lived in the Viet Nam Housing area (a government housing area next to the 29th Street Housing Project, between Avenue D and Avenue F just off 29th Street). I liked attending C. A. Moore Elementary School whenever I did. I made some good friends from the 29th Street Housing Project. Yet during the two years I attended C. A. Moore Elementary, I felt out of place, maybe because I did not have my old gang with me from the Lincoln Park area.

During the spring of 1968, while I was in the second grade at Chester A. Moore Elementary School, my second-grade teacher was Mrs. Simpson. She was a very sweet, beautiful, and articulate young lady. I know I gave her the blues in class, yet she never admitted it to me. She tried her best to work with me, but I was very rebellious at the time and could not hear her wise counsel. Before she died, I would see her from time to time, and we would reminisce about those glorious days when I was in her second-grade class.

Nearly every day I came to school, she would have her class pet to take the attendance roll to the office, and often it was David. I loved David, because he never looked down on me. Oh yeah, his name today is Dr. David Washington, and he is one of my dearest friends. Oftentimes, David Washington would be the one to escort me to the principal's office when I got into trouble in the classroom.

David Washington, Karen Mims, and Reginald Marshall were the model students in the class. They were smart and well behaved, so they received the special privileges of running errands for the teacher, such as dropping off the attendance sheets and delivering other paperwork to the front office for the teacher. They also were the students chosen to take messages to other teachers for Mrs. Simpson.

These students were well-dressed, courteous, smart, and very obedient when it came to following classroom rules. I was often asked why I couldn't behave like the well-behaved students. Mrs. Simpson tried her best to get me on the right track, but there would be no compromise on my part.

* * *

Alvin Miller Sr., D. Min.

My third-grade teacher was a real shocker for me: the first Caucasian teacher I'd had or seen during my first four years of attending school. At the time (1968–1969 school year), the school district was still well-segregated, and it was having its own racial issues that exploded in 1970 and 1971 with racial protests and school riots, especially at Fort Pierce Central High School.

You see, Fort Pierce, as well as other communities within St. Lucie County—such as White City, Port St. Lucie, North Beach, and South Beach—were bent on fostering a white society where desegregation was off-limits and would not exist in the public schools. For me to walk into class and see a Caucasian female with a smile and a warm hug of compassion greeting me and other students was beyond my world and expectations. I had never experienced this type of compassion by a teacher other than my second-year first-grade teacher, Miss Johnson from the state of Alabama.

All I can say is Mrs. McGahee was the real deal when it came to teaching and putting in the extra time to prepare her students. She made everyone feel special in her class, regardless of the way they looked or how smart or deficient they were. She did her best to work with me on catching up with my peers with writing, reading, and arithmetic.

Mrs. McGahee recognized that I was way behind my peers academically. So she gave me special one-on-one session with my math and then signed me up to go to reading sessions while I attended C. A. Moore Elementary. I am more than convinced that Mrs. McGahee knew something was wrong in my life. She would often tell me that she was worried about me and she wished the best for me. Well, Mrs. McGahee, if you can hear me, I want you to know that I am all right today, and I can now read and write on a level with my peers.

While a student at Chester A. Moore Elementary School, even with Mrs. McGahee spending an overwhelming amount of time trying to get me on the right track, I could not stay focused on the fertile ground she was trying to lead me to. Mrs. McGahee's spirit and support were a breath of fresh air for me considering the way I was treated by my first-grade teacher at Garden City Elementary.

Mrs. McGahee was a teacher who loved her students. I can also remember the gift of love shown to me by Miss Johnson (my second first-grade teacher, after I failed my initial year of school). Miss Johnson was a beautiful young lady from the state of Alabama who I believe may have graduated from either Alabama A&M or Alabama State University. Then I had this teacher who was the Charleston, South Carolina, Queen. Her name was Mrs. Bertha Sullivan, and she tried her best to help me, but I refused to listen to her wise counsel.

As a sixth-grade student at Dan McCarty Middle School, I had Miss Athea Bailey, who were originally from Nassau in the Bahamas. She was a good teacher as well, but I was too out of control for her. Finally, the champion rose to the top and hit a grand slam home run: Mrs. Rita Johnson, my seventh-grade teacher, who put in the time to turn my life around. It is Mrs. Rita Marie Watson-Johnson's support, encouragement, and investment into my life that inspired me to write this book and tell my life story.

I enjoyed being in Mrs. McGahee's class because she made every student feel special, to the point where each student was the most important thing in the world at that particular moment. She was very patient and kind to her students. She was full of laughter and fun to be around. Over the years, I have tried looking her up, but I've had no success in finding her.

* * *

There was something very special about those glorious days when I attended elementary school. I was just too young and ignorant to understand the great beauty of what it meant to be a youth. I attempted to rush time when I was young, but now I have learned that time moves at its own pace and waits for no one.

During most of my childhood, I behaved as though time was my enemy. I could not grasp the fact that time was really a dear friend to me. It was not until I slowed down in life that I began to recognize the beautiful treasures time was trying to offer me through my life's experiences. Time had been trying to tell me all along that it was my friend instead of my enemy, and at the appropriate time, time proved to me what a friend I had.

As a footnote, I would be remiss if I did not mention two of my dearest boyhood friends, Terry Booker and Leon Hill, who invested so much in me to keep me out of trouble. Leon encouraged me to come with him and join a basketball league at the white YMCA when I started transitioning my life from bad to good. At the time, Leon, Victor Mobley, and I were the only African American youth who crossed over the canal and played basketball at the white YMCA.

As another footnote, during my high school years, my friend and brother at Goodwill Presbyterian Church invited me to go to church with him, which I did and was later baptized at Goodwill by Rev. Morgan. I felt like Terry wanted to ensure I stayed clear of the trouble that was looking for me. Terry did an awesome job of keeping me in church, which was his way of keeping me out of trouble as well.

One of the unique things about Terry Booker is that he made sure I would come over to his home on Friday and Saturday nights, and we (Terry and his three sisters, Gloria, Cheryl, and Yalonda) would talk and watch television into the early mornings before all the channels went off the air.

Last but not least, Lorenzo Davis, a dear friend, was my next-door neighbor for nearly twenty years in the government housing project (Coco Village) on 23rd Street (1007 and 1009) in the city of Fort Pierce. Lo was a very polite and well-mannered young man who was always looking to avoid trouble. He was Miss Francis's baby, and he was determined not to disappoint his sweet and loving mother. Many of the clothes I wore to school while I was in elementary school were hand-me-downs from Lo by his kind mother. Of course, that was whenever I decided to go to class.

After I made the decision to travel on the right side of life in the seventh grade under the guidance and supervision of Mrs. Johnson, it was guys like Terry Booker, Leon Hill, Lorenzo Davis, and Michael Campbell who would guide me in the right direction, once I returned to the neighborhood after leaving Mrs. Johnson and her family.

Listed below are my formative school years:

- **1965–1966**—first grade, Garden City Elementary School (6–7 years old)
- **1966–1967**—first grade (repeat), Garden City Elementary School (7–8 years old)
- **1967–1968**—second grade, Chester A. Moore Elementary School (8–9 years old)
- **1968–1969**—third grade, Chester A. Moore Elementary School (9–10 years old)
- **1969–1970**—fourth grade, Garden City Elementary School (10–11 years old)

- **1970–1971**—fifth grade, Garden City Elementary School (11–12 years old)
- **1971–1972**—sixth grade, Dan McCarty Middle School (12–13 years old)
- **1972–1973**—seventh grade, Dan McCarty Middle School (13–14 years old)
- No eighth grade—did not attend the eighth grade
- **1973–1974**—ninth grade, Lincoln Park Academy (14 years old)
- **1974–1975**—tenth grade, Fort Pierce Central High School (15 years old)
- **1975–1976**—eleventh grade, Fort Pierce Central High School (16 years old)
- **1976–1977**—twelfth grade, Fort Pierce Central High School (17 years old)
- **June 6, 1977**—graduation, Fort Pierce Central High School (18 years old)
- **1977–1981**—undergraduate student, Eastern Kentucky University (BA in sociology)
- **1985–1988**—graduate student, Southern Baptist Theological Seminary (MDiv)
- **1992–1999**—doctoral student, Oral Roberts University (D. Min., 1999)

I have been told it is not always how you started the race or the journey that counts but how you finish it. As you can see, I started off my educational and socialization journey in life behind my peers. With all the other things I had going on in my life, it is amazing I did not end up as an elementary school dropout. I admit I started off running in the wrong lane, and I could have been disqualified at any time during the race. Yet I am very thankful the judges did not disqualify me for stepping over the line more times than I can count.

* * *

In elementary and middle school, I acquired a truancy record with a deviant activity report that was second to none. I was engaging in various crimes as a youth and was constantly being chastised by the school district and juvenile court for my deviant behavior. Neither the spectators in the stands of life nor I myself had any idea that I could catch up with the rest of the runners (my peers) and even pass some who had made fun of me at the beginning of the race.

Somewhere along the way during the race, I was given a turbocharger in my engine that fueled and boosted my life to another level. The boost I received after meeting my seventh-grade teacher, Mrs. Rita Johnson, gave me superhuman powers to not only run but to win a ribbon in the race of life. I realized that the gate leading to a positive future was open for me to walk into prosperity and success. I walked through the gate of champions.

From the very first day of first grade to the last day of high school, I watched my life move from the road of destruction to a freeway of opportunities. I watched my excitement and expectation for education go from the valley of despair all the way to the mountaintop of hope and prosperity. I watched my life lifted from the gutters of hopelessness to the vast oceans of opportunities and positivity like never before.

I watched my dreams go from a devastating nightmare to a life filled with overwhelming joy. The reality of my hopes was much greater than my expectations. Things were changing so rapidly that I felt like I was in a transformational time machine. I was able to witness the dynamic positivity that was occurring before my own eyes.

I was living in three different worlds: catching up from the past, competing for a good spot in the present, and preparing for the glorious future that awaited me. I became so busy with productive actions that time consumed me with rewards. It was like I was trying to make up for the wrong I had done in my previous years as a youth.

I would be the first to say that education opened doors to a world I had only dreamt about as a child growing up in government housing. While picking tomatoes, oranges, grapefruits, potatoes, apples, and other sorts of produce as a migrant laborer, I would daydream about this wonderful world of opportunities where kids could be happy and not have to work like slaves. As a child working in the groves and vegetable fields of Florida, South Carolina, Virginia, Maryland, Pennsylvania, and New York, I would fantasize about some of the wonderful things life would allow me to experience.

Many of the wonderful gifts and rewards that have come my way over the years, I had no idea existed. As I stated earlier in the book, I was trapped in a small box that I thought was the big world. I thought I was educated about life and the world.

Yet in all reality, I knew nothing about the world or life in general. It is only through education that I have been granted the opportunity to chart my own course and destiny in life. The field of education and its faithful servants changed my perception and turned my life around so I could acquire a new beginning. This marvelous gift came to me after one of the unfaithful subjects of education tried to destroy my dreams and relationship with education.

Bad Choices Lead to Destructive Consequences

As a child growing up under the reins and shackles of the segregated South in Fort Pierce, Florida, I can remember some of the most respected names within the African American community. These names may not mean anything to you, but when I was a lad, they were our heroes and heroines in my little migrant town. These are the men and women we respected and feared with reverence as neighborhood kings and queens. Just to name a few: our family's social worker, Ida Morgan; Coach Robert Jefferson; Coach Floyd; and the city and county law-enforcement officers like Pat Duvall, King Strong, Oliver Walker, Jimmy Blakely, "Gig" Minus, "Hamp" Chester, Officer Regan Ellis, and Officer "Gib" Gibson. All of these great community heroes are now deceased.

We encountered officers who were bent on tracking down the Miller Truancy Group (me, Gary, and *Stewbeef*) with the hope of taking us back to school. Sometimes they would come to our apartment during the wee hours of the morning to catch us asleep. The law-enforcement and truancy officers tried their best to catch us, but we escaped their reach every time.

We thought there was a method to our madness. We deceived ourselves into thinking it was worthwhile. But you can never go right by going wrong in life. If you choose to keep going wrong, you will always end up at the wrong destination. North is always north, and south is always south.

As ignorant kids, we thought we were much smarter than the social workers, truant officers, and policemen who were chasing us. We thought it was some type of game. Yet even to this day, as I reflect over my life and the lives of my brothers, I just wish we would have listened to wise counsel and good instruction. We made bad choices that ended up having painful and even deadly consequences.

Remember this: whatever you do as a child will more than likely follow you into adulthood. So do everything within your strength and power to do the right things in life. As the elders use to say, "Life is nothing but a circle; the question is, can you complete the circle?"

During my elementary school days, I made up my young, inexperienced, and unwise mind that school was not important to me. I convinced myself that I did not need an education in order to survive or make it in life. I had no thoughts about my future or a sure plan for how I would provide a living for myself.

Boy, was I fooling myself—playing Russian roulette with deadly fire. What a terrible mistake I was making for playing such a destructive and foolish game with my life and future. I had no idea of the trouble I was planting for myself when I started out in first grade and through middle school, until I met my seventh-grade teacher, Mrs. Rita Watson Johnson.

All I knew at this particular point in my life was that I did not like school, and I was not going back. It is amazing how you think when you are a child living in a fantasy world with make-believe characters and dreams. I had a false perception that people would have my best interest at heart, especially as a youth.

One day, I found out that some of the same people who were encouraging me to act out really were not my true friends, as I had thought them to be. They were only wolves in sheep's clothing, just waiting for my demise. Remember, true friends do not tell or encourage you to throw your life away.

Always remember, true friends will never root for you to light a match while pumping fuel at a gas station. True friends will never tell you to hang yourself while you are hurting due to a loss, disappointment, or other type of failure in life. True friends will come to your aide and console you in the midst of your pain, disappointment, and shame. True friends will sincerely ask you, "What can I do to help you?"

I cherish my life experiences as a child growing up in poverty, although growing up poor was very embarrassing and deprived me and my siblings of many opportunities that some kids take for granted, like birthday parties, birthday gifts, Christmas gifts, toys, annual medical checkups, toothbrushes, and dentist visits. Times that should have been filled with fun and joy were filled with pain, shame, and heartache for me and some of my brothers.

Even in the midst of the shame, pain, and poverty, there were times that were filled with laughter. To me, all of my past life is better than living in a make-believe world with superficial problems and issues. Even as children, somewhere along the way we got to a point in our lives where we knew we were poor and depended on the state of Florida welfare system and other governmental agencies to help us survive the dreadful monster of poverty.

Yet we still found ways to squeeze fun out of our debilitating and stressful financial situation and environment. We knew our clothes and shoes were raggedy, but we had nothing else to put on. We knew birthdays, Christmases, and other incentives might live in other homes, but not in our houses. So we just had to live with the dream and pretend we were just like all the other children. We played the role while growing up in order to conceal the daily shame and pain. I would not wish my growing-up experiences on any child or person.

* * *

My constant absenteeism from elementary school cost me dearly. As you read this manuscript, you may note that I received an education beyond college and think that I did well for myself even after my rough beginning in life. Please listen to me very carefully and clearly: there are some things I still struggle with simply because I missed some of the very basic foundational educational techniques in math, English, and reading during my elementary school years.

I believe that one of the reasons I have problems with standardized testing is my absenteeism from elementary and middle school. My absence from school is like a ghost that continues to haunt me even in the present and into the future. Learning educational techniques and concepts does not come easy for me as it does for some people. I have to work hard and read things over and over to make sure I comprehend what I am reading, and still often there is a void in my comprehension.

Regardless of who you are and what you think, there is always some type of loss when you do not follow the rules of life and society. I believe there is a serious penalty we shall pay sooner or later when we attempt to take shortcuts in life. Many times, people think they can get better results for not obeying the rules than they can for following the rules.

Just remember to do the right things in life regardless of your age, education, economic status, or affiliation. Doing right in life is your greatest defender of the truth. The greatest guarantee of success I know, regardless of the stage you find yourself on, is to do it the right way from the beginning. Believe it or not, following the right rules from the beginning prevents us from having to do it all over again, and sometimes even then people can fail to get it right. This is what the term "skid row" is talking about whenever you hear it.

I do not want to sound unappreciative or too technical, but as I look over my life from past to present, not staying in school as a child is one of my biggest regrets. I am not crying over spilled milk, especially after what life has brought me and allowed me to accomplish with so many of the odds stacked against me. But I believe that if I'd had conscientious parents, mentors at an early age, or relatives who understood the value of education, I may have been further along with my choice of professions than I am today. I wanted to be a lawyer when I was in tenth grade. I believe my inability to make a good score on the Law School Aptitude Test (LSAT) had a direct connection to my years as a delinquent juvenile.

Furthermore, my truancy while in elementary and middle school has haunted me for my entire adult educational cycle. I am grateful for the accolades I acquired as a result of my educational journey. Yet I wish I had followed the attendance policies and classroom rules while in elementary and middle school. The good thing about my past is that I was given the opportunity to get it right and write about it with the hope of encouraging you.

One thing I know for sure about my life is that I was chosen from my mother's womb to do what I am doing today. I say this because I drifted very far off of the road to near destruction. I was allowed to make the correction with a complete turnabout. I witnessed many travelers turned over in ditches, ending up in fatal wrecks, stranded on the side of the road without hope, losing their way simply because they refused to follow the rules on how to travel the roadway of life.

I missed out on so much during the most crucial years of my education. All the tutoring in the world would not make up for what I lost during my early and middle childhood years. My educational loss is like a never-ending pain from losing a very precious piece of gold or a rare diamond you spend a lifetime looking to find. My absenteeism from school was my greatest downfall during my educational pilgrimage.

I believe if I had gone to class at least half of the time, I probably would not have been so far behind my classmates and peers. It is a mystery that I am as academically inclined as I am today. I am thankful and grateful that I made it this far in life with the help of Rita Johnson. Words cannot begin to express the gratitude I have for my seventh-grade teacher for inspiring me the way she did.

* * *

When I tell people I was retained (flunked) in the first grade because I missed about ninety days of school, they look at me as though they have seen a ghost. Then I share with them that I missed about the same number of days the next year while repeating first grade.

During my second time in first grade, my attendance was a little better, but I still continued to practice my magical disappearing acts from class. Amazingly, I was socially promoted to the second grade. Social promotion is probably not as common a practice today as it was when I was a child attending school. There are so many different options (such as tutoring and after-school programs and educational camps) in existence today to help disadvantaged, troubled, and struggling kids excel in education.

The term *social promotion* means a child is being advanced to the next grade level for the good of society, although that student does not meet the academic criteria for promotion. Though moving on to the next grade, the child is not being promoted based on merits or good academic standards in accordance with district policies and state guidelines. I had a double whammy against me: bad grades and bad behavior. What a losing combination.

To make matters worse, I had a despicable attitude that no one could stand or wanted to deal with. Believe me on this: it is always better to be nice, respectful, courteous, and compassionate to other people than to be mean-spirited or cold-hearted, or inhumane or ugly. You will never win or reap the accolades of life being self-centered and mean to other people. Trust me; I have lived life in both lanes. Being kind to people gains you more respect, rewards, and friends than all the places in the world.

As I stated earlier, when students are socially promoted, they are passed through the system to the next grade level. The school district allows the student to receive a pass for the good of the school district, the community, and society as a whole. Someone in a position of authority in the school district makes the decision to allow trouble to move on and rush the student through the school system.

It is the local superintendent who makes the decision that it would be in the best interest of society and the school district for a particular student to be given a waiver or special pass to move from elementary school to middle school, or from middle school to high school. The social promotion process is intended to minimize the burden or destruction a student may potentially cause to an educational system. It was the school district's way of counting its losses by the process of attrition, while at the same time protecting its interests, assets, and most valuable resources: students, teachers, and staff.

Over the next six years, after repeating the first grade, I was given the same rite of passage to the following grades: second, third, fourth, fifth, sixth, and on to seventh grade, with very little effort to improve myself academically. I must say that my second-, third-, fourth-, and fifth-grade teachers tried to encourage me to put forth my best effort. But I had other things on my mind. Miss Johnson (my teacher when I had to repeat first grade), Mrs. Simpson, Mrs. McGahee, Mrs. Harper-Simmons, Mrs. Bertha Sullivan, and Ms. Althea Bailey all tried to help me become a model student. Yet I was more determined to become a street thug than a scholar.

Sadly, all of their seeds fell on rocky soil. Or should I say, maybe good seeds were being planted and I just did not know it. I was totally unaware of the fact that one day, their planted seeds would take root and produce a harvest.

You never know what a seed will do once it falls to the ground and the natural process of nature takes over. Somewhere along the way, at the right time in the nurturing process, the kind actions of others begin to blossom. The truth of the matter is that it takes an entire village to raise a child. No parent can do it alone.

When we plant seeds of faith with compassion into the lives of people, especially our youth, we can only hope for a productive harvest. The proper rain, sunshine, fertilization, and soil will indeed produce a wonderful harvest that makes us proud of all of our hard labor.

Our crops do not become good and healthy for public consumption without the involvement and care of nurturing farmers: teachers, coaches, and other people in the community. When we plant positive seeds into the lives of young people, they need the same kind of nurturing that good crops receive on farms in order to grow productive lives.

* * *

When I entered middle school, I was nearly a hopeless case. But there was no lack of hope in the eyes of my seventh-grade teacher, Mrs. Rita M. Watson-Johnson. In sixth grade, it was a miracle if I made it through a full week without being suspended from school. I stayed on Dan McCarty Middle School's weekly suspension list with either a three-, five-, or ten-day suspension for fighting, disrespecting teachers, or being a disruptive influence.

When I was in sixth grade, one of my teachers bargained with me, which blows my mind even to this day. Today, as a mature adult, I can better understand her reasoning behind asking me to allow her to teach her class. She went on to say to me that if my group kept the noise down, we could continue playing cards in the rear of the class.

I thought I was doing something big when Mrs. X came to me with the proposal that if we stayed quiet, we could continue our card games. I had no idea I was paving the way for my own destruction in the penal system or in a cold grave six feet below the earth. What a shame! I thought I knew everything when in all reality, I did not know anything about education or life.

Furthermore, I had no idea that this teacher knew something I did not know. I believe she was well aware of the fact that there would be no educational benefit for me if I chose to play cards while she taught her class. I was too ignorant to understand that playing cards and disrupting a class had nothing to do with me and the other students getting a quality education.

I believe Mrs. X knew that if I continued being disruptive and following the path I was on, I would end up being another statistic in the negative column of life. She knew that guys like me eventually ended up as school dropouts, or in jail, or in prison, or worse, in a grave. Since we behaved like animals in the classroom, she allowed us to have our bones as long as we did not bark or disrupt her class. I sensed she was very intimidated or afraid of "out of control" African American males and females. If we said *boo*, she would jump with fear.

In retrospect, I will be the first to admit that the way I was headed would not lead to a good ending. People often told me that if I did not slow down and correct my direction, the handwriting was on the wall. What they were telling me in a very practical way was that if I did not change the way I was living, I would end up as another graveyard or prison statistic.

At the time, I did not know anything about the decimation of African American males within our American society. I was so blinded by ignorance that I could not see clearly or straight. I almost completely robbed myself of the opportunity to learn the things I needed to know in order to sustain my life and the lives of others.

As a juvenile, I thought I knew just as much or more than adults. Tell me what kids don't think they know as much as or even more than adults. I thought the good old days were over for all the old folks, and it was in with the new era for us kids. Life really doesn't change; it's the people in life who have to adapt in order to evolve as we transition from birth to death.

Little did I know that the rules in life did not change because I was born. Only the players in the circle of life change. The game of life is still played by the same principles and rules. There is nothing new concerning human behavior, good or bad. We all still struggle to control our destiny through the process of life.

As a juvenile, I really thought I was running the show, when in reality, I was only acting like an out-of-control monkey in that show. I thought I had the freedom to do whatever I wanted to do and say whatever I wanted to say. Yet I had no idea I was only plotting my own route to failure and destruction.

Alvin Miller Sr., D. Min.

I was a loose cannon aiming in all directions except the right one. Deep inside my subconscious, I knew I needed a lifeline. But I had no idea who would be the one to throw the lifeline to me. All I can say to anyone wanting and willing to change for the betterment of self and humanity is that there are people around you who will help you reach your goals. I guarantee you, there are people around you to help you cross over the bridge of life to achieve a prosperous presence and an enjoyable future.

* * *

When I was in the sixth grade, most of the teachers at school seemed to avoid making contact with me. I was shunned, like a person with a terrible case of the flu or a contagious disease like COVID-19. Many of my teachers at Dan McCarty Middle School felt like the only teachers who could control me were the big strong African American males.

So, during my sixth-grade year and the first semester of my seventh-grade year, coaches like Origen Colebrook, Roy McGriff, Matthew Bethel, and Curley Burch from St. Lucie Middle School were the teachers and coaches I respected the most. It was a relationship like big lion and little cub. The little cub had to give the big lion his respect. I followed their instructions without any reservations. This little cub, with a powerless bite and roar, knew I was out of my league with the kings of the jungle.

I believe it was a physical education teacher named Mrs. Beatrice Williams who figured out a way to bring some calmness to my madness. I do not know how she figured it out, but she was right in her thinking. Mrs. Williams recommended that the male coaches allow me to go out and play the sport or game of my choice. Of course, it was always either football or basketball that I chose when I was allowed to come to school.

As I look back over my life, I was just another angry African American kid looking for an excuse to get suspended or expelled. I harbored anger and blamed others. I listened to people around me complaining about their conditions rather than listening to my own inclination to do right. Within myself, my feelings were telling me, *Everything they are saying is untrue!* Adults have to be very careful what they say around children and especially teenagers, because if they are not careful, children can end up wearing the painful stripes of others as stripes of revenge.

As a child listening to adults' conversation, I too began to blame others for things that occurred in my life. This was a very selfish way of attempting to justify the wrong in my life. Even today, there are many people trying to justify the wrong in their own lives simply because of the ill or wrong treatment inflicted on them, or someone close to them, or someone they love. Such selfish thinking is only a scapegoat to justify a person's actions to hurt or harm others.

At this point of my life, I had not met Mrs. Rita Marie Watson Johnson. I was still in the sixth grade, and I was doing my very best to get expelled from middle school. Each day I went to middle school, I had this rage inside of me that stimulated me to be angry at the world.

The demeanor I had in middle school was not good for a child or adult to have to live with day to day. A life lived being angry with people is not a good life. This way of thinking is the bondage that oftentimes shackles young and old alike. Living with anger forcefully pushes people's minds into corners of isolation with either lost or crushed dreams.

I felt like I was angry about nearly anything and everything a person could get angry about. I would even think about the clothes I was wearing to school and how they did not belong to me but to my brother Gary or my cousin Terry. I became angry because I had no decent clothes to wear to school. Nearly every day while in middle school, I would wear my older brother Gary's clothes or Terry's clothes.

Can you imagine how this made me feel by the end of the day after the students would pick at me for having on clothes that were too big for me? Regardless of the clothes I would wear, between Gary and Terry, they all were too big for me. It seemed like everyone in the middle school noticed I was wearing someone else's clothes that were too large for me. By this time, I had become a freelance comic show in the classroom for the students and teachers. I had not yet come across the lady who would help me and my mother change my life forever.

* * *

I believe it was during my fifth- or sixth grade year that the Honorable Judge Jack L. Rogers told me that if I ever came back to his courtroom, he was going to make sure I went to reformatory school for a long time. Although I never returned to the judge's courtroom, I did not abort my lawless behavior until a year after his stern threat to me. All I can say is I never returned to Judge Rogers' courtroom, mainly because Mrs. Johnson started implementing her behavior modification plan on me.

As I stated earlier in the book, Judge Rogers was well known on the streets of Fort Pierce, especially amongst the juveniles and some of their parents. He came across as a tough and mean man who would incarcerate a person with the maximum sentence. Some of the older teenaged boys used to say Judge Rogers was a cruel, coldhearted, and ruthless person with a hammer in his hand. While on his bench, he looked as though he was angry and hardly ever cracked a smile. You knew he was there for business and only business with some of the worst juveniles in St. Lucie County.

Just knowing you had to stand before Judge Rogers' bench struck fear into the hearts of some of the most notorious juveniles in the neighborhood. I thank Judge Rogers, because he gave me one of the greatest breaks in life. I needed this reprieve.

I believe I first meet Mrs. Johnson, my seventh-grade teacher, while still slacking on the job according to what I had promised Judge Rogers. You see, as a young student, I made a plea of hope to Judge Rogers that I would indeed obey the orders of the court. But my promise only lasted a few minutes after leaving the courtroom.

While I was standing before Judge Rogers' bench, the fear was real and most intimidating. Once I left his presence, however, I relaxed and let down my guard. It's like the old cliché "out of sight, out of mind."

It is only by fate that I never retured to Judge Rogers' courtroom, because I went right back to doing the same detrimental things that had gotten me into the unstable situation that did not look good for my future. Judge Rogers had released me from the hot water, and then I turned around and jumped back in. This was a catastrophe waiting to happen.

The End of My Social Promotion Days

I was passed along for another year, from sixth grade to seventh. I remember talking to the Big Man over the summer. I asked the Big Man to help me do right in school and allow me to change my destructive behavior.

Furthermore, I asked the Big Man to give me the strength to do the right things in school, even though peer pressure was telling me to do all the wrong things. Peer pressure seemed to give me somewhat of a false sense of fame and hope. What I did not know at the time was that peer pressure was pushing me along on a catastrophic trajectory that would end in pain and shame.

Around 1971, after a long summer on the migrant trail, I returned to Fort Pierce to attend middle school. At first, I tried to resist the urge and temptation to play the bully gangster role. But my vices were too controlling and powerful for my little powerless mind. It seemed the more I tried to fight for the freedom to do right, the more I became pushed by the wind to do wrong.

I returned to doing what I knew best: disrupting classes, breaking and entering, and other criminal activities. Attending school was the least of my priorities. My thoughts of doing right never connected with my actions of doing wrong. It is like I was fighting with a force that was determined to conquer me as it pushed me to keep doing wrong in life.

The mold had already been established by my peers as to how they expected me to behave. They expected me to resist the establishment by refusing to become a conformist to the system. While many of them stayed in the ranks of conformity and progressed with their education, they expected me to break the ranks by defying the authority of the adults who were in charge of my education plan. In my warped mind, I thought I was doing something big in life, but in all reality, I did not have a clue as to what was going on behind the scenes.

I began to buck the public-school system like a wild mustang in the free Wyoming country. Little did I know this would be the last time I would run wild without a saddle or rider on my back. I thought I had escaped the axe of expulsion during my sixth-grade year; but little did I know what was cooking on the stove for me.

Within the Oval Office of Dan McCarty Middle School, a meal was being prepared for me. I knew nothing about the planned meal, so I came to school my seventh-grade year thinking I was going to conduct business as usual. I would have a rude awakening during the second half of that year. I would be hit by a bomb that I never saw coming my way.

* * *

During the fall of seventh grade, I got suspended several times. This was a great improvement from the year before. Yet it was not good enough for someone to say progress had been made. I thought it was a drastic change from previous years. I was doing my best to hold on to doing the right things in life, especially while at school, but the temptation to do wrong was a constant daily battle for me each day at school and in the neighborhood.

This particular school year (1972–73), I became determined to win the battle against delinquency and truancy. It clicked in my mind that it was a bad habit or vice that I needed to conquer before it defeated me. A positive feeling came over me that I no longer wanted to go to prison, or become a school dropout, or work in the tomato fields and orange groves for the rest of my life. I wanted a way out, but I did not know where to turn in order to release the shackles that had me bound for so many years.

More importantly, I no longer wanted to end up on death row or dead like some of the people I once knew and had grown up with. I was willing to make whatever changes I needed to make in order to keep from throwing my life away. I wanted a better life than what I had become accustomed to living.

I knew that somewhere out there was a dream for me to fulfill. I was determined to find the dream that offered me a ticket out of the ghetto and poverty. I was hoping for a dream that would free me from the shackles of a life that offered me nothing but hand-me-downs. I was sick and tired of being on welfare and wanted relief from a life of dependency on government subsidies.

Somewhere deep within me, I was looking for a way out of the projects, the street life, and the destructive path I had etched in the hearts of people around me. I saw myself rebelling against people who tried to help me. I was angry with the way my life was going and did not have the wisdom or insight to stop the downward tumble.

Somewhere along the way, I came to the realization that I was the only person responsible for controlling my destiny. The choice was up to me, and no one else had the power to map out my future success. I realized that all the complaining about and blaming of other people and things was not going to change my condition or situation. I had to make the move in the right direction if I was ever going to make it to the next level of success in my life.

* * *

When we look around us and constantly see in the news the images of Black-on-Black crime, especially amongst our young African American males, we have to ask the question, where did we go wrong? You may say, "I did not go wrong; only they were the ones who went wrong." Then I say to you, crime in any neighborhood in America affects the peace, stability, tranquility, prosperity, economy, and cultural issues at all levels and in all ranks of life, including your neighborhood. I hope people will understand that crime in one neighborhood is a threat to all of America. This is why it is so important to lend a helping hand to others in need of guidance, if they will allow it.

We have to always ensure that our youth can live, learn, and thrive

Alvin Miller Sr., D. Min.

educationally in compassionate and nurturing environments. All adults must make the nurturing of our youth in an environment where they can feel safe, loved, and protected a top priority. Somewhere along the way, we have to pay the cost for some the deviant breakdowns caused by others within our society.

Many African American males are angry at their fathers and end up taking their anger out on themselves and people who have not done anything to contribute to their anger or rage. Many of these males learn about their fathers from their mothers, other relatives, and/or people within the community. A lot of the stories and information children learn about their noncustodial parent are not good.

When kids think of their fathers and mothers as their superheroes, they have a more positive outlook on life. When they are constantly bombarded with comments and perceptions that their parents are nothing but deadbeats, their perception of their superhero parents becomes tainted. Once confusion or a distasteful thought incubates in the mind, anger sets in, and on many occasions, disappointment festers into hate.

If we are going to play a pivotal role to help save our children, our family heritage, and even our nation, we must take proactive action to build up our children. We must never talk bad about their mothers or fathers, even when we think the negative talk is warranted. The poem below addresses some of the hidden thoughts and emotions that African American males have against their fathers within American culture. Below is a poem I wrote because my daddy never gave me his name!

Daddy Never Gave Me His Name

Conceived in sin and shame,
Daddy never gave me his name,
That's no claim to fame,
For a child who is not to blame.
Like a good Mother Hen,
She did her best with her ten,
But chance seldom gave her a grin.
Although much time has passed,
Yet the question still lingers,

How long the pains of
Yesteryears will last?
Thank Creation for love, grace, and mercy;
It has allowed me to move on to a different place.
Today, I am no longer mad or sad
About the name I never had;
All because Daddy never gave me his name!

I must confess that not having my father's last name bothered me back when I was a child in elementary school. Even today, sometimes the thought of not having my father's name nibbles at me. At sixty-plus years of age. I still find myself asking the question of why it is that my daddy never gave me his name.

Please tell me why my daddy gave me embarrassment and shame instead of a name that offered me some type of fame? Now, I remember that this is what the elementary-school teacher was talking about when she said to me, "Oh, you are the fatherless child who is causing all the problems around here at school." It was at Garden City Elementary that I met this particular teacher while on my way to the boy's restroom.

Now that I am at a different place mentally than I was over fifty years ago, it is not about how I was conceived. It is more about what I became after I was born. I am more concerned with the question, *Do I become an asset to society, or do I become a liability to humanity? Do I have the courage, faith, and strength to go back into bondage to help others come out of their shackles of shame, disappointment, poverty, illiteracy, complacency, shattered dreams, and destruction, and help lead them to the Promised Land of hope, peace, prosperity, and joy?*

If good-hearted people do not stand up and help lead our young generation to the ocean of vast opportunities for success, then tell me, who will do it? Someone came to my rescue, and now I must do the same for other kids and people who are in distressing living conditions and situations. Or should I sit idle and watch people struggle with some of the same issues that nearly took me under the ground without lending a helping hand to save them from some of the bondage I had to endure? It is much easier for people to look the other way or act like, *It is not my fight, so why bother with other people and their own personal issues?*

When I was conceived, my daddy was married to another woman. I often tell people that there are some scars you can cover up with makeup and makeovers; there are some scars you can have removed from your body with medical procedures; but there are other scars that lurk under the surface that age, time, doctors, changes of geographical location, or a new identity cannot remove. Neither can any of these things heal the scars or scar tissue embedded into the roots of the mind, including emotions and feelings.

Some scars in our lives are constant reminders that we do not want to return to the place where we received them. Some scars are simply too painful for many of us to remember. Let us move forward so we can avoid the scars that have caused us such grief. There are some scars and painful experiences that we cannot avoid. Hopefully, we can gather up the courage and strength to excel and win in life even with the scars and pain that come with it.

* * *

Around 1973, between the age of thirteen or fourteen, I began to process that if I wanted out of my cave and the shackles of despair, I needed to change my behavior. I began to understand the basic fact that if I expected a positive change to occur in my life, I needed to become the change agent that would usher in the positive environment by producing positive actions. I had to produce encouragement in order to earn the support and respect of others.

Mrs. Johnson would often tell me that if I expected to be embraced by the people who held the keys to my success, I needed to change my way of thinking and acting. Although she did not use these exact words, I got the message. I needed to connect with the people who held power and influence. Mrs. Johnson's advice to me was more than right on time. Her good advice was the proven truth that opened the doorway of success for me to walk through with jubilation.

The year 1973 was like no other school year I had experienced. For the first time in my life, I began to say to myself that I no longer wanted to travel on the same dirt roads. I was expecting that some invisible hope would invade my life in some kind of mystical way. I would fanaticize how in my own little way, I could foster a positive change in my life.

Yet I was realistic about the fact that I was carrying a lot of baggage that could become a stumbling block for me. I knew I had to keep the dangerous baggage at a safe distance where I could subdue it. I knew that in order to reach my destination, I needed to dump everything that could hinder me from achieving my desired goal in life.

Like many young African American males, I was laying the foundation for a wasteful life. Over the years, I have come to the conclusion that the rebellious attitude of many young African American males comes about over a succession of years while growing up. The seeds for the troublesome behavior many of our youth are experiencing today are planted way before they get to the point of carrying out their destructive actions.

Many of the youth from my neighborhood learned from members of the previous generation, who were a lot more advanced in age and experience than we were. Many of the people in the previous generations taught us how to play a game that would end up sending us to prison, or into a life of drugs, crime, violence, gang activities, and delinquency. The anger, rage, and hate within many of these young men started when they recognized there was something uniquely different, or wrong, or unusual in their relationships with their fathers.

On many occasions, you can see mothers and grandmothers doing their best to support, nurture, and provide life-sustaining instruction to young African American males. Sometimes you even see these stalwart matriarchs chastising young males, when necessary, in order to keep them from becoming the next homicide statistic in the local newspaper. You may ask: where are the fathers or daddies?

To make matters worse, when young boys realize their last name is not the same as the man who claims to be their father, they may go to their mothers and ask the question, "Why is my last name _____, and my father's last name is _____? If he is my father, then why do I not have his last name?"

To a child growing up without something that would make him proud is devastating. Having a father is pertinent to the self-esteem of a child, especially a male. When boys look for their identity, they look for a strong male image in the family as a model for building their own self-esteem.

All children, especially those living in deplorable conditions as I did, need a hero in their life who can encourage them to dream beyond their present condition. Who can a boy dream to be like when he has nothing worthy of his mother's praise? Struggling children living in poverty and substandard conditions have to be able to dream and see a different and better world than the one life has dealt them.

I believe the greatest hero for a boy growing up is his father. He loves his mother with overwhelming compassion, yet he would reverence his father if given the opportunity to develop a genuine father-and-son relationship. Boys need strong men to bond with as they grow from childhood to adulthood. Young African American boys need African American men to become the plumb line in their lives to help them walk the straight and narrow way.

I will repeat this idea that boys need men (good mentors) in their lives over and over, because it takes stalwart men with impeccable moral character to coach and mentor boys into manhood. Without good men on first base, it becomes very difficult for young boys to make it to home plate. They may be able to run some of the bases in life with a hit, but to make it to home plate, boys need wise and strong men with integrity to guide them through life's journey.

A father is so important in the life of a boy that even in the father's absence, the boy will act like the father is present when he is not. The father is totally absent from the boy's life, but he will do everything within or beyond his power to make you believe that his father has some type of strong presence in his lonesome life. The boy will go so far as to make up stories about his relationship with his father, as though they are actually going fishing, hunting, and playing sports together when it is not true.

The male child will even make up stories about himself and his father watching sporting events in the community, just to feel a sense of belonging. Whether he admits it or not, the lad has an overwhelming desire to be loved by his father. It is very difficult to find something to fill the void of an absent father in the life of a son. Even with all the lies and storytelling about my father, I was never loved, protected, nourished, or provided for by him the way I wished I could have been as a little boy growing up without a father.

Knowing that I had to live each day with a lie about my father was probably one of the biggest hurdles I had to endure as a child. Growing up as a boy, each day for me was a great big shame. Why should I be blamed and ridiculed for something I had no part in doing?

Probably the one thing that created more anger in me than anything else as a child was growing up to see a man disrespecting my mother and other women by striking or putting his hands on them in an abusive manner. A male child without a father in the house or anywhere around takes it upon himself as his duty to protect his mother and younger siblings. When I would see men disrespecting my mother, I would begin to plan and plot ways to covertly retaliate with vengeance and anger. My brothers and I refused to allow men to beat on our mother even if it meant us getting hurt in the process of defending her.

Also, this predicament adds fuel to the fire that the boy is feeling against his father. The boy's anger toward his father is elevated because in his mind, it is his father who has put him in the awkward position of defending his mother against a grown man! Little boys should never have to go defend their mother against abusive men! A lion cub should never have to defend its mother against an adult male lion. It is a suicide mission all the way around.

So when a little boy or girl comes to your school or class and is acting out, and you do not seem to understand it as a teacher, it may be a good idea to do your best to understand and explore the child's home life. Believe me on this: children will most of the time bring unfinished business at home and in the community to school with them. The things I saw and witnessed as a child, I would not wish upon my greatest enemies. Some of the things I had to endure as a child, I will not even share in this book or on this side of the grave.

All I know is that the mercy of the courts, the help of some good-hearted people along the way, and the cooperation of my mother, Mrs. Johnson, and Dr. Skinner, gave me another chance in life, which I desperately needed. It is the compassion of other people that allowed me to hang around and begin to share the story of my last chance to win in life. I am more than grateful for this opportunity to share a portion of my life story about the people who helped me turn my life around for the betterment of humanity and my existence.

PART THREE

The Atmosphere for a Positive Change

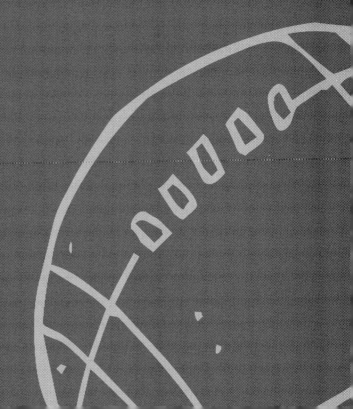

Last Chance

I will give you probably the pivotal thing that occurred in my life to bring about my transformation, which many people doubted at the time. Here is the beginning of how positive change occurred in my life. Mr. Nolan G. Skinner was my middle school principal when I first arrived at Dan McCarty Middle School. During the second semester of my seventh-grade year, I was given an ultimatum by Mr. Skinner to change my ways or suffer the devastation of getting expelled from middle school.

We'd previously had discussions about my out-of-control behavior; but I had ignored his scolding. Yet this time, I knew there was a greater threat behind his verbal chastisement. He looked at me behind those glasses he wore with a different type of sternness. I felt the cold chill even in his glance telling me that he was fed up with me, and this would be our last conversation concerning this matter.

The unique thing about Mr. Skinner's demand is that he not only gave me the choice to change my ways from bad to good but also gave me a support system through Mrs. Johnson that I desperately needed to become a transformed person. At the time, I knew I was sick, but I did not have access to the right medication for my sickness.

Little did I know that Mrs. Johnson was not only the right medication for my illness but also the perfect treatment for it. She knew behavioral modification techniques to use on me in order to attack the stubborn virus that had been ailing me throughout my elementary and middle-school years. Metaphorically speaking, Mrs. Johnson was the right physician and could prescribe the necessary medication for my behavioral diagnosis, and Mr. Skinner believed she could do it.

When Mr. Skinner offered the heavy burden of helping me to change my life to Mrs. Johnson, I was clueless about the deal and the details. Just think, if Mrs. Johnson had declined the offer from Mr. Skinner, I would have used my last mercy card for remaining in middle school. Just the thought of being put out of middle school would have been devastating to me.

More than likely, it would have put me at a point of no return. I was already tumbling down the hill of life, and an expulsion from school at this point would have been detrimental to me. As I look back, I recognize I had used my last pass for redemption. There were no more freebies for Alvin. This was my last chance.

* * *

I believe it was following my seventh-grade school year that Mr. Skinner became a district-level supervisor (director of elementary education for the district). During his tenure at the district office, he became the superintendent of schools. I believe it was during the spring semester of my seventh-grade school year that Dr. Skinner earned his Ed.D and moved into a position at the St. Lucie County school district headquarters on Delaware Avenue next to the Florida National Guard building off of 29th Street and Delaware Avenue in Fort Pierce.

Somewhere around the late fall or early spring of my seventh-grade year, it was solely Dr. Skinner's idea to approach Mrs. Johnson about helping me. To my understanding, Dr. Skinner told Mrs. Johnson that he was in the process of submitting my name to the board of education for expulsion from school. Yet he was willing to give me a stay of expulsion if Mrs. Johnson could turn my life in the right direction.

I did not find out until years later that Dr. Skinner had told Mrs. Johnson that before he submitted my name to the school board for expulsion, he wanted to try one last thing with me that required Mrs. Johnson's participation. Dr. Skinner wanted Mrs. Johnson to have a chance at reforming me, and if it did not work, then he would make sure I was expelled.

It was somewhere around this time that Dr. Skinner was notified of his new position at the district office. In retrospect, after Dr. Skinner was moved to the district office, I thought, *What difference would my behavior make to him?* But although he was no longer the principal, he was now the supervisor of elementary and middle school education for the district. The "out of sight, out of mind" concept would not have worked in this case, because I still would be a thorn in his side or his caseload.

* * *

During the time when Dr. Skinner was negotiating with Mrs. Johnson about my future, I had no knowledge of it. Neither did I know anything that was actually going on about my life as a student at Dan McCarty Middle School. I did not know anything about Mrs. Johnson. As a matter of fact, I had never heard her name until the day I stepped in her class.

I had no clue of what was baking in the oven for my life! The thing I remember most about the deal between Dr. Skinner and Mrs. Johnson was that one day, out of nowhere, nearly all of my classes were changed. I had been added to Mrs. Johnson's English class without any prior discussion or notification.

All of this was done without my input or any prior notice. I was put into Mrs. Johnson's class for English, where I learned more about the subject in one semester than I had learned in nearly eight years of school. Also, the psychological warfare was on and popping from the very first day I entered Mrs. Johnson's class. I do not need to tell you who won!

Mrs. Johnson cut me no slack when it came to her classroom rules. She would even position my seat in the front of the class. I did not like sitting in the front of the class. It brought too much exposure to me and placed me on the carpet of accountability.

I wanted to sit in the back of the class so I could throw paper, make smart-aleck comments, and hide behind the crowd. In order for students to be successful at their devious games, they need to have opportunities to hide behind a crowd. Little did I know, but the day had come when I could no longer hide behind a crowd.

Yet I allowed Mrs. Johnson to win battles and confrontations between the two of us, even the ones in front of the class. After all, she had graciously signed up for a dubious job that no one else wanted. No other teacher on campus was willing to take on the mission or challenge of transforming a little tyrant from the hood to good.

My reputation was so bad that the attempt to mentor me was too risky for other teachers at Dan McCarty Middle School. Many had children and families of their own, and the risk was too great. No one but Mrs. Johnson was willing to take time with a delinquent juvenile who was projected to drop out of school, or face incarceration in prison, or end up as another statistic in the cemetery as a young man whose life was cut short by the decision to walk on the wrong side of the road. Some people had even predicted I would end up on death row by the time I was twenty-one years old.

After the initial shock of the transition and resistance to changing my schedule, I was able to regroup and accept the change. Somewhere within my psyche, I saw a flashback of me over the summer wishing for the opportunity to have a better life. I believe even the worst of children and people in general wish for good things to happen to them rather than bad things. I was receiving the gift of life that I had asked for in my heart and mind.

I believe that people would rather do good than bad. They just get caught up in the moment when the current situation or environment will dictate the actions. Many youths and adults who have committed heinous crimes will tell you that if they had to do things over again, they would have done them differently. Over the years, I have met people who are living in a state of shame and regret for the things they did as youths. Some are still stagnated by the lawless youthful acts of the past.

Some probably would tell you that peer pressure encouraged them to do the wrong thing and become something that was beyond their scope of thinking. In many instances, peer pressure or environmental relationships won out over my ability to do right. As a youth, I struggled with whether to live up to the hype from the peer pressure or submit to following the rules at school and in society.

* * *

It is amazing how, when good things began to happen in my life, the pessimistic version of myself would often come back and agitate my mind for making the decision to do the right thing. Sometimes this negative force would show up as some of my so-called friends and attempt to torture my mind by calling me a sellout.

I did not want to be a sellout. In all honesty, I just wanted a better life than the one I was currently living. I was sick and tired of doing wrong. I did not want to disappoint Mrs. Johnson or my mother. I was determined not to relapse or have a setback on my journey to transformation.

The enemy from within my mind would tell me, *Man, you are a chump for letting that woman handle you like that. Alvin, you better rise up and give her a piece of your mind. Show your classmates who is in charge. Man, you have gone soft and become a coward.* By this time, I recognized I had to make the decision to swallow my pride and live my new life as a change agent, or become a disaster for the crowd. A self-destructing shadow was lurking around the corner waiting to pounce on me like a wild jungle cat pounces on its prey.

In retrospect, I realize that, prior to meeting Mrs. Johnson, I was gambling with my life. The odds were stacked against me. I was dealt a hand that gave me nearly no chance to win with the cards I held. During my gamble with life, I became aware that life is a gift that we have to shape with precision for our own future. Longevity is not promised to anyone, but life becomes an outright gamble if you live it the wrong way.

We have to make the best of the time we have to live on this earth and leave the rest up to the big clock that records our time and actions. At times, we have to be driven by our faith and hope for the best results and actions. Even when you are convinced you have made the best choice or decision, still, all things are not promised to turn out in your favor or as you desire.

Life is full of turns and twists, storms and obstacles, problems and disasters that we have to maneuver through or around in order to make our lives enjoyable. We have to be willing to bring our desire and ability for hard work with integrity to the table. We have to be willing to lay out a practical platform of success for our lives to navigate and achieve as we journey.

Yet life to some people is nothing but a gamble and will remain a gamble throughout their entire lives. The more opportunities they receive, the more they will foolishly bet and even raise the stakes for winning. I no longer wanted to gamble my life away. I came to a point in my life when I was determined to submit, commit, and achieve the best life had to offer me. I never knew the American dream could be so beautiful.

Even with all the gambles we take in life, there are odds that are always against us. We have to learn to override our fears and allow trust and faith to guide us to the city of hope. Although I had some fear about where Mrs. Johnson was going to take me, I also knew she was my greatest hope at the time.

I knew I had to override my fears and allow Mrs. Johnson to help me get to my destiny. Here is the bottom line: at the time, Mrs. Rita Johnson was my only chance and hope for success. I had the choice to either take it or leave it. This was an obstacle course I could not pass by myself; I needed a team leader to guide me. I am glad I was given the best guide to help me complete the course to all I ever could have ever imagined.

Can you believe that fear and the old crowd from my past told me to rebel against Mrs. Johnson? On the other hand, faith and trust told me to hang in there for the sake of the wonderful destiny that awaited me if I just kept the faith as I traveled with hope. Pride tried to convince me to abandon ship and the voyage to the world of total transformation. Meanwhile, trust told me to stay on board, because the ship was not going to sink.

Ignorance tried to convince me I was a hopeless case of childhood delinquency, while wisdom came my way and told me, "It isn't over until it's over!" Then I looked around and became strengthened and motivated by the commitment and determination of Mrs. Johnson.

I noticed that Mrs. Johnson refused to quit even when I foolishly tried to sabotage the entire process. Mrs. Johnson was the schoolteacher who refused to slumber. This is the bottom line to the story: Mrs. Johnson's motivation was to assist me in crossing the finish line of life. She seemed more determined not to abort the challenge than I was to excel in life. She motivated me many times when I could not see the direction in which I was traveling.

The Teacher Who
Would Not Quit

Mrs. Johnson was a tough warrior to crack. First, she defeated me in games of psychological warfare. It took me years to figure out how she was able to get me to conform to her wishes. All I can say is she outwitted me for my own good, and I am glad she did.

Being from the Desire Projects in the 9th Ward of New Orleans, Mrs. Johnson was more advanced in psychological warfare than I was pretending to be. She had a cunning shrewdness about her mission to achieve success, like the great Harriet Tubman did during the American slavery era. On one of Harriet Tubman's journeys to freedom, it is said that she told one of the slaves in her band that she would kill him rather than allow him to return to the plantation and divulge her secret plans of the Underground Railroad.

Right off the bat, from day one, upon my entering Mrs. Johnson's class, it seemed like she smoothly went for the jugular to get the upper hand on controlling me. She sophisticatedly struck up a class conversation about the things boys did with their fathers. I can remember the discussion in our seventh-grade English class like it was today.

Mrs. Johnson used her questions to put me on the defensive and disarm me all at the same time. Mrs. Johnson's questioning process forced me to start telling lies in order to keep from being exposed and embarrassed before the entire class, or so I thought. She moved across the classroom with precision and purpose, like a skilled entertainer captivating an audience with an unbelievable show of gifts. No one in the class knew where Mrs. Johnson was going except Mrs. Johnson. She mesmerized the entire class with her act. "Tell the truth or tell a lie," she said. "I already know the answers!"

Here's a word to the wise: do not tell lies. Lies end up building fires you cannot put out until you tell the whole truth and nothing but the truth. Even then, much of the damage is already done and cannot be undone. Standing on the truth is the first step to a new beginning. You cannot go wrong by telling the truth.

Lies make people vulnerable, because it removes them from their greatest protective weapon: the truth. Once a person gets backed into a corner of lies, only the truth can begin to set that person free. There may be some serious consequences for telling the truth, but a good reward is that once the truth has been told, the healing process can start if the damage is not too earth-shattering or overwhelming. Some lies are so devastating that even time or people will not heal them during this earthly mission.

I can remember one day in English class; Mrs. Johnson popped a question to the class during an open discussion: "Do you all go fishing or vacationing with your father? Raise your hand if these applies to you."

I raised my hand, knowing I did not have any type of a relationship with my father but not wanting to admit it.

Next, she asked, "How many of you in here have your fathers take you to baseball games, basketball games, football games, or some other sporting event? Please raise your hand."

I again raised my hand, knowing I was telling an untruth but not wanting to be exposed. I was exposed. Mrs. Johnson had only asked the question to see how I would respond.

When the questions finally ended, I was exposed by my lies, and after my confession of the truth, I became redeemed. Only after telling Mrs. Johnson the truth about me and my father's fictitious relationship did I become liberated from my lies. It was after class; she had asked me to stay behind after the other students were released.

When we were alone in the classroom, Mrs. Johnson said to me, "Alvin, why did you raise your hand when you and I both know you were not being honest?" She put a nail in the coffin when she asked me which games we attend together, or where did we go fishing and what type of fish did you catch? She sealed the coffin when she asked me when was the last time, I had seen my biological father!

Sadly, I could not remember the last time I had seen my daddy. My daddy did not ever establish a relationship with me. It was only a hello and goodbye relationship in passing. This seems to be the same song among many African American males across America. No matter where you go in Black America, the sheet music of the absentee father can be heard on radios, televisions, and social media venues.

The funny thing about the whole class exercise is that she knew I was lying from the second I lifted my hand. The entire purpose of the event was to disarm me by taking the will to fight right out of me. Once you disarm a person's pride, there is very little that person has to fight about. Like a mission-oriented drone, she zoomed right in on me. I never saw it coming until the strike had hit its target and the mission was accomplished with success.

Like a lioness smoothly going for the windpipe of its prey in order to take the fighting drive away, Mrs. Johnson left me without the strength to fight. After a few in-house disciplinary actions, she was well on her way to taming a savage beast that many teachers and people had said could not be tamed. Many people said Mrs. Johnson was wasting her time by trying to help me transform into a law-abiding student and citizen.

Mrs. Johnson and my mother tag-teamed to prove all my critics wrong. It is a terrible thing when adults wish for failure to fall upon the lives of children. Adults should be solid and stalwart bridges for children struggling to find their way in life. I am so thankful that my mother gave Mrs. Johnson permission to work with me and discipline me.

* * *

Not too long after agreeing with Dr. Skinner to mentor me, Mrs. Johnson started tutoring me. She mostly worked with me after school at her home. I became an intricate part of her family. She was determined to get me caught up and on the right track.

How can a child and teacher work to make up nearly eight years of educational deficiency in four years? When Mrs. Johnson started tutoring me, for the first time in my life and school career, I made an A on a class assignment. It was the first time in my life that I had ever earned an A or a B on a report card. Mrs. Johnson's hard work was paying off in more ways than one: I was no longer showing up on weekly suspension lists or at the principal's office for violating school codes.

After meeting Mrs. Johnson, I never again got suspended from school. I experienced immediate dividends after Mrs. Johnson started tutoring me. It was on an English class scrapbook project that I received my very first A for an academic project. With the support of my mother and the help of Mrs. Johnson, I became excited again about learning and began to apply myself in the halls of education.

I became so excited about my educational progress that I challenged Mrs. Johnson to a deal of faith. As we were riding in her vehicle, I had this feeling come over me to make a bet with her. I challenged Mrs. Johnson to do something that had never happened in my young life. I told her I was feeling really good about my academics, and I got her to agree to give me seven dollars for every A and five dollars for every B on my next report card.

At this time, I believe my class load was around six or seven classes. I had never made any honor roll in my entire educational life. When the grades came out after the next nine weeks, I earned a whopping forty-five dollars by making five As and, I believe, two Bs on my report card. I was on my way to turning my life around for the betterment of myself and humanity. Oh boy, what a great feeling of satisfaction for me to make the honor roll!

Not everyone was happy about the positive progress I was making in school and in my life. There was an unbelievable story in the making, but some people were of the opinion that my story was still a great disaster in the making. Some of my enemies believed that my success was just a fluke and that in time, I would revert to the old untamed guy from the projects that I was pretending not to be. Even to this day, I can hear some of the negative comments. People are still in disbelief and angry that I made it out of the projects and past the potholes in life, including the shackles of poverty and ignorance.

Students I thought were friends of mine became jealous of the progress I was making in school. As teachers at Dan McCarty Middle School and schools across the district began to talk about my possibly short-lived success, I felt both the joy of victory and the pain of rejection. But regardless of how others felt about me, I was beginning to feel like I was on the road to recovery. For the first time in my life, I felt good about myself for the right reasons.

I was more excited than a butterfly dancing in the spring breeze on a windy day for the progress I observed in my life. Once Mrs. Johnson led me to the right track, it did not take long for me to catch up with some of the other students and surpass the majority of them. From the first day I started school in first grade, I had felt inadequate and so far behind my peers. Yet when Mrs. Johnson started tutoring me, with the mindset of helping me to bridge the educational gap, I knew I was on the right path to total transformation. I sensed that the tutoring would be a dynamic game changer.

* * *

In the meantime, the school year was coming to a close. Dr. Skinner was leaving Dan McCarty Middle School to go to the district office as the new director of elementary education. It had been rumored that the incoming principal had a problem dealing with African Americans, and especially young African American males, who he thought were aggressive and unruly. I fit the perfect description of a person he would use to send a signal to all students that he would not tolerate troublemakers on any level.

A teacher and a principal who celebrated my newfound success in education feared for my destiny under this new incoming principal. The teacher seemed to think the new principal knew of my reputation and was prepared to bring me the justice he thought I deserved. I was later told that some of the teachers who supported my new direction in life would discuss ways for me to avoid ever coming into contact with the new principal.

In reality, there was no way for me to avoid the man. Although I had changed my destructive behavior, the reputation I had established across the district preceded all the good I was accomplishing. One of my physical education teachers told me that I was the number-one student on the incoming principal's chopping block. She told me that the new principal knew who I was and was determined to make an example of me.

However, during the summer break of 1973, something happened that changed the course of history for me. As I was preparing to return to Dan McCarty Middle School for the eighth grade, my education curriculum folder was mysteriously put in the stack of folders with the incoming freshmen class attending Lincoln Park Junior High School. I had been prepared and excited to attend the eighth grade at Dan McCarty Middle School. Yet something awesome happened that was beyond my control or imagination: I was given a grade-lift.

I'm sure you've heard of a face-lift and how the procedure is designed to improve a person's look. Face-lifts are a very common practice within our society. Many Hollywood stars talk publicly about their various face-lifts. Face-lifts are used to make people look younger and more beautiful and appealing to the masses.

A grade-lift is designed to give a person a chance at catching up with his or her peers in an academic setting. It is meant to improve the student's self-esteem, morale, academic progression, and peer affiliation. I jumped over the eighth grade like the cow jumped over the moon in the Mother Goose nursery rhyme.

Do you remember earlier when I told you what happened to me in the first grade? I was a constant no-show at school and even went AWOL on several occasions. I was not promoted to the second grade with the rest of my class for two reasons: I could not do the work, and I refused to attend school.

Not being promoted from first grade to second grade with my class was one of the most embarrassing things I endured while in school. Many of the students would remind me how dumb I was by referring to the fact that I failed first grade. Someone once asked me, "Alvin, how in the world could anyone fail the first grade when the answers are practically given to you?"

"I never got the memo!" I responded jokingly.

Until I entered ninth grade, I had always been a year behind my class. Over the summer when I was scheduled to go to eighth grade, it seemed like I could feel and see students across the city meeting mail carriers at their mailboxes to find out their homeroom teachers and class schedules. Well, this particular time when I ran to the mailbox with excitement to see who would be my homeroom teacher and my class schedule at Dan

McCarty Middle School, I was in for a big shock! My paperwork was for ninth grade at Lincoln Park Academy, the junior high school for all county ninth-graders.

I was more than shocked—I was thrilled and tickled to the bone with disbelief. After my initial reaction of jubilation, however, I was sure that some big mistake had occurred in the system. When I inquired about the matter, I was told to keep my mouth shut and move on.

To this day, I still consider that awesome promotion a gift that came in the wind. When we make up our minds to do the right things in life, doors of opportunities will open in directions and places we have never considered. Doing right in life will not allow people to go wrong. If you drive off the road, right will guide you safely back.

Not only did I receive an unexpected gift by passing over the eighth-grade into the ninth grade, but I excelled in ninth grade, nearly making the honor roll once. Ninth grade was an eye-opening experience for me. For the first time in my life, I saw this gigantic world that I could possibly become a part of if only I applied myself and stayed on the right track.

I began to see opportunities that I could not see when I was fighting the same system that was trying to equip me with the necessary tools to save my life. I was unaware that it was this same system that was trying to help me become a productive citizen in society. Once I began to understand what was actually taking place in my life, I started dreaming about things and a world that I had not dared to dream about in past years.

I started realizing things about myself that I had limited or no knowledge about. I started thinking about the good and wonderful things I could achieve on the positive side of life. I had this feeling that if I continued to look at life as an asset rather than regretting my upbringing or concentrating on the negative things that happened to me as a child, my ending would be much better than my beginning.

* * *

I will be the first to tell you that since ninth grade, I have made some bad personal decisions in my life. The terrible choices I made when I was still walking in arrogance were not a good way to live or even travel in life. At one time in my life, I chased empty winds with fictitious clouds of hope only to end up with disappointment.

I will be the first to tell you that I have made mistakes, so that someone reading this book might take my advice and not make the same mistakes. I have brought shame, embarrassment, and hurt upon myself for relationships I knew were not good for me. Sometimes it is a good thing to listen to the opinions of others so you do not end up acting on your personal impulse.

It is of the utmost importance that we exercise and follow good decision-making. It will lead us in the right direction to the fountain of wisdom, compassion, respect, fairness, honesty, and a good contribution for the building up of humanity. If the advice or instructions you receive or your decisions do not lead you down the road to peace, joy, and success, then abort the journey by any means necessary.

I admit, I have experienced great joy beyond the pitfalls of my self-inflicted wounds. I have experienced overwhelming joy in my life from sports, military service, education, writing, and ministry. I still believe I have a long way to go in life with a short time to get there. Each day I live, I do my best to recover some of the precious time I lost as a young renegade.

I constantly ask myself, *Are my mistakes bigger than my drive to succeed?* No, they are not. I ask myself, *Am I greater than my mistakes?* Yes, I am, because as a human being, I have been equipped with a great power that allows me to overcome my natural and personal obstacles.

I know my obstacles have been put in my life for two reasons: to prevent me from excelling in life and to test my faith and perseverance so I *can* excel in life. Passing the test means an elevation in life. I believe life has given me the very best to give even in the midst of a crisis or storm.

Also, I believe it was the early storms in my life that gave me the skills and power to weather and overcome future storms in my life. It is called *resilience*. It is the drive and ability to overcome adversity with faith and sheer determination in order to succeed that lifted me above the storms. Always remember, you are the captain of your ship until you let someone else take control of the rudder.

Just because storms come and go does not mean you have to be consumed by them. You just have to make and mold the storms or events that enter your life so that that they are beneficial to you. You can either ride the storms or allow your storms to bury you. As for me, I have decided to ride the storms out rather than allowing them to ride me down below the ground.

It is your choice, because you are the captain of your own ship and the master of your destiny. The question is, which direction will you travel in life when the storms arrive at your address—up or down? My encouragement to you is to learn how to maneuver through the storms with wisdom, hope, faith, and the assurance that things will get better if you keep hope alive.

Never forget: failure is when you are in the position or state of mind of saying to yourself, "I quit!" Regardless of how rough and tough the road is or may get, don't ever give up! Even if you cannot see a way out, still do not give up. Oftentimes, a breakthrough shows up when you least expect it.

I have learned that success is always reaching down to help someone else stand up. It does not matter if the person is up or down in life, success wants to be your friend. Failure comes to disrupt our communication, shatter our dreams, and destroy our hope for an enjoyable life.

We cannot give failure this kind of control over our lives. Success pulls people up, but failure pushes them down. Failure does everything within its power to keep people down as low as they can go. Success is a friend to humanity, whereas failure is an enemy to all of us.

Whatever situation you may find yourself in, always remember to stay positive and focused on a good outcome. Regardless of your income, always remember, you have something to say about your end results. The ability you have to remain positive is the key and serves as the light you need to lead you through your tests or trials. Your determination to succeed gives you the authority to have more to say about your successful outcome.

You may not be able to control how you came into this world, but you sure can have some control over how you live in this world. The way you live your life might have a lot to do with how you leave the world as well. Please do not allow your situation to control you. You need to be the one person who steers your situation in the direction you would like to see it go.

You must become the pilot of your own destiny. Having a positive attitude, faith, and positive people in your life becomes the medicine and motivation for having a good day. Believe it or not, you have the strength and power to work with others to move yourself from a dark place into the beauty of experiencing great opportunities. There is a wonderful world beyond your wildest dreams and imagination, but only if you desire to truly succeed in life.

Over the years, I have come to the conclusion that we are much greater than the mistakes we make in life. The fact that your past did not kill you is proof that you have been equipped with the necessary tools to survive and overcome the mistakes of your past. Life has not guaranteed us that we will live to see the next day or finish the current day. Yet faith guarantees the hope to plan for a day we have never seen before.

Our mistakes and failures in life should be good examples of what we need to do to make things better for ourselves and those around us. It is amazing how our mistakes never seem to disappear once we have given them life, energy, and a platform. I believe our mistakes and failures are meant to serve as tour guides, constantly reminding us not to go back the way we came.

Many of our past failures remind us of the great travesties associated with life. We have to learn how to manage the bad things in life with the good things. We must understand how to allow the bad to serve as motivators and not agitators.

Over the years, many people have learned how to process recycled goods and items that were once considered unusable trash. We must learn to treat the storms we encounter during our lives. We have learned from recycled trash that you can take failure and turn it into success.

In years past, people did not recycle items like plastics, trash, wood, and metal. Yet in recent years, the process of recycling has played a significant role on our pathway of achieving success in life. At one time, without a thought, we would have discarded things that we now recycle as trash. Just think: many of the things we are currently recycling would have been thrown away in yesteryears.

So, we are reusing what was considered a negative influence for our country and world, turning them into a positive thing for our society and world. Scientists found a way to turn this negative concept that was destroying our planet into a positive so our planet can benefit. Now many of these items are considered friendly to the ecosystem rather than destructive. One of the greatest joys for me is to conquer negativity with positive accomplishments.

Making the right decisions in your life will always bring you to a crossroad during the "meeting of the minds" process. We must come to a place in our lives where we have a made-up mind to avoid setbacks. Our past is given to us to serve as an imaginary detour sign that reminds us to turn away from the direction in which we are traveling and to proceed with caution. Our past is given to us in order to help us monitor our present state of being and future.

Whenever you are surrounded by loving, positive, and supportive people, this is the strength you need to conquer mistakes, failures, and the damaging things in your past that have been given the mission to destroy your present and future. I recommend that we stop giving our past so much power, control, and credit over our lives. We must stop allowing our past to decide whether we go into the future or not.

We should not allow our past to dictate the way we live in the present as we approach the future. Your future demands that you approach it with a pure heart and joy. We must learn to give our future a fair opportunity to prove itself, because you have never met it or been in its presence before. It is all new to all of us.

Finally, some of the things in this manuscript, I have never shared with anyone. I feel compelled by a greater source to confess because it may help some struggling kid or adult handle situations that arise. The personal testimony I share today might encourage some father, mother, grandparent, teacher, or somebody in need of the strength and courage to overcome obstacles.

If life gave me a second chance, surely life can do the same for you! I believe life will continue giving opportunities to humanity in order to correct the misfortunes and mistakes we have made in our lives. Our lives are given to us for more than just doing what we like and enjoy, or only focusing on the things we want out of life. We are also given our lives to help others achieve some of the things they desire to achieve, and to make other people feel good about their own lives as well.

PART FOUR

Lessons Learned on the Migrant Trail

The Loading Ground
Experience

Somewhere between the 1940s and the late 1960s, America probably witnessed the height of its migrant exodus or crusades for African Americans with fruit and vegetables contractors. During this wintery time of year, you can see ducks, geese, birds, and other fowl hitting the big, blue, and beautiful sky in search of life-sustaining substances. During the winter months, you would see a very special group of people heading to southern states from northern states where they had labored during the summer months but now were faced with Old Man Winter's cold spells.

You would often see workers riding up and down the highways in school-like buses and flatbed transport trucks. The larger trucks would transport either a van, pickup truck, or car on their flatbeds. The buses were loaded with people from all walks of life. Passengers riding on the buses made their living by laboring in the fields of America's southern and northeastern states (Georgia, South Carolina, North Carolina, Virginia, Maryland, Pennsylvania, and New York).

For many people, working on farms in potato, cucumber, okra, and tomato fields on the eastern front was an anticipated annual event that was welcomed with joy and excitement. With each exodus, the residents of the various labor camps would leave with the hope and expectation that the next move would offer even greater rewards than the previous one. Nearly every person, including small children first grade and up, could be found working in the fields. This is considering the absence of a labor inspector.

Some of the contractors saw dollar bills instead of the children's ages or child labor laws. If a child could take a potato or tomato and drop it in a basket, then to the contractor, it was more money in his pocket. I worked many days in the fields when I was a minor child, and no one got into trouble, even when we were "up the road" during times when school was in session.

Back in the 1960s and early 1970s, no one seemed to be pushing labor laws like they do today for children. When I was growing up, it was very common to see African American and Mexican children in the fields working during school hours. Only once or twice did we ever got a visitor from the Department of Labor checking to see if school-aged kids were in the fields when they should have been in school.

Many years have come and gone since African American migrant workers from the state of Florida roamed the east coast of the United States looking for work. The farms and fields are only memories of the past. Over the years, many residential and commercial establishments have anchored their stakes in the ground of what were once labor camps, vegetable fields, and orchards for the pickings.

The laborers who toiled in the fields and farms of Southern and New England states across America have returned permanently to the land they once nurtured and treasured as home. As time gravitates beyond events, people, and places, many of the people living today have very limited knowledge about the role African Americans played on the migrant labor frontier in America.

As I look back over my life, I must say that I am both humbled and appreciative to know that my family was a part of the migrant trail. I too got my boots dusty and hands messy. Although it was hard work and the living conditions were not always good, the experience of living and working on the migrant trail has given me a work ethic that is second to none.

It was on the migrant trail that I developed an appreciation for hard work and a deep respect for hard-working people throughout the world.

Like the Buffalo Soldiers of the American Western Plains during the late 1800s, who proved themselves to be some of the greatest warriors to ever live and serve in the America's armed forces, the migrant workers around the middle of the 21st Century were also the cream of the crop when it came to working the fields from Florida and along the eastern coast of the United States.

The stamina, perseverance, endurance, commitment, and devoted work ethic of migrant workers between the 1940s and 1960s will forever be engraved in the fabric of American history, and is to be appreciated and celebrated by all of those to come with similar experiences. For me, it was a great honor and privilege to have the opportunity to work among some of the finest laborers in America. I would be willing to do it over again just for the fellowship and experience I gained in the migrant labor camps. What an awesome experience it was for me to be a migrant worker.

* * *

It was during the spring of 1968, in the month of May to be exact, when we began to load up the wagon train for our annual northern movement on the migrant trail. May was basically the conclusion of the fruit and vegetable season in the Deep South, especially in the state of Florida. Normally, by the end of May and the early part of June, most of the migrant workers were either moving to the north or already at their first campsite in South Carolina, Georgia, Virginia, or Maryland. In order to find work and sustain a living, and avoid the summer drought in Florida, labor crews had to follow the crop-growing season by moving north.

As spring arrived in Florida, the flowers blossomed, and you could smell the sweet and awesome aroma of the Cape Jasmine (the Florida gardenia) permeating the air. Butterflies were dancing across the big and beautiful blue sky. The butterflies' awesome colors shined like sparkling fireworks on the Fourth of July. Birds were chirping songs of new beginnings, and the local migrant population was hustling to load trucks and buses with equipment and human cargo so the migration north could begin.

Until recent years, this human migration process was called "going up the road" or "going on the season." Sometimes people would call our buses terrible names as a way to belittle the poor migrant workers. Nevertheless, we were on a mission, and we were determined not to allow any negative

Alvin Miller Sr., D. Min.

comments or behavior stop us from working and earning an honest living in groves, fruit orchards, or vegetable fields across the eastern coast of America.

I was only about eight or nine years old at the time, but it seems as though it happened just yesterday. I can remember going to the loading ground with my uncle (Dennis Clark Sr.). I had some idea why we would be going to the loading ground. Yet I did not think it was time for us to leave on our pilgrimage up north. I was confused as to whether we were about to leave for the north simply because I knew we had not packed our boxes and suitcases onto the trucks.

I figured since my uncle was a driver for one of the ten-wheeler flatbed trucks, we could load our belongings later. In the meantime, something in the atmosphere was telling me that the time was drawing near for the migrant train to be heading north. As a lad, the migrant train movement was always exciting to me. It was a time for me to meet new friends, experience different things, and travel to see different parts of the country.

As my uncle and I walked across the loading ground, I heard a loud voice yell out, "Hey Sammy! Man, wa' you been? Man, ahhhhh Um gonna go up da road tomara. Ya goin'?"

My uncle responded, "Hey Mr. Bo-Dilly, Man, hi ya doin'? What da matta' wit' choo?" My uncle then told Mr. Bo-Dilly that he was fine, and he was looking for "Cigar" because he owed him some money.

Mr. Bo-Dilly and my uncle hugged, and then shook hands, and left each other's sight. That was the last time I ever saw Mr. Bo-Dilly or heard mention of his name.

* * *

I guess by now you are wondering, "What is the loading ground?" Well, the loading ground was like a marketplace or a large parking lot where people would go if they wanted to work. The fruit contractors would load the people onto their buses and transport them to the various fields, groves, or orchards to harvest the crops. All the people who wanted to work, and all the contractors who needed laborers to work for them, would meet at the loading ground each morning to pick up and transport laborers, starting around four in the morning or earlier. By six in the morning. the loading ground would be empty of all buses, trucks, cars, and personnel until the crews started returning back to the loading ground around six in the evening or later.

During my lifetime, the loading ground was located at the Bob Casey Grocery Store on the corner of Avenue I and 13th Street and at the Lincoln Theater on the Avenue D and Douglas Court in Fort Pierce, Florida, in the African American community. The loading ground was like a fairground experience with various rides of your choosing. You chose the contractor you wished to work for, and the contractor had the right to accept you or not as one of his laborers.

It was a beautiful operation, like a very sophisticated assembly line that never misplaced parts nor caused disruptions. Crop-harvesting depended on migrant workers from the loading ground to the packing houses, to the stores, and all the way to the dinner tables in people's homes all across America and probably the world.

At the loading ground, the buses would be parked and waiting to transport workers to the work site, and then return them back to the loading ground at the end of the day. Most of the time, the laborers would leave home in the darkness of the morning and return home in the darkness of the evening. The reason the workers had to be at the loading ground so early was because the work sites were oftentimes far away from the loading ground. Travel time was anywhere from one and a half to two hours plus, depending on the harvesting field or grove.

Before there was an unemployment office in my hometown, there was a loading ground. The unique thing about the loading ground was that it guaranteed every person seeking employment opportunities would be given a job on the spot. One thing I loved about the loading ground was that you did not have to submit a résumé for employment. You did not have to have job references before you could work. It was nearly always up to workers to select their employer in order to fulfill their right to work. And as long as you had on clothes, there was no such thing as a dress code until you got started picking lemons. Trust me, you needed long sleeves (preferably double or triple long sleeves and some good thick gloves), unless you were a superman or superwoman.

For many, the loading ground was a meeting place where friends and acquaintances would come together and share laughs, stories, ideas, hugs, food, thoughts, and a sense of pride and belonging. You could hear the loud laughter and conversation from blocks away. You could feel and even see the family ties and traditions that bind the people together. The workers showed an excitement and love for their occupation and their fellow laborers. The industry thrived and survived off of trust, commitment, integrity, and an unbelievable work ethic, from the workers to the supervisors.

The Migrant Camp
Experience

I was awakened by the loud humming noise of a bus engine. The bus was hot, every seat was occupied by a potential worker, and there was an unpleasant musty odor coming from the people riding on the hot bus. I tried to stand up in my seat and put my head out the window so I could get some fresh air, but my aunt woke up and made me sit down.

By this time, the bus driver yelled out, "OK ya'll! Dis da lass stop 'til we git to da camp in Souf Ca'lina. Ya'll com on an use da baffroom." All I can remember is when he pulled the bus over to the gas station, I was the first person in line to get off the bus for fresh air. Keep in mind, air-conditioning was unheard of on a migrant labor bus or truck in the late 1960s and early 1970s.

Nearly everyone got off the bus and ran straight for the restrooms. Although a small few stayed on the bus and slept, the majority of people either used the restrooms, bought food and other goods, or stretched their legs and bodies from being cramped while riding on a jam-packed migrant bus for about four hours. Just think about riding on an old school bus without air-conditioning, and a temperature around 90 degrees on the outside of the bus. It was probably another 10 degrees hotter on the inside.

The bus windows had to stay down at all times to allow air from the outside to circulate throughout the bus. Even though it was hot air, some air felt better than no air at all. Many of the migrant workers dreaded the ride on the bus once the sun came up. It was like riding in a torture chamber.

The night rides on the buses were much cooler than the day rides. During the daylight hours, it was so hot on the buses that our driver kept wiping sweat from his forehead as he drove so it would not run into his eyes. For a child between the ages of nine and twelve, it was both a fun and tragic experience for me to ride on the migrant trail.

It is fascinating to me that during our pit stops, some of the people remained on the bus sleeping. I assume they either had no money to buy anything or were recovering from an alcoholic hangover. Maybe sleeping through the night would help them deal with the agony of being penniless, hungry, and drunk. For many of the migrant workers, sleep was a time when they could escape from their misery, rest from their labor, and dream about a better world.

It was common to walk through the camp or the fields and hear migrant workers discussing their dreams. Many would rely on their dreams when making decisions and looking for direction in life. They believed dreams had a mystic appeal that could give them some type of warning or direction.

I know this may seem strange or odd to some, but for many migrant workers depending on their dreams was a way of life. Dreams become very important to people, especially when their lives have been hijacked by failure after failure. Sometimes dreams offer relief from the darkness of what is actually real. All I know is I dreamed as a boy for me to excel in life, and my dreams did come true.

* * *

During the 1960s and early 1970s, many of the migrant workers who became alcoholics also became indentured servants to many of the contractors. Some of the contractors would keep the alcohol-dependent migrant workers as their servants by encouraging and allowing them to purchase alcoholic drinks on credit, which would in turn keep them on the contractors' debit list (sometimes referred to as bill, tab, credit, card, or check), sometimes until the workers died. I witnessed this over and over again as a child.

Many of the migrant workers would not stay sober long enough to work in order to pay off their debts. This was like a circus or fair game called spinning the wheel. The majority of the players who spun the wheel end up losing rather than winning. At the end of the day, month, year, or lifetime, such migrant workers ended up losing way more than they put in or gained. Some of the migrant workers would become indebted to the contractors for life. Some of the contractors would even take out life insurance on the migrant workers, and when they died, the contractors would collect.

The migrant camps were set up like one-stop shops. Contractors provided nearly everything a migrant worker would need at a much higher price than the regular economy. If the contractors thought the workers needed it, they would find a way to provide it. The idea was to keep the money in his reach and on his camp.

Whatever your needs were, the contractor usually had it for a marked-up price as high as 500 percent of the retail price. Whatever the contractor did not have, we would be allowed to make a weekend trip to the nearest town from time to time to purchase. This was not allowed too often, because it could be detrimental to the camp canteen's ability to reap revenue from the laborers. If a contractor allowed people to frequent the local markets at will, it would drive him right out of business due to his markups. It was a sad thing watching people being ripped off without any type of recourse for justice.

It was obvious these people were being taken advantage of, because the more things they purchased on credit, the more of their freedom they gave up to the shackles of the contractor. It was like being trapped in a spider's web—the more the prey wiggled to get out of the trap, the more entangled it became in the web. The migrant workers would cry out for help in the late hours of the night, or while being beaten in the fields or in the camps, but no one in authority could help them or bring about justice that would alleviate their pain. This was the life on some of the migrant camps where I lived and worked.

* * *

Even with all of this, weekends on migrant camps were the most memorable for me. They were as wild and fun-filled as Halloween or Fourth of July party. The air was filled with loud music from jukeboxes. You could hear screams, laughter, and loud noises coming from the ragged wooden camp social hall, where most of the camp's residents would eat and socialize.

The weekend's excitement and celebration radiated throughout the entire labor camp. People were dancing and singing, gambling and drinking, fighting and cursing, and puffing and smoking nearly everywhere you went. These were only a few of the weekend highlights.

Migrant workers looked forward to the weekends because most of the time, it was when they got paid for their week's work. Some Saturdays, we would work half-days, depending on the landowner's needs. Also, the weekend was a time the laborers could withdraw from the pressure and stress of hard work in the fields or orchards and enjoy the fruits of their labor as they attempted to relax for a few hours.

The South Carolina Migrant Camp Experience

In the midst of dealing with the sweltering South Carolina heat, sometime during the early afternoon, we arrived at the labor camp. The camp had many little white buildings that were connected in rows like a bunch of small storage sheds. The roofs were flat, and the white paint on the buildings was dull and chipping off the sides like tree bark from trees. Most of the time, the campsite was located miles away from the next town or civilization.

I once overheard two men talking under a large oak tree. The one man said to the other that we were in a place called Johns Island, South Carolina. He went on to tell the man that he had been coming to the same camp for over fifteen years. At that time, fifteen years seemed to be very long to me.

Keep in mind, I was only eight or nine years old when this conversation transpired. But I knew more about life and crime at the age of six than most twelve- or thirteen-year-old children could imagine. This is not to brag about my disobedient and lawless past. It is to give you a look at what happened to children who grew up on the migrant trail.

I looked forward to each year's migrant camp experience because when it got closer to time to travel up north, I would almost always overhear some of the adults discussing the places we would be traveling. I heard at least two of the field foremen saying that we would be traveling to South Carolina, Virginia, and New York. The year before, we'd traveled to Exmore, Virginia, where we picked potatoes, cucumbers, tomatoes, and beans; and Pittman, Pennsylvania, where we picked tomatoes on the state's rocky hills. It was a brutal experience crawling on your knees with the rocks scratching and cutting you without mercy.

* * *

Prior to the nearly two hundred migrant workers and their families arriving in South Carolina, the camp had probably been empty for at least eight to nine months. It was common to walk into a room and find some critters—including snakes, turtles, rats, mice, raccoons, opossum, skunks, and insects—living in your potential space. When the migrant workers were not living there and taking care of the campground, it was not unusual for these little critters to move and set up camp themselves, until a crew came along and chased them away for a while.

I got a thrill from walking through the various labor camps and watching different families and people unload the trucks and move their belongings into their rooms. I would even volunteer to lend a helping hand. My willingness to help was never viewed as work. It was the kind act of helping a neighbor, as my grandmother often did.

Looking back, I cannot help but compare migrant workers to the wagon trains of the 1800s in America. Both traveled on faith and in search of hope—the hope that their lives would get better through a strategic movement for survival. Both traveled with few belongings, and both could be packed up and ready to go at a moment's notice. Both were hard workers and dependent on the land for survival (farming and grazing). Finally, both seemed to enjoy life even though their journeys were hard, bumpy, and sometime brutal.

Once at the camp, the migrants organized a setup and cleanup crew. Each person or group would clean, dust, sweep, and mop their rooms. These rooms were usually very small, and two people slept in each room, which was around ten to twelve feet long and around six feet wide. At the end of the day, almost every bed frame in the camp had been pulled from the rooms, and burning newspaper torches were used to remove bedbugs and other insects from between the iron coils and frames of the bed springs.

Bed mattresses were taken out of the rooms to have the dust beaten from them. They were cleaned with disinfectant and left outside so fresh air would circulate through them to "refresh" them. This was done to rid each bed of dust mites, bad smells, and microscopic insects that migrant workers called *chantches* but, in reality, were bedbugs. I believe some of these insects were actually a relative of chiggers.

Whatever critters were hiding on the bed frame or in the mattresses were taken care of by the smoke and fire from the bonfires. After the beds were cleaned and made ready, every migrant worker took out the linen they had brought with them and put the sheets and covers on their beds. Keep in mind, no one actually knew how old the dingy and soiled mattresses were. One could tell by visual inspection that the mattresses were old, sour smelling, dirty, and dusty. Yet we had to make the best use of whatever we were given.

This always reminded me of how slaves on plantations had to survive with whatever was issued to them by the slave owner. Other than being locked up as a delinquent juvenile, the migrant experience is one of the closest events in my life to surviving as a slave.

One of the good things about this particular camp, unlike some others I lived on, was that it had running water (although there was no hot water). It had a public shower located outside in the center of the camp, and it had community toilets located behind the camp.

Some of the other camps located further north did not have running water or flushing toilets. Community outhouses were used instead of toilets with running water. We used wash tubs to wash our clothes and bathe in. During the years I served as a migrant worker, there were only a few camps that had outdoor community showers.

* * *

I remember hanging around many of the migrant workers and listening to them talk about some of the wonderful contractors they loved working for. The men and women sharing their experiences would often bring up the following names as being good humanitarians who had a heart for people, treating them with respect, dignity, and appreciation: Raymond Gordon

Sr., Larry Lee Sr., Raymond Gordon Jr., Vernon Dixon, Duke Robinson, and John Albert.

The experience I gained and lessons I learned from my journey on the migrant trail were unlike anything else I experienced as a child. Living on the migrant trail was like growing up and living in a Third World country in America. Many of the labor camps were located off the beaten path so the camps' conditions would not become an eyesore to the local communities.

The more hidden a camp's location, the less the community would see and know about it. I guess many of the local communities felt like the old cliché "out of sight, out of mind" when it came to migrant labor camps. They were not some neat and pleasant sight to look upon. Trust me on this, back when I was a little boy, they looked like some of the slave plantations I had visited in the south.

Now that I am an adult looking back over the years in which I lived in migrant labor camps, I feel motivated to tell the story of the migrant workers and their journey. I am encouraged by the fact that having survived hard times as a migrant laborer, I can press my way through tough times as a free laborer. Just think, I was less than twelve years old when I witnessed things and events without any discretion or consideration for my age or life as a child.

Probably my greatest takeaway from my migrant labor camp journey is my tenacity and ability to work hard regardless of weather conditions, resources, the environment, or the odds that I face even to this day. The migrant camp matured me to some degree and taught me how to focus on working hard. I had the lowest position in the labor camp while working in the fields picking tomatoes, cucumbers, or potatoes. I was at the bottom of the totem pole.

I was even given the job as the water boy for the crew when I started off at around eight or nine years old. I worked the entire day, about eight to ten hours, and I never received any type of pay for my hard labor. Even when I turned twelve or thirteen and started loading the nearly hundred-pound potato sacks onto the trucks, I still did not receive any compensation. Believe me, I worked hard in the sweltering heat like the adults, but I was never paid a cent for my work by this particular contractor.

* * *

When I was about twelve, we were in a migrant labor camp near Melfa, Virginia (right off of Highway 13 in Accomack County). Melfa had a population of around 387 in the 2017 census count. The loading of the potato sacks was a great benefit for me as far as my physical training and development. After all, I did want to become a football player when I grew up.

I developed more physically this particular summer than I had in any other summer. I became strong enough to lift the potato sacks that were made from burlap bags without any assistance from anyone. People around the camp started talking about how muscular I was getting as a twelve- or thirteen-year-old. I too began to notice the strength I was getting from loading potato sacks on the flatbed trucks. I left my hometown of Fort Pierce a boy, but after loading hundred-pound potato sacks nearly every day for two months, I returned home a man—or so I thought.

I am convinced that what I learned from my journey on the migrant trail was the ability to work hard. That experience taught me to love work, with a personal devotion to my duties, whether big or small. Also, working in the fields gave me a sense of pride that I was accomplishing something valuable and meaningful in life.

Looking back, I recognize that I had the ability to do something well without being ridiculed or harassed by others. I received praise for my hard and dedicated work in the migrant labor camps as a boy. My dedicated work ethic may have started in the migrant fields of Florida, South Carolina, Virginia, and Pennsylvania, or in my grandmother's garden on 18th Street right off of Avenue D in Fort Pierce. My grandmother's drive for me to work hard was to make sure I would not become a lazy bum.

What I learned about work while on the migrant trail seems to be part of the drive that fuels my engine for working hard even to this day. I am impressed by people who value hard work with an honest purpose. We have to be true to ourselves and the purpose by which we live and survive. Good people who work hard with uncompromising integrity are jewels in life. They are a gift to others and life as a whole.

Even though I knew I had my share of problems at school and in the community, I became convinced that working in the fields and living in the migrant camps was a great part of my therapy and part of my great desire to clean up my act and straighten up in life. I began to develop an awesome respect for people's value and property as I labored and sweated in the sweltering heat on the migrant trail.

As I worked hard in the summer heat, a revelation came to me that other people worked hard for their belongings and properties. I received a great epiphany about how wrong it was for me to steal from people and other entities just because I felt the need to do it. So, I stopped the practice of breaking and entering people's homes and stealing their goods because I felt the need to be devious.

It was on the migrant trail that I ceased to take from others without asking permission. It was in the migrant labor camps that I constantly pondered the idea that I needed to change my deviant ways before I ended up incarcerated or dead. It was in the migrant labor camp that the idea came to me to do an about-face with my life.

I realized that in my life, the writing was on the wall. I either had to make a change for the better or face the devastation and destruction life had to offer me. I was more than convinced that if I continued down the wrong road, there would be no good ending.

One of the reasons I knew a positive change had to occur was because I had run out of options. Yet deep down in my soul, I was begging for positive change to occur in my life. I knew when good and great people came along and extended life-saving hands to me, I had to reach out and allow them to help me.

Dr. Skinner and Mrs. Johnson were willing to offer me a second chance to turn my empty life around. It was all for my good and the good of humanity. These are some of the wonderful things I learned during my personal journey on the migrant labor trail.

Fort Pierce and St. Lucie Country, Florida—

Thank you! I love you!

Appendix 1

A Tribute of Inspiration

The Fort Pierce, Florida, legacy of great athletes helped inspire me to excel from a loser in life to a championship warrior. During the years of segregation and even today, some of the most awesome athletes come from Fort Pierce and St. Lucie County. Fort Pierce is known as the Sunrise City, and it has a reputation for being a diamond mine when it comes to producing some of the best athletes in the country—football players in particular. Fort Pierce is unlike any other city of its size on the Treasure Coast of Florida. How can a city so small produce such greatness in the wide world of sports?

Many of the high school athletes who played prep football in St. Lucie County went on to play in the National Football League (NFL), Major League Baseball (MLB), the Women's Basketball Association (WBA), and the National Basketball Association (NBA). Fort Pierce had an athlete (Eddie Edwards, Cincinnati Bengals) who went number-three overall in the 1977 NFL draft and another player (Khalil Mack, Oakland Raiders) who went number five overall in the 2014 NFL draft. Also, Khalil Mack was named as the NFL's 2016 Defensive Player of the Year.

Who would have thought that a city so small would be so powerful? I feel honored to know that some of the greatest jewels in the world of sports came from the same soil where I grew up. Let the world know that Fort Pierce not only has beautiful beaches but is a city that has great talent.

The greatness of the citizens will one day make its way to the big screen for the entire world to witness these precious jewels and talents. What a wonderful gift to the world of sports that Fort Pierce has graciously shared with others across the globe. The sun has truly shined on Fort Pierce like no other city on the Treasure Coast. I encourage citizens to celebrate the athletes and the rich history they have given to us.

As you scroll through the list below, you may be surprised by some of the names I have included, as some of the greatest athletes that have walked and played on the dusty roads of Fort Pierce, Port St. Lucie, and St. Lucie County. These former student athletes are from one of the four high schools that still exist in Fort Pierce and Port St. Lucie: Dan McCarty High School, John Carrol High School (a private Catholic school), Lincoln Park Academy High School, and Fort Pierce Central High School. Remember, not all the athletes listed played professionally, but all of them gave us a great ride and something exciting to talk about during their playing days.

From the age of seven or eight years old, I can remember either seeing some of the greatest players or hearing stories about these legends from former athletes, teachers, educators, school administrators, community leaders, people in the community, and people from across the state of Florida. Nearly everywhere I went across the state, the name or names of some great athlete from Fort Pierce would come up in the conversation. Even today, as I sit down to write this book, I hear NFL commentators talking about a Fort Pierce native named Khalil Mack as one of the best defensive players to ever to play the game of football, and it brings jubilation to my soul.

To date, Khalil Mack is the only NFL player to be named to two all-pro positions in the same year: linebacker and defensive end in 2016. After Khalil Mack made all-pro at the linebacker and defensive end positions, the NFL ruled against allowing players to make all-pro at two positions during the same season.

The list below identifies African American athletes who grew up or lived in the predominantly African American neighborhoods of Fort Pierce. Most of the guys and young ladies listed below lived south of the Mason-Dixon line in a literal sense in a segregated African American neighborhood. Although some of the players are beyond the era of the 1980s, their impact on sports were so significant it would be a disservice to the readers of this book not to include them in the history of the greatest of the greats from Fort Pierce.

There are many more heroic athletes from my hometown, but I just want to highlight a few so future generations will know that greatness passed through their hometown way before they came:

- Roy "Chick" McGriff, football/baseball, Lincoln Park Academy High School (LPA) Fighting Greyhounds
- Lawrence "Tiske" Williams, LPA Fighting Greyhounds
- Alvin "Noo-ney" Chavis Sr., LPA Fighting Greyhounds
- Calvin "Speedy" Williams, football, LPA Fighting Greyhounds
- Lee "L. A." Hayes, football/basketball, LPA Fighting Greyhounds
- Isaac "Ike" Jones, LPA Fighting Greyhounds
- Curley Burch, LPA Fighting Greyhounds
- Clyde Harris, football/basketball/track, LPA Fighting Greyhounds
- Freddie Harris, football/basketball/track, LPA Fighting Greyhounds
- Charles "Hawk" Walker, basketball, LPA Fighting Greyhounds
- Joe "Sloppy Joe" Ford, basketball, LPA Fighting Greyhounds
- Jimmy Louis Johnson, baseball, LPA Fighting Greyhounds
- Robert Bennett, football, LPA Fighting Greyhounds
- Charles "Ice Man" Henderson, football/wrestling/track, LPA Fighting Greyhounds
- Henry "Hulk" Green, Dan McCarty High School Fighting Eagles
- Joe White, basketball, Dan McCarty High School Fighting Eagles
- Hardy Pelt, football/basketball, LPA Fighting Greyhounds
- Marcellus "Shorty" Brown, football/basketball, LPA Fighting Greyhounds
- Robert Crutchfield, football/track, LPA Fighting Greyhounds
- Tracy Nobel, football/wrestling/track, LPA Fighting Greyhounds
- Iverson "Trapp" Williams, football, John Carroll High School
- Eugene "Bea" Dixon, football, Fort Pierce Central High School (FPC) Fighting Cobras
- Ray Isaac, football/basketball/baseball, FPC Fighting Cobras
- Wayne Monroe, football/track, FPC Fighting Cobras
- Columbus "Mut/Muck" Allen, football, LPA Fighting Greyhounds
- Tommy Barber, baseball (major league), FPC Fighting Cobras
- Harvey Lee, baseball (major league), FPC Fighting Cobras

- John Cobbs, football, FPC Fighting Cobras
- Lloyd "Big Daddy" Cobbs, football (FAMU), FPC Fighting Cobras
- Don Latimer, football (NFL)/basketball/track, FPC Fighting Cobras
- Harry Williams, football/track, FPC Fighting Cobras
- Jerome "Bootleg" Groover, football/track, FPC Fighting Cobras
- Godfrey Saunders, basketball, FPC Fighting Cobras
- Harrison "the Cat" Freeman, football, FPC Fighting Cobras
- Willie Smith, football, FPC Fighting Cobras
- Gregg Pressley, football, FPC Fighting Cobras
- Danny Pressley, football, FPC Fighting Cobras
- Henry "Hank" Melton, football/track, FPC Fighting Cobras
- Clint Melton, football/track, FPC Fighting Cobras
- Chapel Branch, football/track, FPC Fighting Cobras
- Ronald "Blue" Evans, football/wrestling/track, FPC Fighting Cobras
- Ronald "Ron" Argrett, football/wrestling/track, FPC Fighting Cobras
- Ronnie "Superstar" Green, basketball, FPC Fighting Cobras
- Terry "TR" Miller, football, Dan McCarty High School Fighting Eagles
- Mike Latimer, football/track, FPC Fighting Cobras
- Larry "Bumpy" Lee, football, FPC Fighting Cobras
- Cleaver Hayling, football, FPC Fighting Cobras
- Alvin Swoop, football, FPC Fighting Cobras
- Roosevelt Duncan, football/baseball, FPC Fighting Cobras
- Jackie "Too Tall" Robinson, football/basketball, FPC Fighting Cobras
- Alvin Chavis, football, FPC Fighting Cobras
- Terry Jones, football, FPC Fighting Cobras
- Wilbert Phillips, football/track, FPC Fighting Cobras
- Vernon Phillips, football/track, FPC Fighting Cobras
- Elvis "Red" Rolle, basketball (NBA), FPC Fighting Cobras
- Willie Redden, basketball (NBA), FPC Fighting Cobras
- Larry Sanders, basketball (NBA), Port St. Lucie High School

- Dock Luckie, football (NFL)/track, FPC Fighting Cobras
- Robert Weathers, football (NFL)/track
- Clarence Weathers, football (NFL)/track, Fort Pierce Westwood High School Panthers
- Willie Broughton, football (NFL)/track, FPC Fighting Cobras
- Jeff Blackshear, football (NFL, nine years)/track
- Jerry Johnson, football (all-state, all-American, NFL)
- Jamar Chaney, five seasons in the NFL
- Larry Sanders, five years in the NBA
- Elvis Rolle, NBA
- Willie Redden, NBA
- Randy "Sweetback" Walker, football (NFL)/track, FPC Fighting Cobras
- Jerry "Fleet-Footed' Brown, football/basketball/track, FPC Fighting Cobras
- Goldie Anderson, football/track, FPC Fighting Cobras
- Terrence McGriff, football/baseball (MLB), FPC Fighting Cobras
- Charles "Bump" Johnson, baseball (MLB, twelve years), Fort Pierce Westwood High School
- Sophia Weatherspoon, basketball (WBA), FPC Fighting Cobras
- Wonder Monds, Canadian Professional Football League and the NFL
- Mario Monds, football (NFL), Fort Pierce Westwood High School
- Wonderful Terrific Monds III, baseball (minor league)/football, Fort Pierce Westwood High School
- Ryan McNeil, football (NFL, eleven years), Fort Pierce Westwood High School
- Luther Robinson, football (NFL), Fort Pierce Westwood High School
- Craig Swoope, football (NFL)/track, Fort Pierce Westwood High School
- Ronnie Gilbert, football/track, Fort Pierce Westwood High School
- Cedric Stubbs, football/track, FPC Fighting Cobras
- Leon Hill, football, FPC Fighting Cobras
- Stacy Noble, football, FPC Fighting Cobras
- Dennis Clark Jr., football, FPC Fighting Cobras

- Jerome Rhyant, football/track, FPC Fighting Cobras
- Willie Lanier, football/track, FPC Fighting Cobras
- Mike Ingram, football/track, FPC Fighting Cobras
- Robert "Bobo" McDowell, football/track, FPC Fighting Cobras
- Terry Booker, football/track, FPC Fighting Cobras
- Stephan "Stony" Barriner, football/track, FPC Fighting Cobras
- Luther Ray Sandifer, football/track, FPC Fighting Cobras
- Peter Barriner, football/track, FPC Fighting Cobras
- Wyman "Wap" Phillips, football/basketball/track, FPC Fighting Cobras
- Forrest Harper, football/track, FPC Fighting Cobras
- Larry Mitchell, football/track, FPC Fighting Cobras
- Terry King, football/track, FPC Fighting Cobras
- Albert Wilson, football (NFL)/track, Port St. Lucie High School
- Khalil Mack, football (NFL)/track, Fort Pierce Westwood High School
- Ledarius Mack, football(NFL), Fort Pierce Westwood High School
- Michael Brantley, NFL, FPC Fighting Cobras
- Jamar Chaney, five seasons in the NFL

Champions are made before the contest begins; they just have to show up and convince others!—Alvin E. Miller

Appendix 2

The Photo Gallery of a Competitor and a Champion

Alvin at age 13 while in middle school 1972

Alvin Miller #44 running w/football in right hand and fans sitting on side of hill.

Photo Of Coach Roy Kidd and team members holding NCAA-1AA
National Championship trophy with Alvin Miller in background

Alvin Miller kneeling and praying in endzone after touchdown with football in hand.

Alvin Miller #44 running with football in left hand while
opponent #44 watches from the ground

Alvin Miller taking handoff from quarterback Chris Isaac #16 (deceased)

Alvin Miller #44 holding football in right hand in the endzone while
referee signals touchdown (both hands raised high in the air).

Alvin Miller and player from opposing team on ground after Alvin is tackled with football in left hand. Officers, cheerleaders, and EKU fans in background.

Alvin holding football out in right hand as he crosses goal line for a touchdown, referee, cheerleaders, and fans in background.

Alvin Miller running upfield with football in left hand as defenders (#92 and #22) tackle him. EKU players #63 and #88 in background.

Alvin is running upfield against Nevada Reno with Begley Drug Co. in background.

Promotional photo of EKU Colonels 1979 NCAA National Champion
team with Coach Roy Kidd holding championship trophy.

Alvin Miller #44 running to left with football in left hand with #15 looking on.

EKU players giving Alvin Miller #44 a team hug
in endzone after a Miller touchdown.

Alvin Miller is resting on his back in endzone after scoring
a touchdown. Referee signaling touchdown.

EKU promotional flyer depicting various snapshots of football moments from 1979 football year - OVC runner-up and national champions.

EKU'S Coach Roy Kidd and team members holding 1979 NCAA-1AA National Championship trophy.

Alvin Miller holding hand with former team mate.

Personal photo of Alvin Miller near football trophy box.

Alvin standing by Eastern Kentucky Univeristy
historical marker while visiting EKU.

About the Author

Dr. Alvin E. Miller Sr., a native of Fort Pierce, Florida, earned a bachelor's degree from Eastern Kentucky University in 1981 (Sociology). When Colonel (Retired) Miller arrived at Eastern Kentucky University, he was a walk-on football player. After playing in high school at Fort Pierce Central High School, he received numerous awards for his outstanding play (3rd Team All-State, All-Central Florida Team, All Sun Coast Conference Team, and the *Palm Beach Post* All-Area Football Team).

While at EKU, Colonel Miller earned a football scholarship and began to ink his cleats into the history of a winning legacy at EKU, which became a winning football dynasty in NCAA football during the 1970s and 1980s. In 1979, Dr. Miller led EKU in winning the first national championship (NCAA 1-AA) in football. During the semifinal national championship football game and the national championship games, ABC Television and Chevrolet Corporation selected Alvin Miller as Most Valuable Player for each game.

Along with his football accomplishments came other life-changing experiences. While a student at EKU, Alvin joined the EKU ROTC battalion and excelled as a cadet. He became a member of Omega Psi Phi Fraternity, Inc., Delta Sigma chapter, on the beautiful EKU campus.

When he received his degree in 1981, Alvin became the first family member from his grandparents and great-grandparents to graduate from a college or university. Upon graduation, he received his commission as a second lieutenant by the Department of the Army. After his initial tour of active duty, he was honorably discharged and then was invited to attend an NFL free-agency football camp with the Houston Oilers during the Spring of 1984. After not making the team, he later returned to Fort Pierce Central to teach and coach football at his alma mater.

In August 1985, Alvin entered the Southern Baptist Theological

Seminary, where in December 1988, he earned his master of divinity in chaplaincy and pastoral care. In 1989, Alvin accepted a job on Florida Governor Robert "Bob" Martinez's staff as the governor's drug-free communities coordinator. In 1990, Alvin returned to active duty in the United States Army as a chaplain at Fort Sill, Oklahoma. During this particular tour of duty, Alvin enrolled in the doctor of ministry program at Oral Roberts University in Tulsa, Oklahoma. On May 1, 1999, Dr. Miller received his doctor of ministry degree from Oral Roberts University.

Dr. Miller is the author of three books and other published professional articles. He has received numerous awards and honors during his distinguished career. Among his many awards are the US Army Meritorious Service Medal, US Army Commendation Medal, National Defense Medal, Who's Who Among America's Teachers, Outstanding Young Men of America, St. Lucie County, Florida, Sport Hall of Fame, and a host of other accolades.

Most recently, in 2018, Colonel (Retired) Miller was inducted into the Eastern Kentucky University ROTC/Military Science Hall of Fame. In 2019, Dr. Alvin Miller was awarded the Distinguished Alumni Service Award by the Eastern Kentucky University International Alumni Association. In 2020, he was inducted into the Eastern Kentucky University Sports Hall of Fame and currently serves on the Eastern Kentucky University International Alumni Board. In 2010, Dr. Miller became a member of the Honorable Order of Kentucky Colonels.

Currently, Dr. Miller is married to the former Dominique Haywood, and they reside in Nashville, Tennessee. Together, they have five adult children and six grandchildren. He is the pastor of St. John Baptist Church in Clarksville, Tennessee.

#EKU

Colonel Nation Football

Contact Information

- https://www.facebook.com/BishopAlvinEMillerSr
- https://www.facebook.com/RevDrAlvinEMiller
- email, radicalbishop@gmail.com

When I Die
by Alvin E. Miller

When I die, do not weep over my body;
Because it is only the flesh, and I gave life my best.
Do not say good things about me if they are not true.
Do not bring me any flowers, because my nose is at rest.
Do not feel sorry for me, because I enjoyed life to the best.
So, I charge you to rejoice this day, because
I have made it to a better place.
I have nothing else to say! May my labor to
humanity speak for me When I Die!

Printed in the United States
by Baker & Taylor Publisher Services